Life Goes On

Photo by John P. Schaefer

Life Goes On
Twenty More Years of Fortune and Friendship

by Lawrence Clark Powell

Checklist
of publications: 1919–1986
by Robert Mitchell and
Betty Rosenberg

The Scarecrow Press, Inc.
Metuchen, N.J., and London
1986

The chapter on Portugal has been revised from its first appearance in *Southwest Review* (Spring 1968).

The lines from W. B. Yeats' "Coole Park, 1929" on page 11 are reprinted with permission of Macmillan Publishing Company from *The Poems*. Copyright 1933 by Macmillan Publishing Company, renewed 1961 by Bertha Georgie Yeats.

Library of Congress Cataloging-in-Publication Data

Powell, Lawrence Clark, 1906-
   Life goes on.

   Bibliography: p.
   Includes index.
   1. Powell, Lawrence Clark, 1906-   —Biography.
   2. Powell, Lawrence Clark, 1906-   —Bibliography.
   3. Authors, American—20th century—Biography.
   4. Librarians—United States—Biography. I. Title.
   PS3531.0954Z469   1986   020'.92'4 [B]   86-3943
   ISBN 0-8108-1890-6

Copyright © 1986 by Lawrence Clark Powell
Manufactured in the United States of America

TO FAY

sail and anchor

Contents

Foreword by Eric Moon	vii
Preface	xvii
I	1
II	21
III	29
IV	39
V	60
VI	74
VII	84
VIII	115
IX	125
Checklist of Publications by Robert Mitchell and Betty Rosenberg	133
Index	165

Foreword

ABOUT A COUPLE OF YEARS AGO two young librarians (almost all librarians are 'young' to me these days) were visiting us in Sarasota. We were sitting out on the porch, enjoying Bombay gin and watching that marvelous Florida sunshine subside gently into a pinkish dusk. The talk turned, as it inevitably does when librarians gather, to gossip about libraries and librarians. Somewhere during the conversation, inevitably, I mentioned Larry Powell.

Like an over-trained Greek chorus, in mystified unison they said: "Who's Larry Powell?" I remember only one other occasion when my eyebrows had been sent soaring so high by a question. It was shortly after my arrival in America, when my children were very young. Talking to them and some of their friends I had dropped another name. The answering chorus then was: "Who's Lindbergh?"

Had I mentioned Gandhi or Lloyd George or Smuts or even so recent figure then as Aneurin Bevan the vacuum behind that question would not have had the same power to surprise. One only needs to listen to the pronouncements of some of our political leaders, or to read the letters columns in any newspaper, to become aware that a knowledge of the history of other nations, other parts of the world, is not one of the strengths of most Americans. Too often, what is taught as history in our educational institutions is *American* history—and even that may be truncated to *U.S.* history.

But if the attachment of such blinders may be attributed

to a certain parochial nationalism—by no means a uniquely American phenomenon—how does one explain the education for a profession that leaves its graduates ignorant of its *own* giants, those who have shaped or given character or inspiration to that profession? As I pondered such questions in the wake of that response to Powell's name I thought back to my own days in library school in Britain and realized that one would have to have slept through almost every class to have emerged into the profession without an awareness of the achievements, not only of such figures of British library history as Panizzi or James Duff Brown but also of such more recent, then still practicing giants as Lionel McColvin, Ernest Savage and Frank Gardner. More importantly, in the context of our professional heritage, in our pantheon there were also many names from across the Atlantic. They included not just the obvious lions of the past—Dewey and Cutter and Winsor and Dana and Putnam—but more recent giants, like Joe Wheeler, or then emerging ones such as Powell, Shera, and Shaw.

Such thoughts may be attributed purely to (and perhaps a bit rosied by) nostalgia, a popular pursuit among those who have more years behind them than lie ahead. But if it is true—and I think it is—that without learning the lessons of the past we are ill-equipped to deal with the problems of the present, let alone the unpredictable future, there is more to it than nostalgia. A profession like librarianship, engulfed today in change of unprecedented rapidity, if it operates without the stabilizing forces, the values and thinking and creativity, that have brought it thus far, may well find itself rudderless, making decisions out of expediency rather than accumulated wisdom, accommodating to change without a foundation of purpose or belief.

That innocent question from two librarians on a porch in Sarasota reinforced my belief in the project that Scarecrow Press began a few years ago. It may not be a significant contribution to publishing profits but it is, I believe, an important contribution to the profession to persuade such people as Robert Downs, Ronald Benge, Ralph Ellsworth, Guy Lyle, Will Ready and Johanna Tallman—and yes, Lawrence Clark Powell—to leave us some personal record of their lives and beliefs and achievements. Powell's introduction to librarianship course, incidentally, came about as a result of his teaching at UCLA for six years, one semester a year plus summer sessions. He always included a week on "library leaders." In a recent letter he told me: "I have always revered our giants and tell my students to."

"People, librarians no exception, are forgotten. Books remain." No need perhaps to tell you who said that, but what Larry Powell didn't add was that one of the supreme contributions of the books that remain is that they can remind generations to come of what those otherwise "forgotten" people (librarians no exception) did, what they contributed to bring us to where we are, and of how much less we and our institutions and services might be had they not been a part of our history and development.

The question that provoked all this serious contemplation also reminded me of how the tempo of change today seems to have telescoped time, to the point where you can go into Sam Goody's and find both The Beatles and The Rolling Stones in a bin labeled "Golden Oldies." Twenty years ago I had persuaded Larry to write his autobiography, *Fortune and Friendship*, which was published by Bowker in 1968. If twenty years ago seems to some members of the now generation like the Middle Ages, perhaps one should not be surprised that that volume, despite the wonders that technology has brought to bear upon bibliography and cataloging, is in a sense no longer accessible. It was with all this in mind that Bill Eshelman, Scarecrow's president, and I began our barrage of persistent persuasion that led to Larry's writing this second volume with its optimistic (or resigned?) title, *Life Goes On*. Larry is current, a "now" person again.

●　　●　　●

As I was writing this Foreword I read the news that Lee Iacocca's autobiography had just become the best-selling hardbound non-fiction book of all time. It's not an entirely new phenomenon: examine the best-seller lists over a period of time and you will find that half of the titles, or more, are autobiographies. What is it that makes this literary form so popular? The author, of course, his or her fame or notoriety, is a large factor. But I think an equally large part of the fascination may derive from curiosity about the author's connections—with events or, more importantly, with other people—and what he or she has to say about them. A person writing about himself tells an empty story if his pages do not record the links with those who have influenced his life and work and with some of those upon whom his ideas and personality have had an impact. That Larry is aware of this is evident in the title of his first autobiography, *Fortune and Friendship*. "Friendship"—one kind, an important one, of connection.

When you know the author, reading an autobiography can be even more fun, because you are reminded of your own connections. As I read the anecdotes in this volume about such library luminaries as Ralph Shaw, Jesse Shera, Luther Evans, and Sir Frank Francis, episodes from my own life and career, connections with each of them, danced into memory and I wanted to add my own anecdotes to LCP's. But it is not because of those shared acquaintances that I am writing this Foreword. Bill Eshelman assigned me this pleasurable task, I suspect, not just because I had persuaded Larry to write his first autobiography and had helped to dragoon him into this successor volume but because he knows of the many and interesting ways in which Larry and I have "connected" over the years. He knows, too, of my great (but far from uncritical) admiration for this man who, when he was awarded the American Library Association's highest honor, was described so aptly as "a magician."

Our first connection, Larry's and mine, was in 1957. I had just become one of the two founding editors of *Liaison*, the official news organ of the (British) Library Association, a weapon we had devised to counteract the determined dullness of *The Library Association Record*. My partner, Bill Smith (now a successful bookseller) and I were setting out to bring newspaper vitality and technique to library literature. I had heard that three famous figures of the American library world were to be present at the Library Association conference in Harrogate, Yorkshire that year, and was eager to pull off a scoop by interviewing all three for our fledgling publication.

Discovering them all together one evening, ensconced in armchairs around a large fireplace and sharing drinks and conversation with some of the greyer eminences of The Library Association, our enterprising but brash young reporter, armed with camera, pad, and pencil, charged upon the scene. The three Americans were LCP, Quincy Mumford, the Librarian of Congress, and Howard Haycraft, president of the H.W. Wilson Company and master analyst of detective fiction.

I have often wondered since what it was that made me choose Larry as my first target—perhaps blind luck, or fate, if one is inclined to believe in that. At any rate I planted myself in front of him and said something like: "So you're Larry Powell. Why don't you come outside with me for a few minutes and tell me what makes you so great?" Amid dark frowns all around—bad British form and all that—like a burst of sunshine through the clouds there emerged the famous twinkle in the Powell eyes. "Sure, young man," he said, getting up out of his chair, "You have almost as much gall as I had at your age."

That generous, spontaneous response to a young, unknown (and in this instance, certainly undeserving) individual, though I did not know it then, was typical of Powell. So too were the humor and humanity that warmed our corridor conversation in the following minutes. When I told him that I was going after Quincy and Howard during the week, he grinned and said: "I wouldn't advise the same approach." It was the first time, but not the last, that he would give me very sound advice.

The connections were renewed when I came to the U.S. in 1959 to assume the editorship of *Library Journal*. In our correspondence before my arrival Dan Melcher, Bowker's president and *LJ*'s publisher, suggested, since I had no experience of America or American librarianship (other than through extensive reading about both—a demurrer of which I'm sure Larry

xi

would approve), that we appoint a board of consultants, comprised of eminent American librarians upon whose advice and experience I could call during my first couple of years. The first person I told Dan I wanted was Lawrence Clark Powell. Another person featured in this book who was part of that impressive assembly was Luther Evans, who often broke up our gatherings with huge Texan belly-laughs over my accent and my "un-American" pronunciation of certain words.

Subsequently I asked Larry to become a columist for *LJ*, and for a year (all he would agree to), among his myriad other activities he ground out his "On the Grindstone" column, always coming in—a real rarity among columnists—ahead of deadline. It was over this column, though, that we had our first major disagreements, though not confrontations, as you shall hear. I wanted Larry to bring to bear his power and influence upon some of the critical issues with which *LJ* and I were so deeply involved in the sixties, but I couldn't budge him from his "Passion for Books" message, although he claims to have been "magnificently diverse" and to have tackled what he saw as the issues: they just weren't *my* issues. One tough day when things had not been going well, another of those bibliographic sermons dropped onto my desk. I read it with impatient fury and promptly dashed off a long, angry letter accusing Larry of avoidance of responsibility. . . and then on up (or down) from there. My uninhibited language in that letter was somewhat similar to Ralph Shaw's response to Larry's famous ALA keynote speech, "The Alchemy of Books" (see page 99 of this book). Larry's delightfully unfazed and coy response came by return mail: "You didn't *like* my column?" How can you stay mad at a man like that? What is now clear, in any case, in the context of time, is that both Shaw and I were wrong. Larry had to be *his* man, not ours, and that speech and those columns are still read and cited by many today.

But enough of reminiscences (although they could go on for many more pages). What is it, to repeat that infamous question of mine on our first meeting in the fifties, that makes Larry

Powell so great? Certainly his achievements are undeniable: his transformation of the UCLA library into one of the great libraries of the world; his fight for and establishment of a superb library school with a wondrous faculty including the likes of Seymour Lubetzky, Frances Clarke Sayers, Everett Moore, Betty Rosenberg, Andy Horn, Bob Hayes; and his writings, among the most enduring of any librarian's. Among his greatest contributions, too, were the bridges he built between the library world and the larger world of books—with authors, printers, booksellers, publishers. More than any of this, though, it is his personal qualities that elevate him above most others in our profession, qualities that have inspired and irritated, annoyed and exhilarated, and that have produced more converts and followers and friends, inside of librarianship and out, than most of us could ever dream of.

And that is the hardest thing to capture in writing about him. Like all complex persons he is full of contradictions: he can be ruthless or incredibly kind, caring or oblivious, sneaky or disarmingly open, phony or utterly convincing, sentimental or harshly realistic. All those contradictions, and more, carry over into the evaluations of him by others, including many of those who have known him best, admired and loved him. Consider some of those reactions and judgments:

Andrew Horn, perhaps Larry's closest friend in the library world, asked for his reactions, mentioned *first* Powell's strength as an administrator and manager. This comment is echoed by another lifelong friend, the great antiquarian bookseller Jake Zeitlin, who calls him "a thoroughgoing administrator." This is the same man who has been more often characterized as a bookish evangelist, even a "biblio-simpleton," the same man who will shrug off as unimportant or untrue any reference to his administrative skills (there's some of that phoniness for you). Horn, as usual, puts this particular contradiction into some perspective: "His management style was highly personalized. His definition of management could fit one I've heard, *viz.*, 'Management is getting things done through people'." That indeed sounds like something Powell would say. People, and getting things done, are among his strengths. Just don't call it administration!

Andy Horn was as well aware of the Powell contradictions as anyone. In another note he said: "Sensitive and emotional on the one hand; practical, realistic, and nearly ruthless on the other. Often seems a paradox when analyzed." That word "ruthless" crops up surprisingly often in evaluations by his friends and colleagues, as in the comment by Betty Rosenberg: "Ruthless when the library is at stake."

A passionate man himself, Powell evokes passionate reactions from those around him. A good example is Everett Moore's comment on "this unique man." Says Moore: "I've admired and hated, enjoyed and endured, turned hot and cold in turn, along with many of his associates. I owe him much. I'm grateful for my associations with him."

So how does one sum up this outrageous, contradictory, complex man? He himself, in *Fortune and Friendship*, talks of his "personal, autobiographical, egocentric, didactic, flamboyant, hyperbolic manner." All true. On another occasion I added, if only indirectly, another adjective to that list. During a little celebration to mark the publication of *Fortune and Friendship* I gave a copy to Larry's wife and, as he relates (see page 43), wrote in it: "To Fay, the most objective of the Powells." There is much more than objectivity to this wonderful woman whom Larry calls his "sail and anchor." He's undoubtedly needed both, though almost certainly the anchor more often than the sail. Whatever he is and has achieved, Fay has been an integral part of it. *Her* autobiography would be fascinating.

LCP's colleague of these later years, David Laird, Librarian of the University of Arizona, comments: "As impressive as Larry's careers are in things that show up on a résumé or an entry in *Who's Who*, it is an intangible thing that most impresses me: Larry has that magical spark that we call charisma, or once did before the word went out of fashion. Nearing 75 [David wrote this a few years ago] he still has more enthusiasm for life and love than most folks have at 25, and when he comes in contact with other minds the sparks fly, the wires hum and all systems are GO."

Laird comes close to the essence of Lawrence Clark Powell in that comment. Larry's personality is perhaps his greatest weapon, the ingredient that may best account, along with the passion of his beliefs, for his tremendous impact on so many people over so long a period of time. Important too is his energy, that "enthusiasm for life and love" that Laird mentions. That it continues was evident at the 1983 Los Angeles ALA Conference, at which Larry was the speaker at a Junior Members Round Table session.

To those who haven't know him a long time it appears, before he starts speaking, that this bowed, frail-looking man will just not make it through the program. But he's looked pretty much like that ever since I've known him, and we his fans who were sitting in the front row at Los Angeles knew the transformation that would occur the moment he got behind the microphone. Larry is more actor and performer than speaker, and a microphone and a platform will do more for him than a double martini. He just turns on, lights up and, as David Laird says, "All systems are GO."

On this occasion, in his late seventies, there he was in full histrionic form, urging on the younger librarians to fight for what they believed in and not to be too bothered about job security. The man in the grey flannel suit would not have approved at all. At one point he leaned over the lectern, grinned down at me and said: "We gave 'em hell, didn't we, Eric?" But the moment in the speech that was pure LCP was when he announced somberly: "This will be my last appearance before you at ALA." There followed a long pause, to allow us to absorb the sadness of the moment. . . and then it was broken. Up came the head, the twinkle was back in the eyes, and Larry whispered: "Unless you ask me back." It was coy and corny and funny, but you knew that here was a man who *wanted* to return. He did not want to give up the limelight, the missionary spirit was still strong, the sermon wasn't over—and probably will never be while he is still on his feet.

The essential Powell is best captured, in my opinion, in the citation that Larry received when he was inducted as an Honorary Life Member of ALA. Since many readers of this volume will never have seen it, it seems appropriate to end this Foreword with just a small sample from that splendid statement:

"Author, bibliographer, bookman, essayist, librarian, teacher, dean, and adroit administrator, Lawrence Clark Powell is many things. But essentially he is a magician. He turns young people into readers, students into book owners, scholars into bibliographers, book dealers into colleagues, library workers into librarians, academic administrators into library defenders, university regents into buyers of book collections, and legislators into fighters for library funding. . . He is the profession's best recruiter and its most effective lobbyist. No one knows where his influence ends."

I hope there are a few answers here, and in the pages that follow, to the difficult questions those two young librarians asked me a couple of years ago: "Who is Larry Powell?"

Eric Moon

Preface

TWENTY YEARS HAVE PASSED since I left UCLA and wrote *Fortune and Friendship*. All that has happened since then, much of it unforeseen, came inevitably from what went before. Now at eighty the chain of my life appears cunningly linked. Because of the persistent encouragement of the two Scarecrows, William Eshelman and Eric Moon, I have been persuaded to look at the links between 1966 and 1986.

I have written about what is remembered as interesting and significant. The passage of time lessens the importance and meaning of things. The longer one waits, the more is lost. Although I have kept a journal, I lack the Pepysian desire to recreate the happenings and minutiae of each day while they are fresh. It seemed wise to write before age slowed me any more than it has. If I should live another ten years without having written this continuation, I could not see the past as clearly as I do now.

What I have chosen to write is deliberately selective and professional rather than personal, and yet between the lines a discerning reader might be able to perceive what the writer in his preoccupied blindness can't see or prefers not to say.

So be it. I have little to lose and less to gain. Never lost has been my need to communicate by written and spoken word what life has meant to me, who has lived it according to his nature and character. I have embraced life with its roses and thorns, enjoying the pleasure and accepting the pain. The first five of the twenty years were a search for a promised land where

I could most fully realize my gifts. In the end that land proved nearer than I knew.

In the writing of these pages much is owed to many. Not all of my debts are acknowledged. The dedication is to her to whom I owe the most. As he was when upon his urging I wrote *Fortune and Friendship,* Eric Moon has been my most valued critic, with Bill Eshelman, friend clear back to his student years at UCLA, not far behind. My first drafts by Scripto and Olivetti were made legible through many word processor revisions, thanks to Joyce Goldsmith, devoted friend of my work.

Now I yield to the reader.

LCP

Tucson
Bajada of the
Santa Catalinas

Acronyms & Abbreviations

ALA	American Library Association
ARL	Association of Research Libraries
ASU	Arizona State University
BSA	Bibliographic Society of America
CHP	California Highway Patrol
CIA	Central Intelligence Agency
CLA	California Library Association
GLISA	Graduate Library Institute for Spanish Speaking Americans
HRC	Humanities Research Center, University of Texas
LAPL	Los Angeles Public Library
NAU	Northern Arizona University
NEH	National Endowment for the Humanities
NYPL	New York Public Library
OPA	Office of Price Administration
PNLA-MPLA	Pacific Northwest Library Association-Mountain Plains Library Association
SUNY	State University of New York
U.C.	University of California
UCLA	University of California at Los Angeles
U. of A., UA	University of Arizona
USC	University of Southern California
USDA	U.S. Department of Agriculture

Life Goes On

I

UNTIL THE PANAM 707 cleared the runway and with laboring slowness gained altitude out over the Pacific to make the wide turn and head back over Southern California on the eleven-hour non-stop flight to London, I did not feel the bond break that had held me in a long and fruitful relationship with UCLA. In another week I would be sixty years old. I could have remained on campus another ten years in a gradual relinquishment of authority.

"Why leave before you have to?" I was asked by my contemporaries as they settled in to various degrees of comfort and security. "What will you do? What can you have that you don't have here?" Them I did not, could not answer for I did not know for sure what I was going to do once I got away. I did know that I did not want any more of the success and recognition that had been mine as university librarian, dean, and director of the William Andrews Clark Memorial Library.

Harder to leave were those such as Birdie Ross, a typist-clerk in the university library, who came up to me at the campus retirement party and said pleadingly, "Don't go. We need to know that you are here even though we don't see you." Years before, she and I and her little son also named Larry had met in the university hospital's emergency room, the boy with an injured eye and I with my first painful attack of iritis. The child and I agreed to be brave and not cry, as the mother bit her lip and smiled. A bond was thus formed of lasting human sympathy.

Many such bonds had been formed with staff and students,

as well as with unknown ones by my talks and articles and books. Thus I had become linked with listeners and readers never known to me personally. And so if I made any answer, I said I'm leaving while still loved, quitting while still ahead, or, I want to write more while I still have strength for it.

Two books were uppermost in my mind. The first was one written in 1941, which after being rejected by a reader at Knopf, had been put away though not forgotten. When after I had written several bibliographical studies and Fay chided me for having abandoned an earlier intention to be a novelist, I began almost blindly to write what eventually became *The Blue Train*.

Henry Miller was its earliest reader when we were neighbors in Beverly Glen, and the ardent letter he wrote me then had now led to my taking the manuscript from where it had languished for twenty-five years, and in the six weeks of the summer session, when I taught my last class in the library school, I sequestered myself after lunch at the Faculty Center and in that month and a half, rewriting by hand and then on the typewriter, I recast the book that still had to wait another eleven years before it was published.

Encouragement had come from William Targ, my editor at World Publishing Company for *A Passion for Books, Books in My Baggage* and *The Little Package*, a trio of books about books, libraries, and reading. Now the finished manuscript had gone off to him at Putnam, where he had moved after Times Mirror had bought World and discontinued the bookish series.

The carbon copy was in my briefcase (Xeroxing was not yet on the scene) and as the plane flew all night over the Arctic Circle, Greenland, Iceland, and Ireland to London's Heathrow Airport, I stayed awake while Fay slept, and read through what I had just rewritten with such passionate conviction. Now I had cooled but was no less certain that mine was a book destined to be read after my time and in tongues other than my own. (Thus far French is the farthest it has reached.)

When upon landing at daybreak we learned that our flat in London's apartment block called Dolphin Square, on the river in Pimlico between Westminster and Chelsea, would not be ready until a week later, we hired a car and headed southwest to Salisbury and the White Hart, a country hotel known during my sabbatical year of 1950/51. After dinner of roast lamb, peas, and potatoes and a demitasse in the lounge, we donned our woolens and walked to the cathedral for *Son et Lumière*. There in the ancient close beneath the tallest steeple and spire in Britain, every last care and responsibility fell away. An unknown future gleamed ahead, mine, ours, for the living.

Responsibility for libraries and library school belonged now to those to whom I had given encouragement and example. Since 1961 Robert Vosper, Page Ackerman, Everett Moore, Paul Miles, Louise Darling and Jo Tallman had managed the main and branch libraries, and now Vosper had added the Clark with the continuing assistance of William Conway and Edna Davis. With those around them on the firing line, they formed a sterling management team. Andrew Horn had succeeded me as dean of the library school. Andy and I had brought it into being and were like brothers. To guide the school into the rapidly approaching computer age, we had recruited Robert Hayes from industry and an earlier UCLA doctorate in mathematics. A campus parking permit was the opening lure, at least that's what Bob says. These men and women were ready and able to lead UCLA to a brilliant future, a future in which I had no place except as a founder-father figure. No longer was I what I had been for thirty years: the right man in the right place at the right time. *That* was really why I left when I did, with a sense of timing that had always served me well. At the same time, I recognized the need for change. No change, no growth.

As we wandered north-northwest past Stonehenge to Hereford and on into Wales, country of my father's people, to the coast at Aberystwyth and north to Bangor and a visit to Charles Mowat, who had returned to his native Britain in protest against the university's redundant loyalty oath.

This anti-Communist oath had been adopted by the Regents upon the advice of the Sacramento lobbyist in order to ensure passage of the university budget. It proved disastrous advice, for the faculty, already having taken a similar oath required of all state employees, rose up in angry protest. Mowat was one of several, including historian John Walton Caughey, who resigned rather than sign. After a year of divisive bitterness the courts ruled the special oath to be unconstitutional.

I recalled the opportunities for service elsewhere that had come after the announcement of my retirement: to the University of Arizona as consultant to the president on libraries and library education; to the same at the University of New Mexico; to head the library of Eastern New Mexico in Portales; to Hawaii to organize a new library school on the Big Island and to Alberta to do the same in Edmonton. To all but one I said no thanks. To it I said later.

Charles and Jo Mowat lived in the country a few miles east of Bangor. He now taught history in the University of North Wales where their son and daughter were enrolled. Charles was one of my earliest UCLA supporters. A group of us Young Turks had formed a monthly discussion group of which he was the secretary and leading dissenter. Jo too was English, also a native of Bristol, kindly beneath a stern exterior.

Rain beat on the slate roof of their cottage as we regaled the Mowats with the latest UCLA news and gossip while son John plied me with questions about Henry Miller, of whose scandalous books his parents and sister were safely ignorant. (Our friendship went back to 1931 when I was a student in Dijon at the Faculty of Letters and Miller was the *répétiteur d'anglais* at the Lycée Carnot, living out that miserable winter described in *Tropic of Cancer*.) We were also encouraged by them to take up indefinite residence in England.

The next day we drove over Telford's Menai Suspension Bridge to Anglesey and on to the westernmost point where at Holyhead we watched the mail steamer for Ireland disappear into the mist. Only later did I learn that the opulent seat of the Marquess of Anglesey, Plas Newydd, held a large mural painted by Rex Whistler whose work we had collected at the Clark Library. In Bangor we stayed at the Castle Hotel with every comfort except hot water and heat. Bedtime reading was in *Pierre*, a Melville novel not meant to raise a writer's spirits.

Taking the car out of the garage the next morning, we had our first encounter with a Great Pyrenees dog, a scary sight.

En route to London we stopped in Chester for lunch, then in Shrewsbury and Broadway for two nights. At the latter Cotswold village we luxuriated at the Lygon Arms, an inn of comfort and concern, free of ostentation, finding food and warmth which had been scarce during our stay in the post-war austerity of 1950.

At Rodney House in Dolphin Square we were welcomed as former residents of 1960 and 1963. Flat 620 overlooked the great courtyard garden around which the Houses, all named for British admirals, formed the square. Bedroom, sitting room, bath, and kitchen made up our quarters, with daily maid service. A ground floor arcade held the dry and greengrocers, Lloyds Bank, cleaners, and other shops. There was a large swimming tank overlooked by the Blue Pool restaurant, while underneath the building was a garage and petrol station. The 134 bus line terminated out front. Victoria Station and the BOAC terminal were nearby. The River Thames was just outside the square to the south. We were under the approach to Heathrow as planes landed into the prevailing west wind. When we did not hear them, it meant the wind was from the east or the airport was closed because of fog.

We unpacked and while Fay took the lift down for milk, coffee, bread and butter, veg and salad, I stretched out on my bed, turned on the BBC and heard sonatas by Enesco and Milhaud, then Bernstein's haunting *Chichester Psalms*, and felt an ineffable sense of well being.

It did not last. Fay came back up laden with carrying bags, one of which contained mail held at the desk. It included a letter from Bill Targ. His rejection of my manuscript was absolute. It lacked, he said, all that I had deliberately omitted: drama and tension. It was not the kind of book he was used to and had gone right over his head.

I kept my disappointment from Fay and almost from myself. Targ had been wonderfully supportive on the three books we had done together, yet now I realized I could no longer count on him. I was nevertheless determined to see the book in print however long and as many rejections it took, not knowing that it had another decade to wait until it was published by Noel Young's Capra Press in 1977.

Remembering his 1941 letter, I wrote to Henry Miller in Pacific Palisades to ask if I might use it as an introduction or an afterword. I enclosed a copy of his letter. His reply came by return mail, more than making up for Targ's rejection.

"Anyway, pay no attention to negative criticism, even if from people you believe in," Miller wrote. "Just believe in yourself—completely. Avanti! Fuck the critics, editors and their ilk. I do remember the warm sensuous feel of your book. You'll never lose that. And if I may say so, don't go for perfection. Turn out one after another—time is short. You have dozens of books in you. Bless you, my dear Larry."

He ended by suggesting several publishers, including one in London.

Even before this exchange of letters, I had begun to write the other book that had yielded place to my French novella. Before leaving UCLA I had gone through my files and made a rough outline of an autobiography. On my 60TH birthday, the third of September 1966, the day after we arrived at Dolphin Square, I took a yellow pad and my yellow Scripto and began what became *Fortune and Friendship*, an account of my boyhood, youth, and manhood to June 30, 1966. The flow was unbroken. I missed only one day when we were at my niece and husband's country house at Barkham Square, fifty miles west of London in Berkshire.

She was Marcia, my late brother Clark's daughter, who had married Guy Lawrence and thenceforth made her life in England. She had come to us in Westwood after the war, with her younger brother David, after living through the Blitz. She called me her Wicked Uncle. Soft-spoken Guy, whose manner hid his decorations as an RAF Wing Captain of Wellington bombers, gave her the security lost with her father's death when she was eleven. With her soft English speech, fair skin, green eyes and copper-colored hair, she was taken for an Englishwoman, although born in Berkeley during my brother's senior year in Agriculture. She retained her American citizenship and passport. Guy had risen to be managing director of Lyons, the great British food and restaurant company whose overseas holdings included Baskin-Robbins' 31 Flavors. He was eventually knighted for his service to the government's food program.

By the end of September a first draft was done, and I mailed it off to UCLA where Marian Ellithorpe's familiarity with my handwriting enabled her to make a typed copy. Back it came for me to correct, and by the time we had returned home for Christmas it was ready for Eric Moon (its only begetter) to approve and John Berry, editor of the *Library Journal*, to ready for publication in 1968.

Freedom from responsibility and telephone calls, plus uninterrupted mornings, the first I had known since student years, made it possible to draft the book in less than a month without benefit of notes. It was written in the reading room of the Westminster Central Reference Library and in quiet rooms of the National Gallery on Trafalgar Square and in Forte's coffee bar at the top of the Haymarket.

Although I dedicated it "To Fay, then, now and always," it didn't please her. I had avoided reference to any crises in our long marriage—it was not intended as a personal account any more than this one is—and also took liberties in emphasis and chronology. No two people however closely their lives are linked ever see or say things the same way. Some of what I left out, I later made into allegorical fiction. The book's only other hostile reader was a pseudonymous reviewer who castigated me for not being what I wasn't. I never answered any critic. As for Fay, we took each other for better and for worse, and as everyone knows, I got the best, she the worst.

We were soon back in the English rhythm, spending afternoons and evenings at galleries and concerts and on walks along the riverbank, and in renewing old friendships with booksellers Winifred Myers, Alan Thomas, Stanley and Sally Smith, Harold and Olive Edwards, Bertram and Anthony Rota, Arnold and Dorothy Muirhead, and Ruth Collis; and also with librarians, especially Sir Frank Francis and his wife Kitty.

Sir Frank was high among my library "heroes." As director and principal librarian of the British Museum he embodied qualities I admired the most of bookish administrator, administrative bookman, with freedom from snobbishness. As a visitor to the UCLA library school he won the students by his friendly manner and keen mind. In 1963 he brought together for me in a luncheon at the Museum, England's leading Mozartians, including his predecessor, C. B. Oldman, and Alec Hyatt-King, head of the Museum's music division. After lunch King showed me such treasures as Mozart's manuscript catalog of his own work, beginning with K.449, and the manuscripts of his last ten string quartets including the six dedicated to his musical blood brother, Haydn. In 1966 Winnie Myers, dean of British antiquarian booksellers and one of our dearest English friends, presented me with an inscribed set of Emily Anderson's translation of Mozart's letters. Before she could arrange for me to meet Miss Anderson, that rare civil servant-musicologist died.

In my final years as director of the Clark Library I had concentrated on rounding out two collections begun twenty years earlier—on sculptor-illustrator-typographer Eric Gill and on poet W. B. Yeats. In the autumn of 1965 we held a Clark gathering in *Homage to Yeats* to honor his 100TH birthday. From Leeds we brought the Irish critic Norman Jeffares to speak on the women in Yeats's poetry, while UCLA provided Walter Starkie on Yeats and the Abbey Theatre. It was also my thanks for what his poetry had meant to me. Such poems as "After Long Silence" had become part of my own creative being. His *Letters on Poetry to Dorothy Wellesley*, in the copy once belonging to Hugh Walpole and bearing that novelist's poignant inscription "This beautiful book born dead in the war," was among my most precious things which I gave to the Library that day.

Now using the Gill bibliography, I sought out public works

carved by him. The figures of Prospero and Ariel at Broadcasting House and the Stations of the Cross in Westminster Cathedral (not Abbey), enthralled me. Earlier in the cathedral at Hereford I had seen a memorial tablet whose lettering convinced me that it had been cut by Gill. Only later did I learn that the artist was David Kindersley, Gill's last apprentice.

The quest for Yeats which in 1950 had yielded some rare acquisitions for the Clark led this time to a pilgrimage to his grave in the west of Ireland.

We flew to Dublin early in October on an Aer Lingus four-motor Vanguard turbo-prop, arriving short of the terminal in a driving rainstorm. Upon gaining shelter we were handed towels to dry off and were soon at Buswell's Hotel in Molesworth Street, cozy in the lounge with a coal fire and hot tea.

The next morning we hired a VW 1300 and set out on the 130-mile drive to the West. The rain had passed through and probably settled down over Dolphin Square. The sky was pale blue and the land bright green, the roads narrow, the traffic light. Farmers were carting their milk to the cooperative dairy. Lines from Yeats were jumbled in my memory. This was his native land. After a good nine shilling lunch in Longford and crossing River Shannon, we reached the Great Southern Hotel in Sligo late in the afternoon, checked in and went straightway to nearby Drumcliff churchyard.

I have never concealed my liking for necrological pilgrimages when the buried is a writer or musician, and I confess to being deeply moved as we entered the churchyard. The day was ending with a last burst of golden light. A cold east wind made us glad of Burberrys dating from 1950. We found his grave in a narrow flowerless bed of clean gravel, his name and dates and own epitaph cut in a plain limestone headstone—*Cast a cold eye on life, on death, Horseman, pass by.*

Inside the church a guest book was nearly full with names and places from around the world—Capetown, Panama, Halifax, Hong Kong, to which we added Malibu, all pilgrims drawn by the power of one poet, the man dead since 1939, his work untouched by time. All I could remember of Auden's elegy was "Earth, receive an honored guest, William Yeats is laid to rest." And there above us was bare Ben Bulben's head.

The next day was also devoted to Yeats's memory. We slept late, then set out on a cold gray morning and took the long way to Galway, along the sea road by Ballina and Castlebar, through stony sheep country, a poor green-gray land, the sky threatening but no rain. In Galway we had a delicious late lunch in another railway hotel. There we bought a butterscotch-colored throw rug which we still have.

Nearing Gort I saw the road sign Coole and turned off along a narrow rocky lane through fields to the forest reserve and the ruins of the great house of Lady Gregory, utterly torn down and gone, the gray park walls still standing—trees, shrubs, flowers and creepers, a riot of green in the rain which began to fall as we walked about. We found the huge beech tree whereon the writers had carved their names, now ringed with a high iron grill to prevent vandalism, and heard the whistling of a forest worker and the ring of his axe, and birdsong—and no ghost of the great lady whose house had been a creative sanctuary for Yeats.

At Gort another sign directed us four miles to Thoor Ballylee, restored the year before for the centenary by the Irish Tourist Board, now in charge of a pretty and intelligent Irish girl, dark-haired, rosy-cheeked and blue-eyed. We climbed the circular staircase, pausing on each level to read words of Yeats framed on the wall, and finally to the top, open to the sky with a wide view on the rainy green gray countryside. No one else was there. The season was due to end next week. We had come just in time. I told the girl I would send her the booklet of the Clark's homage to Yeats.

As darkness began to fall, we drove on fifteen miles in the rain to Ennis and a friendly hotel, seeing the cows being driven in at day's end.

Back in Dublin we did the usual sightseeing: Trinity College and the Book of Kells, opened that day, alas, to one of the plain pages in the Book of Luke. In the Municipal Gallery we saw the portraits of all the great ones, including Lady Gregory. In a bank I bought a set of the Irish coinage sponsored by Senator Yeats, the silver and copper coins in a little velvet-lined box: fish, cock, bull, horse, dog, stork, rabbit. To spend? Nay. For the Yeats collection at the Clark, even as Professor Majl Ewing had once brought us a tile from the poet's tower.

That night propped up in bed I read in one of the Jeffares paperbacks of Yeats poetry and prose, these lines from "Coole Park, 1929" in memory of our visit to there:

> Here, traveller, scholar, poet, take your stand
> When all these rooms and passages are gone,
> When nettles wave upon a shapeless mound
> And saplings root among the broken stone;
> And dedicate—eyes bent upon the ground,
> Back turned upon the brightness of the sun
> And all the sensuality of the shade—
> A moment's memory to that laurelled head.*

Before flying back to London we did final shopping in the Irish Cottage Industries shop where Fay bought a coat and skirt of rough green wool, a spidery white scarf, a white Cossack-style hat, and a winter coat of creamy white Donegal tweed. My shopping was for several narrow neckties of mixed autumn-colored woolens. Them I still wear whether wide ties are in or out.

It became clear in spite of the idyllic six weeks of carefree relaxation, that ties with my past were still there, only waiting for time and circumstance to pull them taut. First came an overseas telegram from Paul Horgan, director of the Center for Advanced Studies at Wesleyan University in Connecticut, offering a year's residence fellowship. In earlier correspondence with him and Wyman Parker, librarian of Wesleyan, and in meetings with Horgan in Santa Fe, I knew that such an offer was forthcoming. Now it was for a college house and a study at the Center, a seminar in Southwest literature if I chose to

---

*The Winding Stair and Other Poems, Macmillan, 1933.

teach, and a generous salary. He hoped I would come the next year.

I had to reply that 1967 was to be given over to writing *California Book Trails*, a companion volume to the one on the Southwest I had written in 1963, and to be funded by my second Guggenheim fellowship. Could it wait until 1968 and then for only the spring semester which was as long as we wanted to be away from Malibu? The answer was Yes, followed by a formal offer from President Victor Butterfield. Thus did our future begin to take shape.

Our next involvement early in November was a trip to Zagreb to speak to a meeting of the Croatian Library Association. This came from the presence at UCLA in 1963/64 of Dr. Lela Markić, librarian of the School of Public Health at the University of Zagreb. She had come at the behest of Louise Darling to work in the Biomedical Library and take courses in the library school from Seymour Lubetzky, Andrew Horn, and me. She was an attractive 40ish woman with graying black hair, dark eyes and ivory skin, and a fluent command of English and French.

During her last week before returning to Yugoslavia I had asked Dr. Markić to address the school on her year with us. This she did with quiet eloquence. When it came time to say goodbye she said sadly, "I don't suppose we'll ever meet again for you'll never come to my faraway country."

"Ask me," I heard myself saying as I kissed her cheek, "and you'll find out."

A year later when she heard from Louise Darling that I would be spending the rest of 1966 in London, Lela Markić did indeed ask me and I agreed to come.

So there we were aboard a Swissair flight to Zurich where we were due to lay over before a Yugoslav plane to Zagreb. We had hoped to spend the few hours on a taxi ride around Zurich, our favorite Swiss city where I had taken delivery of a VW in 1960 and a Porsche in 1963. Alas, we were confined to the transit lounge.

After a two-hour flight over a tumult of snowy Alps we

were met by Dr. Markić and her sturdy black-haired husband, another Croatian and a government lawyer. We dined that night in their small book-filled flat while he played Yugoslav folk songs and occasionally broke into song. We loved their Irish setters, Beba and Bijou, mother and son, affectionate sleek red-coated animals with wistful brown eyes. Quite a flatful!

The next day was All Saints and as we toured Zagreb in a government car we saw thousands on the way to deck graves with flowers. We also saw Marshall Tito's villa and the School of Public Health named for its founder, Andrea Stampara. We were accompanied by Professor Bozo Tezać, a chemist in the Institute of Physical Sciences, passionately interested in the new library information sciences and also in a museum of scientific progress in transportation machinery. He was in addition the editor of the Yugoslav *Chemical Abstracts*.

When he pointed out the statue of Tesla in front of the Institute and said it was by Ivan Mestrović, I ventured that I had admired that sculptor's work in the Art Institute of Chicago. Whereupon Professor Tezać lit up even brighter and after a bear hug drove us to the Mestrović museum housed in his former studio, bare, austere, and beautiful, filled with noble works in wood, stone, and bronze, and a piece in marble of lovers in embrace, reminiscent of the Gill erotica I had bought for the Clark Library and kept in a closet away from improper viewers.

Later I learned that five years earlier and within a period of only nine months, Professor Tezać had lost his wife and two sons by suicide, accident, and disease. Whereupon he married a graduate student protégée and they had two children. I was impressed by the big dynamic man of my age, not knowing that he was doomed to die of cancer . . . but not before we met again in California and later in Arizona.

My talk was given in the university's Faculty Club lounge to a gathering of librarians from around Croatia—given in English to be sure, with a running translation by Dr. Markić. I called my talk "The Three H's," meaning head, heart, and hands, the essentials of good librarianship. In an acknowledgement given in English by the city librarian of Zagreb, she said that they had never before heard such an address in either content or delivery, having always been addressed by technicians or historians and not by a humanistic spokesman who reached from heart to heart and mind to mind.

Before going to sleep that night at our station hotel to the sound of steam engines—the Simplon Orient Express, remembered from Dijon years, passes through Zagreb, gateway to the Balkans—I wished someone at the Ford Foundation, with the vision of the Carnegie people who in 1937 had brought Wilhelm Munthe from Norway to make a talking swing around the USA, would send me around the world as a kind of roving library spokesman to librarians everywhere, transcending barriers of language and custom to reach the common ground of bibliobrotherhood. Of course such never came to pass, as matters of organization, techniques, networking, and bibliographical control took center stage and have stayed there. In darker moments I fear I shall not live to see the revival of humanistic librarianship.

Dr. Markić's husband had arranged for us to fly to Dubrovnik for a couple of days of sightseeing. I was eager to see the old Roman town on the Dalmatian coast. Two years earlier in Honolulu in the Bishop Museum we had seen watercolors by Whistler of sailboats on the water at Ragusa, now given its Slavic name.

After an hour's flight we arrived after dark of a cold windy night. A rough bus ride over cobbled roads took us to the town square, thence by taxi to the waterfront Hotel Excelsior, a rambling luxury resort now nearly empty at the season's end. A sleepy waiter rustled up sandwiches and milk for our supper. We slept to the sound of the Adriatic against the seawall and thunder in the distance.

We awoke to sun and blue sky, a view of the ancient walled town and a green wooded island out to sea. They had arranged for a young woman guide with excellent English and French. After a morning tour we were left to our own devices. We took a sundown walk along the seawall to the old town. Its short main street, paved with great limestone flags and closed to all vehicles, was the most beautiful street we had ever seen. Lined with small shops and lit by old-fashioned electroliers, it breathed a timeless peace. We bought two red apples and at a little sidewalk cafe peeled and ate them with wine for Fay and café au lait for me. Across the way an apothecary shop held lighted jars of colored water. In another window of a small museum we saw an 18th-century piano by Stein, the very make played upon by Mozart. It was the perfect ending to our stay.

Flying back with a brief stopover in Zagreb we were met by Lela Markić for another fond goodbye. "Meet us someday at the top of the Spanish Steps," I said to her. "It's only a short flight across the Adriatic to Rome." "Alas," she replied, "it is difficult to leave my job and so expensive." We have kept in touch by letter these twenty years and who knows, might yet keep that rendezvous. She is a dear woman and an ideal librarian.

We made a brief stopover in Paris. Winter had arrived that very day and the city was under the earliest snowfall in a hundred years. We called on C. F. MacIntyre, beloved teacher-poet of our Occidental years, bedridden six years from a stroke, now nearly speechless and tearful. He died a year later. His archives at UCLA continue to grow. I once planned to edit his life in letters. Above the fireplace in Jeffers' Tor House is carved these words: "Time and I against any two." Alas, Time will not fight on my side.

Fay and I were back once more in Paris where we had first been together thirty-six years before, older now, wiser and sadder, yet still together. Again we lunched at Lipp's, finding it as good as ever, on lettuce and cucumber salad, thick carrot and leek soup, roast lamb and white beans; a demi-brune for Fay, a demi-Vittel for me.

Flying back to London on a BEA Vanguard, it was reassuring to hear the crisp cool speech of the blonde stewardess as we came in over a sea of overcast, breaking through to glimpse golden woods, winding river, and the four streaming stacks of the Battersea Power Station, upriver from Dolphin Square.

An accumulation of mail included a cable from UCLA's

Chancellor Murphy and Librarian Vosper saying that the Regents had given my name to the original library building. Thus was fulfilled an epiphany of April 1936 on my first visit to that great Lombardy Romanesque building, when I wrote that night in my journal "This is my place."

Two months had passed since we left California, during which I had lived at my usual pace of writing, speaking, and traveling. Now after returning from the stimulation of Ireland, Yugoslavia, and France, I felt let down. I waited impatiently for the typescript from home so that I could resume work toward another draft. Unfinished business disturbed my compulsiveness to get things done. I needed constant activity of mind and body to keep up my spirits.

Yet I felt no enthusiasm for an impending visit to the Welsh National library school at Aberystwyth. On its faculty was a former English town librarian and library columnist, J. F. W. Bryon, whom I had met at Harrogate in 1957 when I gave the Library Association Annual Lecture. When he heard earlier in 1966 that I would be in England, he had an invitation extended to spend a couple of days at the school meeting with students and faculty. It was scheduled for the last week in November, and on December 1 we were due to fly to Lisbon and on to Madeira before returning home for Christmas.

As the time neared I felt depressed by the prospect of the day long train ride to the Welsh coast. I came close to cancelling because of ill health, although all I had was mild bronchitis. Fay gave me no encouragement.

And so off I went to Paddington station and the Cambrian Express to Aberystwyth via Birmingham and Shrewsbury. The autumn countryside was beautiful as we entered the Welsh hills and followed the Severn up near its source and on over the mountains to Cardigan Bay on the Irish Sea. All day long I lay back, not even reading, gazed out the window and dozed. The only other occupant of the compartment was a girl who read a book, with occasional wary looks my way. Neither spoke a word. By day's end when John Bryon met me at the end of the line, I felt rested and ready.

That evening was spent in the students' lounge bar and games room in the lower depths of the old building. It was jumping with young life as I was steered among the men and women students by Bryon and his principal, Frank Hogg, and their attractive young librarian, Philip Corrigan. The students seemed to be more English, Scottish, and Irish than Welsh. My patronym was explained by me as that of a 17TH-century Quaker dissenter who fled into Devonshire where he captured an Englishwoman and embarked for America.

In their responsiveness those students were of the best. It was great fun and ultimately tiring. I was not up to par. My windowless room in the misnamed Belle Vue Hotel was the size of a large telephone booth. I passed a claustrophobic night thinking of home and Fay. I went down for early morning tea and asked to be moved to a windowed room for the second night.

That morning I rallied and spoke for an hour to the entire class of two hundred, followed by a coffee break and a final hour of Q and A. From where I spoke, my view was across a rocky hill to the site of an Iron Age fort. I was close to my roots.

I kept feeling stronger as the time passed, at home in the ideas and language of a common heritage shared with the present generation. It proved to be one of the best of many such experiences I have had in America, Europe, and Asia, and I knew again that mine was a lifelong commitment to librarianship.

The students surprised me with a keepsake made on their own press. It was a gathering of things said about me by Henry Miller in his books, thanking me for what I had done to feed his insatiable appetite for books. There was also a faculty luncheon attended by the principal of the university and the county and the national librarians, after which Bryon took me to see the monumental National Library on a rocky eminence overlooking the town and bay.

That night at a farewell dinner with Messrs Hogg, Bryon, and Corrigan I was invited to join them as a visiting lecturer for as long as I wished to stay. Although they and the students were warm and attractive, Aberystwyth was not. I am essentially a Mediterranean, and of both shores, civilized and desert, of that inland sea.

I left the next morning on a local train that connected in Shrewsbury with the Glasgow-London Express. It was a little train of few cars drawn by a hard-working steam engine whose hoarse exhaust gave me nostalgic pleasure. I was told that it was the last run of that faithful old engine before being replaced by a Diesel with a smooth exhaust.

In Shrewsbury there was time only for a ham sandwich and tea before the London train arrived. It made a fast run with one stop in Birmingham. As we passed through Princes Risborough, Marcia and Guy Lawrence's first home in England where Fay and I nearly froze to death in the winter of 1950, I caught a glimpse of the Whiteleaf Cross cut in the side of Bledlow Ridge, while on the other side of the train were the beechwooded Chiltern hills.

Fay and hot tea welcomed me home that night, mission accomplished. Some day I shall play the recording the students sent me of that session spent in lively communication, and will remember our great day.

Much was packed into the last days before leaving for Portugal. At the Lawrences in Barkham Square I took long walks along an oak-lined country road, puzzling over what to do next. I kept pressing Fay to consider moving to England to a cottage fifty miles from London on a fast train line, and yet I knew that I needed more worldly engagement. Ambivalent I surely was. In London we saw the film of Nureyev and Fonteyn in Prokoviev's *Romeo and Juliet*, and again I marvelled at the man's panther grace. The doom-laden bitter-sweet music gave me goose bumps while the hair rose on my neck. At the Royal Ballet we saw productions of *Apollo* and *Petrushka*, with their heart-shaking scores by Stravinsky, and at Covent Garden heard Krips conduct *Don Giovanni*. So close were we to the pit that I could see the sweat drip from his brow, and so ravishing is Mozart's orchestra that I found myself listening to it, not to the voices. Winnie Myers gave a farewell supper for us at The Ivy, attended by Harold and Olive Edwards and Dudley Massey.

Upon Henry Miller's suggestion I had submitted my novella manuscript to Calder and Boyars. Weeks passed and I heard nothing. Now on our last day in London I sought out their office in Soho. Mrs. Boyars was vague as to my identity and the manuscript's whereabouts. When she finally unearthed it, obviously unread, with the explanation that they were oversupplied with fiction, I took it and slipped away. I vowed to submit it no more, perhaps privately printing it in Holland and letting it make its own way as I knew it would.

After Fay went to bed that night, I took a turn around the square and along the Thames. Everywhere were lighted windows and the smell of woodsmoke. Traffic was quiet. Now and then a riverboat whistled. An east wind was creaming off the smoke from the Battersea stacks. I paused in my walk to listen to Big Ben strike ten, at the same time inwardly hearing the music of Vaughan Williams' *London Symphony*.

I was on dead center, eager to move off, to return home via Portugal and resume work on the autobiography and the book trails book, and go on to the spring of 1968 in Connecticut. I realized that I should not have sent the autobiography back to California for a typed second draft, but instead kept it close at hand, either making a typed revision myself or employing a London typist. I had not brought the Olivetti portable my last UCLA class had given me, and no one in all wide London could have coped with my handwriting. I learned then never to break the flow when writing something that completely engaged me until it was finished. That lapse in the continuity of ideas and the second rejection of the novella further dragged on my usual high spirits.

I knew now that having left the academic milieu which had been mine for three decades, I needed always to be gripped by something beyond myself. Nor could I settle in some remote place unless I were at the same time moved by an idea, a project, a goal. My having zipped in and out of Ireland, Yugoslavia, and Wales was not enough.

The prospect of Portugal, California, and Connecticut was quieting. Perhaps Portugal would prove the place I was seeking. I returned to the flat and slept soon and well.

II

WIND AND RAIN marked departure the next day from London Airport. The TAP Caravelle climbed steeply through the cloud cover and flew above it all the way to Portugal then slipped through a rift in the weather to land neatly at Lisbon airport.

We were in Portugal, fabled Lusitania, a fulfilment of years of desire, composed of various elements. The maritime discoverer of California was a Portuguese—João Rodrigues Cabrilho. He had probably learned navigation in the celebrated school at Sagres, in the lee of Cape St. Vincent, founded by Prince Henry the Navigator, who had sailed for Spain as Juan Rodriguez Cabrillo.

That was the historical lure of the Cape. The poetical came from Browning, his "Home Thoughts from the Sea," and its opening line, "Nobly, nobly Cape St. Vincent to the Northwest died away," and from Fernando Pessoa, the shadowy Lisbon poet, who wrote under various names in several languages, including English. I cherish a copy of his *English Poems*, given to me long ago by Richard Aldington, with its sensuous "Epithalamium," one of the most beautiful wedding poems in our language.

Lisbon was one of the few European capitals I had never seen. It is like no other. We spent our first week there in mild weather, becoming accustomed to the speech, the rhythm, and the ambiance of a new way of life, finding the Portuguese people cordial and honest. Overpayment to such varied personages as a taxi driver, a waiter in the Hotel Ritz, and a street peddler of bananas, resulted each time in the mistake being pointed out and the coins returned to me.

I brought with me no judgment of the Salazar regime. Personal indignation felt by a foreigner over another country's social and economic system seems to me a waste of emotion. As a student in France a generation earlier, I was naturally involved in various social judgments. Coming now to Portugal as a middle-aged traveler, I felt free to look and listen, to use my senses and my wits to guide me each day as we walked and rode about Lisbon, admiring the public monuments to men of arts and letters as well as to military and political figures. The sidewalks are paved in mosaic patterns of colored limestone pebbles. Streets are cobbled. Taxis are a uniform fleet of Mercedes 180 Diesels, their characteristic knock Lisbon's leitmotiv.

Lisbon is hills and harbor, served by a wide central boulevard with swan pools and papyrus, off which run narrow curving streets and alleys, all dropping eventually to the waterfront, to Lisbon's noble harbor, the wide estuary of the Tagus, ocean's end of the river we had last seen three years before in Spain, where it all but enisles Toledo.

We watched a string of barges arrive from upriver and tie up at a dock. They were full of yellow wheat. A team of dockers with shovels began to sack the grain, then carry the heavy sacks on their shoulders to a scale where a weighmaster entered each one in an open ledger. Then the sacks were loaded into little freight cars. Automation had not reached the Lisbon waterfront.

Farther along the embankment is the monastery church with the tombs of Camões and Vasco de Gama; the Museum of Coaches, an assemblage of eighteenth-century vehicles gorgeously gilded and painted; and nearby, the monument to Prince Henry the Navigator and his followers, a colossal work of concrete and stone sculpture erected in 1960 on the 500TH anniversary of the Navigator's death.

Near this harbor point is the new bridge over the Tagus, Europe's longest suspension bridge. Until it opened in August, 1966, bridging the estuary for the first time, the only way across to the south had been by auto ferry or a three-hour drive upriver to the first bridge.

"Heading south?" they asked incredulously when we hired a Volkswagen and inquired the way from city center to the Tagus bridge. "Tourists always head north."

"My destination is Lagos, Sagres, and Cape St. Vincent," I insisted. "Not Estoril, Coimbra, or Oporto."

"But therés nothing down there. No cultural centers. Only sand, sheep, and sardines."

"And the Prince's ghost," I said, heading south from Lisbon.

The road follows the ridges and valleys of the first range of hills from the Atlantic shore, through forests of eucalyptus and cork oak, the ocean far below on the right and in the east the distant blue sierra between Portugal and Spain. Traffic was light. There are few towns and villages. The flora changes to olive, fig, and almond, orange, and lemon. Sandy earth turns red. Whitewashed, flat-topped farm houses, trimmed in blue, show the Moorish influence. The peasants' carts bear colorful decorations. This is the province of Algarve, from the Moorish, meaning The West.

The Atlantic is reached at Lagos (lagoon), and there on the waterfront is another monument to Prince Henry, depicting the seated Navigator looking over the harbor where his caravels once anchored. It too was dedicated on the anniversary in 1960. A wide sandy beach curves east from Lagos eight miles to Portomaio, a strand strewn with clam and scallop shells—and no people. Here and there sardine boats are beached. They too are brightly decorated. Our hotel was the Meia Praia—the Middle Beach—and in early December there were more employees than guests. Meals were served with courteous elegance. The seafood was varied and cooked within hours of catching. Royalty could not have fared better.

Eastward forty miles to Faro, the capital, the coast of Algarve becomes rockier. The most fashionable resort is Praia de Rocha, but even it has none of the *luxe* that marks the French Riviera. It was still a comparatively unspoiled coast. Back from the beaches the land rises to hills and low mountains, the Sierra Monchique. Fig, citrus, and almond orchards yield to carob groves and then cork oak. The heavy red soil is fertile. Most of the farming is still done with primitive equipment.

Time has lightly touched this sheltered coast. The Moors have long since been driven back across the Atlantic to Africa. Their ancient stronghold of Silves is on a hill a few miles from the shore. It looks like a cubist painter's dream of a city, geometrically formed and planed, all dazzling white with blue and pink tile roofs and a great fortress with an underground reservoir to hold a year's water in case of siege.

We explored no further than Silves, pausing there to look back over the cultivated coast to the rocky beaches and the fishing harbor at Portomaio and the long sandy *praia* sweeping west to Lagos. We cast a longing eye inland and higher to the sierra, where the book on Algarve by David Wright and Patrick Swift describes remote villages of unchanged customs and almost tropical verdure.

Our compass pointed west, magnetized by the cape we had come to see. We drove there on a cool day of the prevailing northerly. Our goal lay about fifteen miles from Lagos through more of the rich red soil planted mostly to figs. The old trees were winter bare, their silvery limbs like sprawling spiders. The approach to the cape is by the small town of Sagres. It was there that Prince Henry's monastic school was located.

The cape is a couple of miles northward across a small bay. It is a rocky headland, the basalt cliffs rising sheer two hundred feet from the ocean. There is deep water everywhere, and shipping comes in close as it turns the corner to and from the Mediterranean. *Aqui é o fim do mundo*, the Portuguese declare. Here is the end of the world. The ancient appellation of Cape St. Vincent was Promontorium Sacrum, the Sacred Cape, from which Sagres derives its name. Here at the final limit of the world, the gods were supposed to rest at night after the labors of the day. The cape owes its present name to the legend that it was here that the corpse of St. Vincent, an Iberian martyr who died in 304, was washed up by the sea.

And here is Europe's farthest southwest. It is where the Navigator lived for the last forty years of his life and trained his sailors in that art of navigation which led, after his death, to the discovery and development of the whole wide world. Vasco de Gama, Cabral, Magellan, and Columbus, that Italian married to a Portuguese and sailing for Spain—these and others owed their discoveries and fame to the sciences correlated and taught in the Prince's cosmopolitan school.

Cabrillo either studied at Sagres a generation after Henry's death, or was taught by someone who had; and so there is that link between Cape St. Vincent and California, discovered by Cabrillo in 1542. Little is known of him, other than what is in the log of his voyage, and his death in 1543 and probable burial on the island of San Miguel off the coast at Santa Barbara.

I stood in the wind on the prow of the headland, trying to remember all of Browning's lines. The only building is the lighthouse. A flock of brown and black goats browsed to the edge, some even surefooting over in search of the tiny foliage in the crevices. The long Atlantic swell rose and fell on the cape's ankle. We counted eight ships turning the southwest corner. Those heading north plunged their bows deep in the swell, lifted, plunged, lifted, all in a slow rhythm with the elements. Seabirds screamed overhead. I felt nostalgia for the sea voyages of my youth, and sensed many ghostly presences, all friendly.

Back in Lisbon we continued to ignore the cultured north and went even farther south than Algarve. On a windy, rainy afternoon we took a TAP Constellation flight to Funchal, capital of Madeira, the volcanic island off the coast of Spanish Morocco. It was discovered in 1418 by a caravel expedition sent out from Lagos by Prince Henry. Now it came on the horizon as cumulus clouds over the peaks, then red rock steeps, heavily wooded (Madeira means wood), and on the westward side intricately terraced and farmed.

The airstrip is a new one, carved out of a ledge near the sea, and the approach is over deep blue water. Funchal is fifteen miles distant by taxi along a narrow cliff road, snaking in and out of canyons which indent the plunging mountainside. The vegetation is dense and colorful. Portugal's bananas come from Madeira. The trellised vines that produce the celebrated wine were bare, and carrots and potatoes were being raised beneath the arbors. Funchal is built in a great natural amphitheater rising from harbor to peak, a conglomeration of colored stuccos and greenery. The earliest settlers from Portugal fired the woods to make a clearing. The resulting conflagration raged over the island for seven years. The volcanic soil thus enriched by ashes is responsible for the present riot of vegetation.

We stayed in the Savoy Hotel, built in 1900 and still offering amenities of the Victorian age. The dining room is of great beauty, paneled in white and green and gold, with a mezzanine all the way around. Multi-course meals were served formally, each table having a carrying waiter and a serving waiter. We counted thirty-five guests and twenty-two waiters. Again the seafood was of delicious variety and freshness. The chef has been at the Savoy for forty-five years, we were told, and is aided by twenty sub-chefs. An orchestra plays for concert and dancing.

The Portuguese of Madeira are as courteous and honest as their kinfolk at home. Tourism has miraculously left them unspoiled. After a sightseeing tour we settled into a quiet routine, the high point of which was the afternoon walk to the harbor to see what ships were in. Funchal is a port of call for the Union Castle Line between England and South Africa and for Portuguese liners between Lisbon and Brazil. They stop only for a few hours. Passengers go ashore and buy lace, basketry, wine, and bananas. A ship from Rio was passengered with every shade of colored folk, lively and laughing. An English motor yacht was in, taking the long way back from Gibraltar to Southampton. The deck officer allowed that the crew was homesick, hoping the owner would change her plan to stay in Funchal for the New Year's Eve fireworks.

A friend at home had charged me to search the English Cemetery for the grave of Emily Shore, one of the many English consumptives who died in Madeira during the first half of the nineteenth century. Her diary was published fifty years after her death in 1842. My friend had read it and wondered if her grave could be found.

First I had to find the cemetery. Up the hill from the harbor was the general direction given me. And so up the hill I trudged along a curving, cobbled street, dwellings and garden walls on each side of such height as to prevent me from taking bearings. Then I saw a clue: several tall Italian cypresses. I threaded and climbed until I came to the high wall behind which the trees were growing. And a locked gate. It was the cemetery. I pulled the bell cord and waited a long while. Finally a young man came, bowed, smiled, and let me in.

I spent an hour in a vain search for Emily Shore's grave. In addition to the cypresses, an ancient pepper tree dominated the graveyard. Shrubs and vines grew in such profusion as to obscure many of the stones and markers. On some the lettering was obliterated. Emily's was probably one of those. I gave up the search and made my way back down hill to the main square. There at a sidewalk café I looked out on the statue of Madeira's discoverer, João Gonsalves Zarco, dispatched from Lagos by Prince Henry to cruise the African coast. In Funchal the Prince takes second place to the island's discoverer—a smaller square, a smaller statue.

The oxen-drawn tourist sleds slid by on the smooth cobbles. Flower and lace peddlers drifted past in courteous solicitation. An urchin shined my shoes for pennies. I studied the shipping news in the weekly paper, as showers of soft rain alternated with sunbursts. Then I saw a double rainbow arching over Funchal.

The good omen heralded our departure on the return flight to Lisbon. We gambled on a punctual arrival, for we had only a forty-five minute interval before the Swissair flight from Zurich and Geneva left for New York. As we landed, we saw the DC-8 taxiing in, a minute ahead of us.

As the great white plane with the Helvetian cross on its tail soared up over the Tagus estuary, our last sight of Lisbon was of the monument to the Navigator and his men and of the noble bridge which had led to Algarve and the Cape. Then swiftly we were over the Atlantic, westbound for America, our ultimate destination and that of Cabrillo, the seacoast of California. *Aqui é o fim do mundo.*

Throughout those two idyllic weeks in Portugal and its enchanted island I realize now that I was unconsciously seeking *the* way to follow in retirement. Should I withdraw from all involvement in the library world and create my own world as a writer—or do what and go where? Fay surely grew tired of hearing the dialogue I was wont to hold with myself. As 1966 came to an end, I knew that more seeking lay ahead before the promised land was reached.

III

WE STAYED IN NEW YORK only long enough to call on Gordon Ray at the Guggenheim Foundation to inform him of my readiness to take up my fellowship and begin work on the California book. What he really wanted to hear was how I'd found the London book market. I had to report that it was my first time there since 1950, that I was not buying books for UCLA and thus had not made my usual rounds. I was now a full-time writer and lecturer and also unsure whether that would be enough to occupy my retirement.

Another call was on Eric Moon, editor of the *Library Journal* and prospective publisher of the autobiography he had persuaded me to write. We discussed illustrations, publication date and I learned that he and his assistant, John Berry, would be rewriting my manuscript enough to keep them from libel suits. I assured him I had mellowed. Then forget it, he said, and let the ALA publish it.

I had come to be fondly admiring of that tough Somersetman who had entered the American scene from Newfoundland to become a conscience voice for us all. As dean of the library school I had sought to lure him from New York to join our faculty. "Not enough action," he said. "I need to be on the firing line." That's where he stayed through his presidency of the ALA, a great mover and shaker. I felt good with my book in his hands, as I do now with this, grateful for his severe and honest criticism. I remembered that during his editorship of *Library Journal* he had persuaded me to write a monthly column called "On the Grindstone" with which he did not always agree, yet never changed.

Next I stopped in at the New York Public Library's Berg Collection to tell John Gordan of my pilgrimage to Sligo, Coole, and Thoor Ballylee. The Clark and the Berg had competed in 1963 for the Lady Gregory papers, and we had lost in a manner that only strengthened the friendship shared by Gordan and me. His death not long after was a cruel loss to the book world. Our friendship went back to 1940 when he and William A. Jackson called on us in Beverly Glen.

That was when Jackson spotted my Steinbeck collection, all fondly autographed by "Salinas John." He said that if I ever wanted to sell it, Harvard paid top prices. I knew he exaggerated, having learned from Jake Zeitlin, today the dean of America's antiquarian booksellers, that Bill was a Yankee bargainer. A year later when my UCLA salary had risen in three years to an even $1800, I sold the Steinbecks to the Houghton Library for $250, enough for a vacation trip to Colorado for Fay and me and the two boys. I also believed that New England would benefit from the cultural cross-fertilization.

We then took the Springfield Express, the New Haven railroad at its worst, to Meriden where we were met by Paul Horgan and driven to nearby Middletown. There we were lodged in a guest apartment at the Center for Advanced Studies for a preview of what we could expect a year hence. We also saw the white colonial house we were to occupy, dined with Paul at his elegant campus residence, the old coach house transformed, and admired his thousands of volumes on belles lettres, art, history and biography. We agreed that a fine year lay ahead for us all.

The next day Horgan drove us back to New York through the snowy woods along the Merritt Parkway. After lunch at the Harvard Club and he and I had withdrawn to the washroom, he surprised me with his check for $1500, explaining that it was half of what he got from the *Saturday Evening Post* for a story inspired by my account of the Malibu fire in my volume *The Little Package*, published three years earlier. When my protest naught availeth, I gave the check to Fay toward liquidating the mortgage on our Malibu property.

Looking back at 1967, my first full year of retirement spent all but a month in California, I have ambivalent feelings. It was one of my richest periods of writing, lecturing, and discovery as I rolled up 20,000 miles of field work on the Guggenheim project. Until then I knew mostly the lengthwise highways; now I discovered the shorter roads that criss-crossed the Sierra Nevada and the Coast Ranges.

Fay's attachment to our Malibu house was stronger than mine. My security came from it and the university; she had only her home, facing the Pacific and backed by the Santa Monicas where we had lived since 1955. And yet there was always the fear of fire from over the mountains. Several times the flames had come close enough to burn our grape-stake fence. In 1956 we had taken cats and dog and fled to the beach below. When the Santa Ana blew from east northeast, that meant fire alert and then I found myself rising in the night to look for a glow in the sky and the sound of sirens. As I aged it became a fearful obsession of knotted stomach and dry mouth. I felt in my bones that we were fated to lose it all to fire. These were warnings to prepare for loss.

And so one night eleven years later in Tucson when the Malibu house had been leased and we heard on KNX that a fire in Malibu was burning down Encinal Canyon to the shore, I said to Fay, "Thank God we aren't there to see it go."

Toward midnight the phone rang. I knew what it was. Fay answered. It was our tenant calling. By the time he and his wife had returned from a day in Santa Barbara, he said, they found the entire neighborhood burned to the ground. They had lost everything except their car and the clothes they had on. The house and its contents were gone—our cherished furnishings, memorabilia, most of Fay's and some of my books. She had not shared my prescience in moving most of my books and records and journals to Tucson.

We gave the now empty ocean-front land to our alma mater,

Occidental College, to establish a Book Arts endowment to which we have continued to add. We have not been back in the eight years since. Once lost, Paradise can never be regained. Our Christmas book that year was called *Farewell to the Encinal*.

In addition to resuming my reviews in *Westways*, written in our absence by my old friend W. W. Robinson, I compiled an annotated Los Angeles bibliography for *Sunset* magazine. For the *New York Times Book Review* I wrote an omnibus review of nine new encyclopedias for young people, including an in-depth sampling of each work. This took me on trips to public and school libraries in the region, with visits to Rosemary Livsey, head of children's work in the Los Angeles Public Library who had been my first boss after library school, and to my former colleague, Frances Clarke Sayers, now living in Ojai. She had headed the children's division of the New York Public Library and was one of the most inspiring of all librarians and educators. I compared the entries on Mozart and Haydn in all nine sets and with some extraordinary results. Of the sets we kept one, gave one to Fay's brother Norman, now an elementary school teacher, and the rest to the Santa Monica Unified School District for use throughout the system. I shall never forget Norman's thanks—he was then a bachelor: "Now I need never have another lonely evening."

Next to the Guggenheim book the most absorbing project was to prepare the annual lecture on bibliography in the series given to the UCLA library school by Jacob and Josephine Zeitlin and concurrently to the Berkeley library school by Warren Howell. William A. Jackson, Frederick B. Adams, Gordon N. Ray, Fredson Bowers, Noel Poynter and Sir Frank Francis had preceded me.

My subject was "Bibliographers of the Golden State," including Alexander S. Taylor, H. H. Bancroft, Robert Ernest Cowan and Henry R. Wagner. I had known only the last two. Although Bancroft's career was well documented, Taylor was comparatively unknown. That meant trips to the Bancroft and

Huntington libraries in search of original material; and most rewarding of all to Mission Santa Barbara, where Taylor had spent his final years and left his papers.

A long day was passed with Father Maynard Geiger, OFM, the mission archivist and biographer of Junípero Serra. I lunched with the brothers on hot dogs and cole slaw and searched in vain with Father Maynard for Taylor's grave in Goleta near the place once known as La Patera, the Duck Pond. Highway and other development had bulldozed his bones into oblivion.

During my librarianship I had served Kenneth Rexroth as I had Henry Miller and he too reciprocated by the gift of his papers. A Malibu neighbor, James Hartzell, who had left industry in middle age to add a UCLA M.A. to his Yale B.A., now took as a project the first bibliography of Rexroth. This the Friends of the UCLA Library published, with help from Fay and me.

When C. F. MacIntyre died we redoubled efforts to build his literary archive at UCLA. His widow Marian embraced the project with the same devotion she had given to Mac during his final illness.

Upon the death in 1983 of the prolific polymath Robert Payne I learned that he had willed James Callahan's powerful oil portrait of Mac to UCLA in my honor. A year later it was formally presented at a ceremony bringing together several score of Mac's friends from near and far, including Ward Ritchie and Gordon Newell, my Occidental classmates and fellow Mac protégés, and August Frugé, former director of the University of California Press, the man responsible for publishing the poet's many successful translations of Rilke, Baudelaire, and the other German and French Symbolist poets. No other teacher had as profound and lasting an impact on my life and that of Ward and Gordon.

One of my last achievements as director of the Clark Library was to bring David Kindersley as a fellow during the spring and summer of 1967. His only obligation was to organize the Eric Gill collection, including drawings, engravings, sculptures, wood blocks, letters, diaries, business records, and several hundred books from his library, together forming one of the finest of all such assemblages.

Kindersley became a favorite of staff and readers and the book arts community throughout California. High point of his stay was a seminar on Gill which brought his brothers—Evan the bibliographer from England and Cecil the doctor from Canada—and also Beatrice Warde, the typographer and printing historian from London. She had been Gill's favorite model and, some said, his mistress.

This was the Clark's finest day since the *Homage to Yeats* two years before and it heightened the Clark's renown as a center for the graphic arts. On Miss Warde's first visit she responded enthusiastically to the memorabilia. We had arranged a portfolio of his life drawings on a table in the reading room, and when she came to one of his nudes, she cried delightedly, "C'est moi! C'est bien moi!" Many years had passed. She was now seventy, with the beauty that comes from vitality. I did not risk showing her the erotic sculpture lest she shatter the library's marmoreal hush.

Kindersley's talk on his apprenticeship to Gill was issued by the library with illustrations from the collection and printed by Saul and Lillian Marks at their Plantin Press, and became the library's most sought-after publication.

Kindersley's residence gave me an opportunity to rectify what I had come to regard as a slight to my predecessor as university librarian. After John Goodwin's death in 1946 it was sought to have the building named for him, a request denied by President Robert Gordon Sproul much to Widow Goodwin's dismay. She refused to have any other memorial to him.

When the building was given my name, I was chagrined. Mrs. Goodwin had followed her husband in death. I asked Kindersley to carve a likeness of Goodwin and appropriate lettering for a stone tablet to be placed in the building. A photograph of Goodwin at his desk, gazing out the window, was the only likeness we could offer for a model. To add to the sculptor's problem, Goodwin wore glasses without which he would have been unrecognizable.

I drove Kindersley to an East Los Angeles stoneyard where he selected a slab of creamy Minnesota limestone, had it cut to size and thickness, and then using the library bindery as workshop—it was the old coach house he shared with printer Will Cheney—he set to work to the enthrallment of occasional observers. The finished portrait was placed on the wall of the stairway leading to the rotunda. Those who knew John Edward Goodwin were amazed by the likeness, including the glasses. I not the library bore the cost. It was the least I could do to honor the man who gave me the chance to grasp the bottom rung of the ladder.

In addition to the bibliography lecture given at both library schools to audiences of bookmen north and south, I talked about California literature on the Santa Barbara campus, and at the Santa Cruz campus on Prince Henry the Navigator. Meanwhile the California book was advanced by running the Porsche to nearly 100,000 miles. It was an ideal car for mountain roads. One early morning en route from Monterey to Sequoia National Park, I drove over the new freeway through Pacheco Pass at an even 100 m.p.h. I had installed a new set of Pirelli tires and felt secure from all but the CHP who fortunately had not risen that early.

Another trip took us up the Kern River and over Walker Pass, southernmost of the Sierran crossings, to the Owens River valley and Mary Austin's house in Lone Pine, now a little museum at the foot of John Muir's Range of Light. On north we went to Reno and a sidetrip to Pyramid Lake and beyond to Susanville and a circuit of smoke-plumed Mt. Lassen.

In that town I sought in vain to find John J. Lund, the county librarian. It was his resignation from the UCLA acquisitions department in 1937 which had opened that beginning position to me. Lund had gone on to Duke where he became head librarian and then to the same position at Caltech. Then he left to become an embassy counselor in Denmark and from there in an unlikely move to the librarianship of Lassen County and an additional post as high school mathematics teacher. His was a peregrination I have never understood, although I have never stopped thanking him for that first move. If he had remained at UCLA he would undoubtedly have succeeded to the librarianship, as the man who determined that succession, Professor Waldemar Westergaard, was a Danish countryman of Lund's. One's fate is sometimes a complicated thing.

That trip ended at Los Molinos in Tehama County in the upper Sacramento valley where Fay's father and mother now lived. Her mother's parents had homesteaded in the 1880s on rangeland near Mary Austin. When I gave my mother-in-law a copy of *The Land of Little Rain*, she exclaimed "That is indeed the way it was!"

From there we took a lonely road through the Trinity Alps and down the Mad and Eel rivers to the coast at Eureka, then back over the Coast Range on logging roads through Mendocino Pass. Another great trip took me alone over the Pines to Palms Highway along the shoulder of Mt. San Jacinto to Palm Springs and Indio, past the Salton Sea to the Casa del Zorro at Borrego Springs where I wrote up my field notes. From there I threaded my way through the Laguna Mountains inland from San Diego, exploring the Mesa Grande where I photographed the granddaddy of eucalyptus trees, one to rival the Ellwood Queen at Goleta, the state's tallest lemon-scented gum.

Perhaps the finest trip of all was through Yosemite Valley at the time of maximum snow melt when the fury of falling water was awesome. The sheer wall of El Capitan brought us to a halt. Was it really rock, polished thus to satiny smoothness? We paused for an unbelieving look, then climbed through the zones of conifers to the highest point of Tioga Pass, land of lodgepole pine and exfoliating granite. From that summit the road drops like a roller coaster down Lee Vining canyon to the Owens Valley floor.

By the end of summer I had laid the geographical base for my book. My vision of the Golden State and the influence of its configurations of seacoast, valleys, mountains and deserts upon its literature had been confirmed, deepened, and expanded.

In September the antiquarian booksellers held their national meeting in Los Angeles. The local chapter asked me to write a brief essay on bookshops for Will Cheney to print as a banquet keepsake at which I was to speak on my book in progress. Young John Maggs said to me afterward that even though a foreigner had not understood my words, their music was enthralling. My hope has always been to make meaning and sound inseparable.

We had been considering a new car for the drive to Connecticut. My Porsche was too small and Fay's Chevie wagon too old. Driving along Wilshire Boulevard to the Ambassador Hotel we were early and stopped at the Citroën agency to look at the newly arrived DS 21 sedan advertised in the morning paper as an ideal long range touring car.

A look was all it took. I returned the next day and ordered one to be delivered at the factory near Paris. Shipping it through the Canal to San Pedro meant a savings of a thousand dollars even after I flew over and back. I was getting restless and Fay did not object to my going.

During three weeks I put 1500 miles on the new car on a swing around France to the Dordogne and back along the Atlantic coast through Brittany and Normandy to the channel ferry at Boulogne. I stayed a few days with Marcia and Guy and with Alan Thomas in Chelsea, drove to Cambridge for lunch with Tim Munby, then turned the car in to shippers and flew home nonstop on Panam.

After a dinner for Patrice Manahan upon her retirement as editor of *Westways*, I met with her successor Larry Meyer and his assistant Davis Dutton. They broached an idea they had been hatching in my absence. It was to begin a new series called "California Classics Reread," admittedly taken from Kenneth Rexroth's *Saturday Review* feature, "The Classics Revisited"— classics of world literature not Californiana. I had been book reviewing for the magazine since 1934 and was near burnout.

Will Robinson would gladly take over that department.

That night as I lay awake I realized what had been planned as a book trails book had suddenly turned into something wider and more interesting, yet none of my reading and field work would be wasted. I rose at daybreak and began to list the works I planned to write about. It meant more space, more readers, and more money. The first installment was due March first, then one a month thereafter. Our series eventually ran for three years and was collected in book form, and has been in print and finding readers ever since.

IV

EARLY IN THE MORNING of January 10, 1968 we packed the new car with clothes and books, destination: Wesleyan. Brother Norman had moved in again while we were gone until summer. Ours was a wistful goodbye. He was now indeed one of the family. I first met him at Occidental in the fall of 1928 at the same time his all but twin sister also came as a freshman. We had seen him through a broken marriage. From ranching on the western slope of the Rockies he had made the painful transition in middle age to school teaching and was again rock steady.

We took the southern route to avoid the cold that was gripping the Midwest, and headed across Arizona, New Mexico, and Texas to the Gulf coast and up the Atlantic seaboard, driving 350 or 400 miles a day. My fellowship did not begin until February 1, and so we had a leisurely trip ahead. Our good fortune prevailed. On the 4279-mile drive we had thirteen unbroken days of fine weather.

It was my fifth time across by automobile. The first was to Boston and back for the ALA–BSA conference in 1941, another was to Colorado and Missouri to visit Fay's relatives, and two were in 1951 and 1957 in a Hillman and a Jaguar shipped from London to New York. The Citroën proved trouble-free, with hydraulic suspension, front-wheel drive, stability, and fuel economy, cruising effortlessly at 80 m.p.h.; and the deep leather bucket seats were like no others we had ever known.

We stopped overnight in Baltimore with Edwin and Rachel

Castagna at a time when Mayor Joseph Alioto of San Francisco was on the phone urging Ed to leave the Enoch Pratt and come clean the Augean stables the San Francisco Public Library had long been. Ed was too savvy an hombre to be lured even by a fellow countryman. He stayed out his tenure in Baltimore, then had too short a retirement before he and Rachel chose to die together after his year-long struggle against encephalitis proved hopeless. They were a gallant couple. He was one of my most fond and faithful colleagues as well as one of the best public librarians of our time. To him, Harold Hamill, and John Henderson, in their time the Big Three of public librarianship in Southern California, I owed much in establishing the new library school.

Wesleyan proved a happy experience for us both. A good omen marked our arrival. The next day was Sunday and Paul Horgan invited us to a piano recital at the Honors College. John Kirkpatrick played the brooding Concord Sonata by Charles Ives to an enraptured audience. Later that spring we heard a lively student production of *The Threepenny Opera*, staged in the bare gymnasium, and accompanied by a feisty combo of violin, trumpet, and drums.

Weather and flora as well as people and customs in the New England college town were new to us. Although I had no specific obligations, my life soon filled up with talks, trips, teaching, writing the California series, and the start of a novel about the struggle between Arizona and California for the water of the Colorado River.

My position at the Center was ideal. In order to finish his biography of Archbishop Lamy, Paul Horgan had yielded the directorship to Professor Philip Hallie of the Philosophy department, although he remained in residence and we saw him nearly every day. The Center came about when President Butterfield, now emeritus, used a multi-million dollar windfall of Xerox stock to found a junior Princeton think tank. He persuaded Horgan to create a program which brought each year in residence a group of creative persons in need of freedom and a minimum of formalities. Some of my predecessors were Edmund

Wilson, William Arrowsmith, C. P. Snow, John Cage, and Leon Edel.

My colleagues that spring were Richard Wilbur, poet-translator, Edward Weismiller, Milton scholar, Gorham Munson, editor, Huseyn Yilmaz, Turkish mathematician, Ralph Young, former member of the Federal Reserve Board, and Arvid Brodersen, Swedish sociologist. Each of us had his own study, and there was a secretarial pool, a lounge with basic reference books and current periodicals, plus a coffee bar. Once a month we dined at the Honors College with invited members of the Wesleyan faculty to present a paper of our own for discussion. The sense of meaningful community was strong.

We could teach if we chose. I offered a seminar in Southwest literature in the English department chaired by Professor George Creager. Four seniors enrolled. We met in my study every Monday evening from six to nine. I was nervous at the first session, for they had taken Horgan's seminar the previous semester in the art and archaeology of the Southwest, and they warned me that his was a tough act to follow. All I can say is I tried—and none dropped out.

The college librarian, Wyman Parker, was an old friend in the Bibliographical Society of America. During my presidency in 1954–56 I had inaugurated regional meetings and had met literate librarians not usually found at the conferences of the ALA which were mostly given over to technical matters and dreary debate.

Parker and his staff, particularly Michael Durkan (now the librarian of Swarthmore) and Brian Rogers (now in charge of the Connecticut College library) and also Elizabeth Swaim, head of the rare books room, made me warmly welcome. Parker included me when he hosted meetings of the Little Ivy League librarians: Wright of Williams, Harwell of Bowdoin, McKeon of Amherst, Lathem of Dartmouth, and Engley of Trinity.

Wesleyan's library resources were supplemented by Yale, Trinity, and the Middletown public library. After the first chapter on Mary Austin, I turned to writers with New England origins: Helen Hunt Jackson and Dana, and later to Stevenson and John Muir. The Beinecke Library held a peerless RLS collection and its assistant librarian, Kenneth Nesheim, was a graduate of our first UCLA library school class. Jim Babb, Fritz Leibert, and Don Gallup of Yale were old colleagues.

Up Harvard way, alas, Bill Jackson had died two years before. Half an hour from Wesleyan was Farmington, the Walpolian stronghold of Lefty Lewis. My *New York Times* review of his autobiography had pleased him. He invited Fay and me to drive over for lunch. Ten years had passed since I had been his overnight guest. After a delicious meal he gave Fay a potted geranium to take with us.

Another day was spent at nearby Storrs (in New England everywhere is nearby) with librarian John McDonald and novelist John Seelye. McDonald's father Edward was the senior D. H. Lawrence bibliographer who set a model for us who followed. When later that spring we were in Philadelphia to receive a Drexel Institute award, I telephoned Professor McDonald, now retired in old age, to thank him again for his work having made possible my 1937 cataloging of the Lawrence manuscripts. There were connections everywhere we went. When I spoke in New Haven at a meeting of the Connecticut Library Association, a member came up afterward and said she was a cousin of Peters Rushton, whose library memorial at Virginia I had cited in my ALA keynote speech at the Waldorf Astoria in 1952. I kept learning that the book world is infinitely interconnected.

As well as to Drexel we made another Pennsylvania trip to Williamsport (home of the Little League) to dedicate a new library at Lycoming College. That is Methodist country and we had a time getting a Martini for Fay. At the following dinner I spoke to faculty and alumni with thanks for an honorary doctorate awarded that morning. Afterward the director of Education for the Methodist church, Dr. Wilkie, congratulated me upon the "texture" of my talk. Although I was not sure what he meant, I liked what he said, a usage perhaps peculiar to Methodism.

Perhaps it is because Pennsylvania contains so many colleges that the law of averages has brought me three honorary degrees from that state: Lycoming, Juniata, and Carnegie-Mellon, plus the Drexel award. At that last occasion I was introduced by Neal Harlow, dean of the nearby Rutgers library school and one of my earliest UCLA colleagues, who had come in 1945 to found our department of Special Collections. Also at Drexel were previous recipients of the award, including Luther Evans and Emerson Greenaway.

On a later visit to the Harlows at Rutgers when I spoke to the library school I was introduced by Ralph Blasingame, former assistant state librarian of California. "Don't be misled by his bookish talk," he warned the students. "LCP is also a damn' good administrator." Those were the kind of words I didn't hear too often, so loudly had my biblio-preaching prevailed.

We were the Harlows' overnight guests at their home on the shore of the Raritan. Eric and Diana Moon joined us at dinner for a fond reunion. Neal had left UCLA to head the University of British Columbia Library in Vancouver and eventually to become the first American to serve as president of the Canadian Library Association. Both Eric and Neal were among my sternest critics, given to looking askance at my sometimes overly sentimental "love of books." Harlow went on to become a good historian, author of works on the maps of San Francisco Bay and the pueblo lands of Los Angeles, and the conquest of California in 1846. I once chided Neal for spending too much time on the apparatus of administration at the expense of historical writing. He proved richly capable of both, making my earlier needling pointless.

Still another overnight trip was to New York to sign copies of the newly published *Fortune and Friendship*. Moon, Berry, and Shirley Havens of the Bowker staff, lunched us royally, and in her copy Eric wrote "To Fay, the most objective of the Powells." True. That copy met a sad fate when Fay, in the only time she was *really* mad at me (with cause), reduced it to bits and pieces. I have been holding a replacement copy, lacking only Eric's re-inscription, and awaiting the propitious moment.

On that trip I also met with Francis Brown, editor of the

New York Times Book Review, for whom I had been writing throughout the 1960s. A Targ-LCP anthology was near publication by the Ward Ritchie Press and Bill gave a dinner for us, the Francises and the Andreas Browns. The latter was the new owner of the Gotham Book Mart, one of my old rendezvous during Frances Steloff's ownership. Toward midnight the phone rang. It was Ben Grauer, calling from Kennedy, saying that he had just arrived on a flight from far off and to wait for him, he'd be along in a few minutes. He was indeed. It was the last time we saw him, senior NBC announcer, musician, bookman, erudite bon vivant, and a loyal and charming friend to Fay and me.

So short are distances in New England that we covered a lot of ground in no time that spring. We made a trip to northwest Massachusetts to visit my cousin Mason and his father (my father's younger brother) and then went on over the Berkshires for my first visit to my father's grave. He had been dead for 46 years. It is in a little Quaker burial ground at his natal village of Ghent, near Chatham in Columbia County on the eastern shore of the Hudson, where he grew up on his father's Orchard Farm. It was then prime apple country and my grandfather's crop of Cox's Orange Pippins was shipped in sawdust barrels to Covent Garden for London's leading hotels and restaurants.

Spring had not reached the Hudson River valley. The trees stood bare among the graves of Powells, Macys, Chases and Townsends. A cold wind was blowing. On the headstone of my father's grave which also held his father and mother, these words were carved: IN LOVE THEY SERVED MANKIND.

We picnicked on sandwiches and milk and as I looked across the river to the distant Catskills, I remembered these lines of Apollinaire:

> *Les souvenirs sont cors de chasse*
> *Donc le bruit meurt parmi le vent*

Still another overnight trip was to Williams College to visit

Richard and Margot Archer. He and Vosper were the first of my professional appointments in 1944, Bob to head acquisitions, Archer as bibliographer at the Clark. In his eight years there he did much to make the Clark a center for graphic arts, and it was he who commenced the Eric Gill collection. A man of exquisite taste and high standards he had gone on to Chicago to complete his doctorate at the Graduate Library School and to be librarian of the Lakeside Press before moving to Williams as librarian of the Chapin Library. Margot was equally sensitive and talented. We had a fond weekend with them, hearing William Masselos in the Williams gym give a rousing performance of the Saint-Saëns G minor concerto, and also seeing the choice Clark art gallery. Alas, Archer was to survive retirement for only a year before dying in Boston after open heart surgery.

Another memorable weekend was with Lillian Dykstra in her home at Orleans on Cape Cod. She was the widow of Clarence Dykstra, UCLA provost after the war and a strong friend of my early efforts. We had last seen her at the dedication of Dyke's portrait by Winifred Rieber, now hanging in Dykstra Hall at UCLA. Acquisition of the portrait by the UCLA alumni association had taken some pushing by guess who. That was when I learned how quickly big men are forgotten by small men.

That spring I brought Brother Antoninus to read at Wesleyan with the sponsorship of the Honors College following my talk on his poetry to the Center's fellows. I had first known the Dominican lay brother as William Everson and in 1939 arranged for Ward Ritchie to print his first book, *San Joaquin*. Limited to 100 copies for presentation only, copies today bring several thousand dollars. As well as Everson's most characteristic book, it is also one of Ritchie's most beautiful.

Antoninus was our house guest. I assured him that the vestiges of Edmund Wilson, that austere critic who had occupied our house when he was a fellow had vanished. The first night I was awakened by the anguished sound of the poet's praying. The next morning we walked in the nearby Indian Hill cemetery while he gathered his forces for the reading. We paused to decipher inscriptions dating to the 18TH century. It was a bitterly cold day. Antoninus was obviously still moved by inner torment which had led to his nocturnal prayers.

We must have made a sight walking across campus to the Honors College, he in a white robe and black surplice, a head taller than I and so long legged that I had to trot to keep up with him. First we saw the exhibit of his books in the Olin Library, held an interview with the student editors of *The Tin Drum*, and paid our respects to Phil Hallie and Paul Horgan.

Then at four o'clock came the reading to an overflow crowd of students sitting, standing, and lying on the floor around the edges of the room. After my introduction he read for an hour and twenty minutes his *Rose of Solitude*. It was a spellbinding performance punctuated by long pauses while he strode the platform and the only sounds were of trucks grinding up the Hartford road.

Caedmon recorded that performance as "Brother Antoninus Reads at Wesleyan," complete with the pauses and the sound of the trucks. It left him drained and the audience enraptured and bemused. We walked back to my study where he lay down on my couch. I slipped out for a word with Hallie who had been at the reading. All he said was, "Christ, what balls the man has!"

The next morning I drove Antoninus to New Haven for the commuter plane to New York. Eight years had passed since we had last met. Too long, we vowed. We sat quietly on a step in the mild sun awaiting the little plane. It was a moving reunion for us both.

Our friendship had flourished for thirty years and survived when I had difficulty in keeping contact after he had been converted to the Roman Catholic faith. Its theology and doctrine do not speak to my condition as a birthright Quaker. I prefer to embrace what is said in the old Shaker song: "Tis the gift to be simple, 'tis the gift to be free, 'tis the gift to come down where we ought to be."

He who was a disciple of Jeffers and had sung of the earth and its sexual power of fecundation, when denied fulfilment in marriage by the church, had sought to annul his sexual instincts.

Such denial produced strong poetry, true, yet from theological doctrine and vocabulary not from his primal root.

The reading he had just given, expressing his torment, as well as the agonized praying I had unwittingly overheard, presaged what came a year later when at the end of a powerful reading on the Davis campus of the University of California he threw off his robe and vows and henceforth embraced the married life the Lord had gifted him for. The poem, "Tendril in the Mesh," is a celebration of a return to his deepest self.

That spring of 1968 came and went too soon. I remember an anti-Vietnam rally addressed by William Sloane Coffin, the Yale chaplain, which re-confirmed our feelings about the folly of our trying to fight a land war in Asia. Disappointing was a chapel talk by Norman Mailer. He read without expression the narrative published later as "Armies of the Night," never looking up from his typescript.

Deadlines were met, trips taken, talks given. Several times we kept Paul Horgan's cat Colette, and I am still urging Fay to write about that charming creature, the most adorably individual of all the many cats who have lived with us. Colette had her own game with a Ping-Pong ball. Taking it delicately in her mouth she would run upstairs to the bathroom, stand on her hind paws and drop the ball in the empty tub, then bat it round and round, until tiring she would take it again in her mouth, trot downstairs and deposit the ball in a corner of the living room. Her other endearing practice was to jump on the window sill when it was raining and the window partly open and sing to the rain, a musical purr rising and falling in a true song.

As the semester ended and we packed to leave, Fay planted a little garden of lily of the valley at Paul's doorstep. Now eighteen years later, he still sends her a few flowers and leaves as they come out in the spring. *Muguet* the French call that fragile lily, and it is also *porte bonheur*, bringer of happiness.

After a farewell lunch at the Center, we drove to Newport, then on up coast as far as Bar Harbor. I had agreed to teach a summer course at the Simmons College library school in Boston, meeting for three weeks four days a week from nine to eleven. The course was one I had developed at UCLA on Research Library Resources. Fay would fly home as we came back to Boston from Maine and I would drive across country alone after the summer session had ended.

First we had two weeks to wander. In Newport to see the Redwood Library, the country's oldest subscription library, we were strolling back to our motel when a car stopped and a young man jumped out, asking if I weren't LCP. He was the town librarian, Richard Combs, who had recognized me from my picture in a recent issue of the *Library Journal* announcing the publication of the autobiography. Whereupon ensued a lively evening with him and his wife Adele, followed the next day by a tour of the great Newport houses and the Vanderbilts' greatest of all, The Breakers. We also were shown Combs' plans for a new library building. I believe this was the first time I realized that I had slipped unknowingly from middle age into elder statesmanship, a role I have yet to master.

The next two weeks were idyllic as we made our way up the Maine coast with a break at Booth Bay harbor and a launch trip out to Squirrel Island. The granite coast was unlike the conglomerate cliffs of Southern California. Here the Atlantic met the shore in close embrace so different from the long rolling surf we were used to.

We had breathing space to recall the Connecticut spring, rich in new experiences, seasons, and weathers. I was so continuously engaged with a variety of things relating to teaching, speaking, travelling, and writing, reviewing old work of others and broaching new work of my own, that I did not suffer again from the dead center syndrome that had flawed the first months after leaving UCLA.

At an old resort hotel in Bar Harbor we took a housekeeping cottage for a few days. We listened for the whistle buoy and bell at harbor entrance and heard the blast of the daily steamer *Blue Fin* to Halifax. At a high point in the Cadillac park we looked out over a gray ocean, a far cry from Algarve, Madeira, and Malibu.

Remembering that a former UCLA colleague, Richard Hocking and his wife Kay, summered in New Hampshire since taking up a Philosophy appointment at the University of Georgia, we located them at the hamlet of Madison and received a warm welcome to visit. They had been neighbors in Beverly Glen during those six years when I was clinging to the bottom rung. Richard too was a clinger, though eventually cut loose for lack of published research. That he was simply a superb teacher and charismatic man was not enough, and so he had moved on to greener fields.

Again we benefitted from New England's short distances. The first day we paused for a break at the Gross family pond in the Maine hinterland. Larry Gross was one of my four Wesleyan students, a shotputter of a man who had married his high school sweetheart and was already a father while still a college senior. His summer job had been as a telephone company lineman in the Maine forests, and for his creative assignment he had produced a short story of what happened when a lineman inadvertently looked in an uncurtained second-story bedroom window. His father was a member of the University of Maine faculty at Orono. We found four generations of Grosses around their pond, the oldest an accomplished whittler.

Reunion with the Hockings was joyful. Their 18TH-century stone house on a mile-square piece of land had belonged to his father, the celebrated William Ernest Hocking whose lifetime accumulation of professional papers was there in a separate study built in the 1930s. Richard was uncertain what to do with the papers. Several institutions, including the Library of Congress, sought them. In addition to that decision, he was unsure what to do with love letters written between his father and an equally celebrated American woman. My advice was to give the papers to Harvard where his father had come to fame and to seal the intimate ones for a generation. I learned later that this was what Richard had done.

Fay and Kay were as happy as Richard and I to relive the past as we now faced our uncertain futures of retirement. Warmed by a log fire and to the sound of rain on the roof we talked and read aloud, Auden's "Down by the River" and Thomas's "In My Craft and Sullen Art." In the morning a low sky obscured Mt. Washington which we had intended to climb. Instead we said what was likely to be a last farewell and headed for Boston.

At Simmons Fay saw where I was to have a proctor's suite in one of the women's dormitories. We lunched at the Parker House with Bill Jackson's widow Dolly, still unreconciled to his untimely death which had left unfinished his lifelong revision of the *STC*.

My three weeks at Simmons were intense and productive. My suite included a kitchenette in which I made my own breakfast and supper. Lunch was eaten on campus in the student cafeteria usually with some of my class. I had eighteen women students, most of them holding library jobs throughout New England and attending the summer session for more units toward their Master's degree. They were eminently teachable and nice.

The library school was well sited on its own floor in the new library building. The director Kenneth Shaffer and his deputy Tom Galvin, their colleagues and staff were kind and thoughtful. I had employed Simmons graduates, and my stay there confirmed my judgment that here was one of the best American library schools. Wisely choosing not to drive an automobile in Boston, Shaffer came to work and left each day by taxi—same time, same corner, same taxi.

A junior faculty member Ken Kister interviewed me for the *Bay State Librarian*. The published result with extraordinary candid photos by Robert Cain was shrewd and penetrating. I also spoke to Kister's class in Censorship on my experience with investigative committees.

My afternoons as well as weekends were my own. I had work to do in addition to the class. For the chapter on Gertrude Atherton I scoured the Boston bookshops for my own copies of her works, although I was concentrating on *The Splendid Idle Forties*. After hunting in Ernie Starr's bookshop I trudged home across Boston Common carrying two loaded shopping bags. I also made a friend of George Gloss of the Brattle Book Shop, the greatest book salesman I have ever known. When he learned that I collected postcards of library buildings, he became my major source up to his recent death. About once a year a batch came (free) from George. No matter that many were of the Boston Public and the Library of Congress, they were taken at different epochs and thus showed the changing styles of the automobiles parked out front.

In borrowing a book from the Boston Public Library I paid my respects to Phil McNiff, not met since the dedication of the Lamont Library at Harvard which he had headed. At the Widener I called on Douglas Bryant, the director and an old California colleague and again in London in 1950 when he was the Embassy librarian. He and I agreed we had been to the library wars and come back alive.

Too late for me to see him came a call from Keyes Metcalf, the old olympian who had pulled our proposed UCLA research library building out of the legislative fire when all seemed lost. I have often wondered how my career would have gone if World War II had not prevented Metcalf (upon Bill Jackson's urging) from offering me, still a junior librarian at UCLA, the headship of the Harvard College Library order department.

I also visited Harvard's Countway Medical Library near Simmons where I was recognized by an English librarian, Mark Hodges, who had heard me speak at Harrogate in 1957. That gracious and efficient building was a monument to Ralph Esterquest, Harvard's deceased medical librarian. I was due later to meet his daughter Shelley, enrolled in the Arizona library school

Still another old friendship renewed was with Jacob Blanck, editor of the *Bibliography of American Literature*, one of the great scholarly works of our time. With him and Harrison Hayford, the Melville scholar, I dined at Anthony's Pier Four on broiled scrod and cole slaw. The view across the harbor was to where, 42 years before, the *President Harrison* of the Dollar Line had berthed, sheathed in ice after a stormy two weeks' crossing from Marseilles. In bringing all things, Time had brought back to Boston as a retired librarian that erstwhile ship's musician. How unlikely life was, how circuitous and inevitable!

With so much free time I was able to spend afternoons in my office, making a first typed draft of the river novel begun at Wesleyan. When I had given my students a creative writing assignment as the course's final requirement, they had challenged me to produce one of my own. Whereupon I used our final meeting to read them the just completed draft of what became *The River Between*. It puzzled them (as it did me), yet held them.

Now I was able to give it the continuous belief that eluded me at Wesleyan. As much as I enjoyed being with Fay, her absence allowed me some deep breaths and to renew my resolve to remain creatively alive regardless of the cost. Such occasional separations were also good for her, although she has never told me so. More of them lay ahead before we finally made harbor.

Another reminder of my past came in the Museum of Fine Arts near Simmons when I recognized a dark carved armoire as the work of Hugues Sambin, one of the Flemish artisans brought to Dijon by the Dukes of Burgundy in the 1500s. The Musée de Dijon contained many examples of their work. Now half a century later I still sense the ambiance of that old town which Victor Hugo called "délicieuse ville, mélancolique et douce." I had sought to permeate *The Blue Train* with that bittersweet quality once so magical for the young man I was.

Life in the women's dorm had its rewarding aspects in the sewing on of buttons and the provision of fresh lemonade in the lounge's fridge. The building formed one four-story side of a walled garden square whose gates were locked at midnight. Errant students who managed to gain entry only to find themselves locked out of the dorm were accustomed to ringing the bell for the proctor to let them in. I did it just once and for a very astonished young woman. I told her to spread the word that I was a dangerous man when aroused from slumber.

With my own little radio the hours were full of music. Each morning I was awakened at dawn by the disjointed song of a robin outside my window. Pre-dawn birdsong was also heard in the music of Bartók, particularly his 3d piano concerto. I was almost within hearing of the Boston Pops.

With the aid of the Rand-McNally road atlas I plotted my drive west. The first stage was to Hanover to visit the Dartmouth librarian Edward Lathem and to meet John K. Wright, brother of Austin, author of *Islandia*. John K. was the retired librarian of the American Geographical Society who had drawn the maps of his brother's imaginative country. In the course of our correspondence he had given me for UCLA a long field letter from his brother written from the islands of Santa Rosa and Santa Cruz off the Santa Barbara coast and which I had published in the *Southern California Quarterly* with the title "An Islandian on the Islands." The rest of the Islandia archives are at Harvard where Austin's father was once the dean.

It was my first sight of the Dartmouth campus. I knew of its library riches from earlier meetings at the ARL with Lathem's predecessors Richard Morin and Nathaniel Goodrich. I wanted to see the fiery Orozco mural in the student refectory and also the Amundsen collection of Arctica, yet what I remember most from that visit was the little apricot-colored poodle that came to work with Adelaide Lockhart, the associate librarian, and slept all day on a pillow beneath her desk.

At a small dinner party chez Lathem we talked about Robert Frost and the Webster papers being edited by Lathem, and I reported on the Wesleyan campus's outraged reaction to the assassinations of Martin Luther King and Robert Kennedy. Of the two ill-fated Kennedy brothers it was Bobbie I lamented more.

John Wright and his wife lunched me the next day at the Dartmouth Inn, coming from the village of Hyme where they lived in retirement. From him I gained new insight into his brother's genius, and his having used the White Mountains of his native New Hampshire for the landscape of the imaginary country, as well as the sailing coast of Maine for the marine scenes in the novel.

In the excitement engendered by my first reading of *Islandia*, a decade after its wartime publication (which meant its rapidly going out of print), I gave many talks about it, ending by urging my listeners to write the publishers please to get the book back in print. This they eventually did, declaring in their publicity that it was LCP who had set the ground swell in motion. I came to know the author's daughters and sons and now at last his brother. I had also heard from fellow Islandians near and far, and from Mark Saxton who together with Wright's daughter Sylvia first edited the book. Saxton went on to write three plausible "sequels" to *Islandia*.

I headed west that very day on the second leg of my journey from the northeast to the southwest, due to add 5140 miles on the Citroën's speedo. After crossing the Connecticut River into Vermont I aimed for the New York State Throughway and ran 285 miles to Syracuse for the night. Thence to Toledo and south to Louisville and four hundred miles west to Columbia, Missouri. On those long drives by freeway I had time to plan the California summer and fall before I was due early in 1969 to give a six-weeks' lecture course on American research libraries at the Loughborough Technical College in Leicestershire. This was in return for its library school dean, Roy Stokes, having come to UCLA as a visiting lecturer.

I had intended to stay overnight in East St. Louis, but upon arriving there by mid-afternoon I did not like what I saw of urban decay. Instead I sought out the Carl Milles fountain at the Union Station in St. Louis which symbolized the meeting of the waters of our two greatest rivers. I had two reasons for wanting to see it. I had once written to Milles to ask if he would consider a commission for a fountain at UCLA. I had no idea of where the money would come from but thought I'd better first sound him out. Alas, he died before my letter reached him. The other reason was that I was including that fountain in the novel I was writing.

An erratic breeze was blowing when I began to reconnoiter the spouting splashing bronze figures and I was drenched from whichever side I approached.

I reached Columbia as darkness fell to dine on panfried catfish and more cole slaw. In the absence of California iceberg lettuce, chopped cabbage was the best salad to be had. I also like it.

My next destination was Aspen via Denver where Hal Bieler, our family doctor and old friend and believer, awaited me at his summer cabin. Paul Horgan was also there at the Aspen Institute, and we all had music under the Big Tent. Paul called ahead to the Santa Fe opera for my ticket to *Der Rosenkavalier*. I took the long way over Independence Pass and down the Arkansas to Alamosa for the night, thence up the Rio Grande to the South Fork and over Wolf Creek Pass and down the nascent San Juan to Pagosa Springs to see again the site where my novel reached climax.

Strauss in Santa Fe and Mozart in Flagstaff (*Cosí fan Tutte*) were heavenly stops en route to Tucson where I had hoped to talk with President Harvill about my spending some time at the university. Since my giving the commencement address in 1961 he had been urging me to come. I found that he had been called away. His wife George met me at Dorothy McNamee's Overland Bookshop for several hours of good talk about the attractions of the university town.

Home again after seven months' absence I resumed work on the California book, researching and writing a chapter a month, depending again on the resources of the state's libraries, especially the Huntington, Southwest Museum, Bancroft, State and UCLA. Smaller libraries also helped, as when in writing about Stewart Edward White I found that the Oxnard Public Library, a short distance from Malibu, held the only recorded copy in California of one of White's more obscure titles.

I alternated writing and yard work, hauling loads of canyon shale for our garden paths, accompanied by Emily, our loving puli, and gathering driftwood from the beach. Carrying an oak log weighing almost as much as I did cost me my first hernia, not operated on until four years later. We made another long trip to Fort Bragg and over the Coast Range again to Los Molinos to see the old folks. I also went to Palm Springs in search of the archives of J. Smeaton Chase and to Yucca Valley to visit E. I. "Eddie" Edwards, the desert bibliographer, for leads to who it was who actually wrote Manly's *Death Valley in '49*. *Westways* reported that my series was bringing more response than anything they had run in years. With Ward Ritchie I planned the published book to include thirty-one chapters, to be followed by a similar volume on the Southwest.

I had been asked by the California Library Association to give the Edith M. Coulter memorial lecture at the annual conference in San Diego. I chose Miss Coulter herself and her career as a reference librarian and professor of librarianship. She had been my instructor at Berkeley in 1936/37. Driving home across the continent I had thought out the form and content of the lecture and when I faced the audience of five hundred, I was ready and eager to pay tribute to that remarkable woman who achieved true faculty rank and status by teaching, research, and publishing. The lecture was followed by an autographing session at which were sold the hundred copies of *Fortune and Friendship* sent out by Bowker.

That was our last visit with another remarkable woman: Margaret Girdner, former head of San Francisco's school libraries and one of the best library politicians I have ever known. Over a drink in the hotel bar she said that she was willing us her collection of Quimper dinnerware from having once admired our few examples, vestiges of my Dijon years. Not too long after, we heard from a San Francisco lawyer that Miss Girdner had died and the collection was on its way to us—a hundred or more pieces, rare and modern, of the beautiful Brittany ware. We eventually moved most of it to Arizona in the early 1970s and it now fills a china cabinet bought especially to house it.

Two kinds of status can be gained by librarians, one professional, the other public. Margaret Girdner had both. Of regal size and bearing, she dressed accordingly. A graduate of Mills College, she was one of the last of the famed "Gillis Girls"—librarians trained and inspired by State Librarian James L. Gillis at the library school founded by him in Sacramento and transferred eventually to Berkeley. From the capital those ardent young ladies fanned out to the uttermost reaches of California to found its county library system which served years later as the model for the new Soviet Union.

During my presidency of the California Library Association in 1950 I came to be impressed by Miss Girdner's universal status. When my board determined the need to raise the dues, I was warned that it couldn't be done without the approval of the school librarians who also belonged to their own association, and that their president, Margaret Girdner, was adamantly opposed. I flew to San Francisco to seek her support. She was then the head of the school libraries system of the city and county of San Francisco. From a bit of advance research I learned that she was a devotée of the arts.

Our meeting was set for breakfast at the St. Francis Hotel. When I went early to book a table, I found the dining room overflowing with conventioners. I met Miss Girdner in the lobby and suggested we go elsewhere where we would not have to wait in line. She only smiled and led me back to the dining room where she held up two fingers to the maître d'. He immediately beckoned us past the line and escorted us to a table in the farthest corner. To her husky-voiced "Thank you, Joe, you're a dear," he bowed and said, "Ever yours to command, Miss Margaret," and poured our first coffee.

I waited for her to speak. "I was the librarian of Mission," she explained, "long before you were born. It was the toughest high school in the city and Joe Belloli was the meanest kid of all—until I learned that he was a reader. You and I know that books too have charms to soothe the savage breast." Her smile disappeared and her eyes narrowed. "Now what's this about your wanting to raise our dues? They're already too high. I don't know why we don't withdraw into our own association and let you brainy ones go your way without us." Again she smiled. "That would really reduce your membership, wouldn't it?"

"Of course it would," I admitted. And then asked, "What would the ghost of Jim Gillis say to that?" Gillis had been one of CLA's founders back in the last century. I took another swallow and continued, "I know as well as you do that without your support, we don't have a chance. I must tell you though that I didn't fly up just to ask for your help. I wanted to hear Berlioz' *Requiem* tonight at the Opera House, but they told me it's been sold out for weeks."

"Nonsense," she scoffed. "Nothing in this city's ever really sold out. I'll tell you what we'll do. I want to hear it too. Pick me up at eight at my apartment and we'll go together."

We had two of the best seats in the house, although a bit too close to one of the four brass bands Berlioz called for in the score. We never spoke again of the dues. When a motion was made at the annual meeting to raise them, it was Miss Girdner who seconded it.

After the San Diego conference we drove to Santa Fe and Taos where I wanted Fay to enjoy the idyllic Sagebrush Inn where I stayed on my way west from Boston. There we renewed friendship with Claire Morrill and Genevieve Janssen of the Taos Book Shop and looked at a house that had belonged to the Taos painter Oscar Berninghaus. In spite of love for our Malibu home, it had become clear that we would live elsewhere at least part of the year. England, Algarve, Funchal, and now northern New Mexico were considered. Neither knew that southern Arizona was destined to be our promised land.

Back home I found an invitation from Chancellor Harry Ransom of the University of Texas to speak to a newly organized Texas collectors' club, meeting in Austin. The Ransom-Powell orbits had been crossing since I met him at Austin in 1954 on my first visit to Frank Dobie. Texas and UCLA had competed for some choice collections, the latter winning some and losing more. Wins included the Ogden and Sadleir collections. Losses I shall not recount. In any case we admired and respected each other. Ransom's achievement in forming the Humanities Research Center was altogether brilliant.

High points of that fast round trip were dinner with Bertha Dobie—it was our last meeting—and an offer from Ransom to come on a split appointment with the library school and the English department which he had once headed. I relished an opportunity to work with an administrator-bookman of the same rank as Gordon Ray and Franklin Murphy and also to use the riches of the HRC in my continuing work on American letters. I also sensed that Texas and Arizona were on collision course for my presence. My having missed Harvill in Tucson seemed to favor Ransom.

My feelings about the future were increasingly ambivalent. A part of me longed for a true retirement, a disengagement from the public life I had sought and relished for years. Our idyllic setting between sea and sierra, the still tranquil beach especially in the off seasons, and the nearness of the wild western ranges of the Santa Monicas, still held me; and also a few congenial neighbors—the Hartzells, Dworskis, and Brents—formed an ideal setting for the contemplative life I thought I sought, and which still held Fay in thrall.

Yet such did not seem to be my lot. My character was still compulsive, driving me toward achievement and recognition. Requests to speak, to review, to write forewords, and a continuing interest in the UCLA libraries and library school to which I had given so much of my life, kept me from any real retirement. I determined henceforth to accept only speaking engagements that required a fresh look at old subjects or that led to new environments and experiences.

Such was the prospect of the spring in London and Leicestershire. I also knew that wherever I went and whatever I did, my need was to be near a research library with old and new books and backfiles of journals to support my research and writing. And I needed the anchorage of Fay.

V

WE LEFT SOUTHERN CALIFORNIA again in January 1969 in a driving rainstorm. Our roof was leaking, our cliff eroding. Again Brother Norman moved in and assured us that he would take all necessary steps to ensure our house being there when we returned by summer. I hated to leave the great drifts of beachwood washed up by the storm and brought down by the creeks. Before flying from New York to Rome we paid another visit to Middletown to thank Paul Horgan and Wyman Parker again for their kindness of the year before. Twenty-degree weather kept us bundled up.

More than thirty years had passed since we were last in Rome. Former Malibu neighbors Stanley and Frances Clarke, now living in Rome, drove us about in their Mercedes 180. Stanley had adapted to Roman traffic and was able to exchange insults in his own rich Italian with threatening gestures. He was also making a chronology of the Roman emperors on 5 x 7 cards. When I asked why, he only smiled. Gold was the thing to buy, he assured us as he and Frances were preparing to move to Kenya. They later went on to South Africa where their children were living in Johannesburg, and there Stanley died.

We stayed at the Albergo Dinesen near the Pincian Gate. It was run by an aged Danish lady married long ago to an Italian. The food was lavish. Strange clanking sounds came in the night from above our second floor bedroom as though a heavy chain were being dragged across the floor. Was it a large animal? Or an idiot aunt? I was afraid to ask.

Marcia and Guy Lawrence arrived unexpectedly on Fay's birthday and we made a walking tour of our favorite fountains including the Triton and Bernini's bees. We went with the Clarkes to St. Peter's Square to receive the Pope's blessing. When he appeared on his balcony with outstretched arms, I held up my Scripto. They also took us to the English Cemetery where Keats and Shelly and Trelawney are buried, and also the author of *Two Years Before the Mast*.

I had been writing about Dana. He came to Rome at the end of his long voyage, and a year before his death in 1882 he wrote to a friend, "This is the land of vines, olives, figs, oranges and lemons, of beauty in nature and art, in human form and movement and voice, in the blue islands, the blue wave, and the violet hillsides. It is a dream of life." It was a vision akin to the one he had of California, half a century before. Was it for me? For Fay? I knew that in addition to harmony between us, we also had to be at home with our environment.

In Zurich we took delivery of a butter-yellow VW Kharmann Ghia, then ran it in on trips to Lucerne, Berne, and the great library at St. Gallen. The charms and cares of home seemed far away. Both the art museum and the zoo drew us, the latter a model of cleanliness and care for the animals. Fay photographed me by the lifesize bronze of Joyce reading a book in the little cemetery park below the zoo. "I buried him there," Norah said, "because Jim liked to hear the lions roar."

Our drive to England took us through Geneva. Then on a sudden decision we detoured to Dijon to see my old master Georges Connes. We had not been back since 1957. It was the last time we saw him. He died not long after from an accidental fall on his ancestral farm in the chestnut forests of the Rouergue. He was one of my three decisive teachers and a representative of all the strongest and best in French culture.

This time we bypassed Paris or tried to, getting disoriented on the Belt road until a vociferous and kindly French driver set us right for the Autoroute du Nord. After Chantilly for the night we made the Boulogne-Dover ferry with no time to spare as the last car on. The Lawrences were in Switzerland and we had their country house and staff to ourselves for a few days before checking in to our old flat in Dolphin Square.

On our last day in Zurich, following the visit to the zoo and the statue of Joyce, I wrote in my journal,

> Thus the days pass in simple living eased by our financial independence, so far from the impecuniosity of my European youth and yet essentially no happier, except that now I have Fay. Then life lay ahead, veiled, beckoning, unknown. Now forty years later life has long been unveiled. I must open a new creative vein; only then can I manage to live on in this violent modern world, must find my way again to a state of passionate belief in what I am doing. Lecturing at Loughborough will help and resumption of work on my California book.

And so it came to pass as we settled in again at Rodney House. The porter greeted us as did the grocers and best of all Queenie, our same maid whose problems with her layabout son gave Fay her daily laugh. I had planned three chapters for *Westways* on writers whose works would be plentiful in English libraries. With Sir Frank Francis as sponsor I was given a card at the London Library, the venerable subscription library in St. James's Square founded by Carlyle. It proved ideal: quiet rooms, open stacks, many current and bound periodicals, and rich holdings of works by Bret Harte, Mark Twain, and Jack London.

A daily routine was soon established. Early coffee and *The Times* with Fay, breakfast of porridge and milk, toast and banana, then by 134 bus to the top of the Haymarket, thence to the library and an unbroken morning of reading and writing. The books (except for reference works) circulated, and I headed home for late lunch with brief case full of further reading matter.

The librarian Stanley Gilliam and assistant librarian Douglas Mathews and desk attendant Pamela Redmond were uniformly cordial. The last-named became one of my most faithful English readers and correspondents when with her husband Terry and their five stalwart sons they emigrated to America, first to New Jersey and then to Southern California. Twice in subsequent years Pam and Terry made lightning round trips to Tucson to see me in my native habitat. Terry, a tough, red-haired Celt from Liverpool, drove a Trans Am with apparent immunity from speeding tickets. On both visits they stayed only long enough for lunch and a glimpse of Mission San Xavier del Bac before heading back to L.A. on Interstate 8. I never did know what Terry did—something about plastics. I once accused him of being a CIA agent. He neither denied nor affirmed. They are now happily back in England, sending me alluring post cards of old barns and Kentish oast houses.

I daresay there are more books by and about Bret Harte in England than in most American libraries, and for the reason that after his first meteoric success with the Mother Lode stories, then failure as a lecturer and loss of his American readers, Harte spend the last thirty years of his life in self-imposed exile in England, his first and only creative vein panned out. He never returned nor lived again with his wife and sons, although they did not divorce. Now his grandsons, John and Lawrence Bret Harte, are Tucson neighbors.

Reading Bret Harte far from the California scene gave me new insight into the nature of his immensely popular stories. In the Mother Lode tales of Truthful James, M'liss, the Outcasts of Poker Flat and the Heathen Chinee are the progenitors of the denizens of Tortilla Flat and of Idwal Jones' tales which enriched the pages of *Westways* long before my contributions were to appear.

When the London Library occasionally lacked a book, I found the Westminster Public Library, headed by K. C. Harrison, to be an unfailing source, with overnight delivery if necessary from as far away as Hull. I regret never having met that library's poet-librarian, the talented Philip Larkin. A year later Ken Harrison was our guest in Malibu. The guild of librarians functions throughout the world whether in Tokyo, Perth, New Delhi, or London, to make a visiting librarian at home. The Book is indeed the best passport.

The search for Harte in England led me to his grave in

Frimley churchyard, a few miles from the Lawrences at Barkham Square. On a windy day in March we were led there by Marcia. En route we gathered a branch of pungent needles from one of the California redwoods—Wellington pine the English call the tree—along the double-planted avenue leading to the college named for the Iron Duke. My chapter on Harte ended with the verses he wrote in 1870 upon the death of Dickens:

> *And on that grave where English oak and holly*
> *And laurel wreaths entwine,*
> *Deem not all a too presumptuous folly,—*
> *This spray of western pine.*

Eric Gill continued to interest me. In Geneva at the Palais des Nations we saw his bold sculpture and on reaching England we went to Guildford to see his work on the façade of the cathedral. I once planned to travel about Britain photographing the memorials and inscriptions carved by him in towns and villages, even to Charters, where Winston Churchill's stone lawnmower bears an inscription carved by Gill. One of the last things I wrote for the *New York Times*, as Francis Browns' retirement was imminent, was an appraisal of David Randall's *Dukedom Large Enough*, the autobiography of the most creative bookseller-librarian of our time. There was troubling news from home of student vandalism in the libraries at UCLA, Berkeley, and Illinois. Again I had thoughts of a full year in England, living outside London in a beechwood cottage, savoring the full round of seasons.

Work on Twain and London went smoothly with momentum generated by the Harte. Justin Kaplan's book on Twain and Harte and books by Franklin Walker and Irving Stone were helpful. It was clear how the roots of Hemingway and Steinbeck reached back into those earlier novelists. I also thought of Melville's "shock of recognition" and of how American literature has been fashioned by such linked handiwork.

Again I relished the freedom from day-long employment which now was mine. Mornings were for writing, afternoons for drives and walks with Fay, evenings for music or theater and dinner guests, or quiet reading when in Rossetti's words "twofold silence was the song of love." Fay once said unexpectedly "How fortunate we are never to have bored each other." Remembered of that spring's reading, borrowed from the London Library, are the memoirs of William Carlos Williams and Nabokov.

We drove throughout southern England as we had the year before in New England, again to Salisbury and the White Hart, with an envious eye on the old stone dwellings within the cathedral close; and also to Avebury and Stonehenge and the White Horse in the Wiltshire chalk and on to the Westonbirt arboretum. Over Leith Hill, highest point in the south and to Hadley Heath where we came upon a bench on a walking path with a brass plate to remember Roy Wilkinson who once walked there. What better memorial? Always books led to travelling and they back to more reading.

Loughborough Technical College where I was due to lecture at the library school is in County Leicester, 120 miles north northwest of London. I drove up every Tuesday morning, lunching with the faculty, then lecturing from two to four and a tea break with the students, a final cup, then back to Dolphin Square at the end of the twelve-hour day.

Getting through the maelstrom of central London at the morning rush hour calls for self-confidence and a blend of offensive-defensive driving. Unlike the vociferous Italians and the vituperative French, the English are quieter and more considerate, especially when they see foreign plates on the offending car. The Karmann Ghia's stylish Swiss plates stood me in good stead when inadvertently discourteous. Earlier driving in 1950, 1957, 1960, 1963, and 1966 enabled me to thread in and out of London from all points of the compass.

My objective on the weekly run was to gain M 1, guided by the reassuring road sign TO THE NORTH. When I finally reached that motorway, most of whose traffic at that early hour was incoming, I quickly gained the fast lane, safe from the lorries that kept to the slow lanes, then set my speed at 75 m.p.h. Two hours out I pulled off at one of the Granada laybys and gave the car petrol and myself tea with milk and sugar.

By the time I had bypassed Leicester and was in country beginning to roll, with snow still on the ground, I knew I had reached the beginning of the true north of Nottinghamshire, Lancashire, and Yorkshire. Beyond the Tyne and the Tweed lay Scotland. By then I had my lecture in mind. It was the perfect way to prepare for class, filled also with a sense of England's continuity. That the Empire was crumbling was not my business. What concerned me was what American libraries owe to their English origins and of how much the westward flow has enriched them.

My experience three years before at Aberystwyth and then at Wesleyan and Simmons had taught me to expect students better prepared in educational background and working experience than the California students I had known. I welcomed again the courtesy I first knew at Harrogate in 1957. It was there that I met Roy Stokes, the Loughborough director. Cordial, witty, fluent, learned, and broadly cultured in Anglo-American ways, Roy was the perfect host, aided by his deputy John Cox and colleagues Leonard Durbridge and Roderick Cave. I was taken at once to meet Dr. Robert Lester, the chemist and principal of the college, for an equally cordial reception.

My students numbered thirty, all with working experience and drawn from throughout the British Isles. My lectures were on research libraries, not special, industrial, or governmental libraries; of their differences in collecting, servicing, and managing, ranging from the completely independent and fully endowed Huntington, Morgan, and Folger, to the partially endowed Clements, Brown, Beinecke, and Clark libraries, with a look also at special research collections in university libraries.

In the opening lecture I made it clear what the series would and would not be about, and that (from ignorance) I would have nothing to say about the new techniques and uses of Information Science. As a result of that confessional opening, half a dozen students did not come back for the rest of the lectures. By the sixth and final lecture I had weeded them to twenty.

A delightful surprise was that Beatrice Warde was a fellow guest lecturer, speaking on types and printing. Thus we resumed the friendship formed earlier at the Clark Library. Our lectures came at the same time, two to four, and in adjoining rooms. At tea afterward that first day, she asked me please to lower my voice when lecturing, inasmuch as her students were listening to me not her. My reply (thought of on the drive back to London) was "her voice was gentle and low, an excellent thing in woman."

The course was broken in the middle by the spring holidays of several weeks. On the Tuesday before the break, Fay came with me and we were overnight guests of Roy and Jeff Stokes and their two little girls. That evening Roy and I and John Cox attended a dinner in Nottingham with a discussion group of regional librarians including Dick Smith, the university librarian and Paul Sykes, the city librarian.

Aware of the Nottingham-D. H. Lawrence connection, I spoke afterward in tribute to the university's Lawrence collection and the editorial work of its professor V. de Sola Pinto. An evening like that with colleagues who shared my idealism and vocabulary led me to reaffirm my commitment to librarianship present and future. I was not sure what the future held, only that reading would continue, whatever form books might take.

It had been a long day since leaving London early that morning, a day of driving, lecturing, talking, and listening, and when I finally tucked in at midnight I fell into a deep, dreamless, and restorative sleep.

We took off the next morning heading to Lincoln and its cathedral met in *The Rainbow*, my first Lawrence novel read in the 1920s. When there in 1957 we had trudged up Steep Hill to the church. This time we let the VW do the work. Our final destination was Harrogate where based again at The Swan we revisited Fountains Abbey and drove east to Whitby on the North Sea. The Yorkshire coast is as gray as that of Cardigan

Bay. Any thoughts of a seaside cottage in the old fishing port were dispelled. On the way back to Harrogate over the snowy moors we saw hang gliders launched from a high hill.

My rushed schedule did not provide opportunity for closer acquaintance with the students, more reserved than their American counterparts, nor did they have a Cellar like the one at the Welsh school. Only two students sought me out after my lectures. One was a Lancashire woman with an extraordinary head of red hair. She wanted to thank me for giving her the needed boost to finish her diploma. Her face showed great sadness and strength, and I regretted having to tell her that I had time only for a cup of tea before heading south. What would she think if she ever read *El Morro*?

The other student was another native of Lancashire who asked me to have tea with him after my last lecture. He had been impressed by my earlier lecture on the value to research librarians of previous experience in the antiquarian book trade. "How do I get such experience?" he asked me. "Talk to a sympathetic British bookseller," I answered. "Such as?" he countered. "Such as Anthony Rota, the son of Bertram Rota." "When?" came the further question. "Ride back to London with me," I said, hardly believing that he would, "and I'll call and ask him to see you tomorrow."

I didn't reckon with Roger Mortimer's get-up-and-go. He had done American studies and geography at Kiel University and was another of those Lancashire redheads I came to realize were a special breed.

He jumped in the Kharmann Gia and away we went TO THE SOUTH. I let him do the talking—after all he had listened to me for six weeks—and he proved informed on everything about the landscape and culture of the regions we traversed on the long drive to London—vegetation, geology, antiquities, folklore, including much about the Roman Wall to the north of us which had enthralled me on first seeing it in 1950 on a long day's train ride from Edinburgh to Manchester.

The upshot of that encounter and my call to Tony Rota was that Roger Mortimer apprenticed the next year with Bertram Rota Ltd of 30/31 Long Acre, W.C.2 and also with Ben Weinreb, London's leading architectural books authority. He then followed his dream across the Atlantic to work in Special Collections at Washington University in St. Louis and finally to head that department at the University of South Carolina. There in 1977 I had the pleasure of seeing him again when I spoke at the dedication of a new rare books facility in the impressive library planned by Librarian Kenneth Toombs.

Home again in California in the summer of 1969 I bore down on researching and writing the final chapters in the Classics book. The field work was done. California's contours and configurations were now with me wherever I went, as I came to perceive the relationships between literature and seacoasts, valleys, mountains, and deserts.

I learned that its writers had done for California something of what Yeats called on his countrymen to do for Ireland: "I would have our writers and craftsmen master this history and these legends, and fix upon their memory the appearance of mountains and rivers and make it all visible again in their arts, so that Irishmen even though they had gone a thousand miles away, would still be in their own country."

Such was my experience fifty years ago when as a student in France writing a book about Robinson Jeffers far from the Big Sur, I found that the genius of his poetry gave me the constant sense of being there on that faraway coast.

We were beginning to see a long-overdue revival of critical attention to Jeffers' poetry which had been unpopular since his outspoken opposition to our participation in World War II. He had been virtually abandoned by his publisher Random House, headed by the wise-cracking Bennett Cerf. Now it became apparent what I had insisted in my 1932 thesis that Jeffers was *the* religious poet of our time. Critical books by Jesuit, Dominican and Episcopalian writers bore me out. In editing hitherto unknown early manuscripts in the Humanities Research Center in Austin, Brother Antoninus established the continuity and growth of Jeffers' genius. Now I cooperated with Anne Ridgeway in her edition of Jeffers' letters, introduced by Mark Van Doren, and I reviewed it together with Antoninus's monograph in the *New York Times Book Review*. I also took part in the establishment of Tor House as a National Historic Monument and in the publication of a Jeffers News-Letter by Occidental College.

Lectures were given on my book in progress on the university campuses of Riverside, Santa Barbara, San Francisco, Berkeley, and Davis, the last two appearing in beautiful typographical format as had my lecture on the four California bibliographers.

Now trips were made to interview relatives of the deceased writers who were my subjects. In Laguna Beach I met Olive, the widow of Idwal Jones, and in Aptos near Santa Cruz, I interviewed Charis Wilson, second wife of Edward Weston, with whom she had collaborated on a California book of great beauty. She was also the daughter of Harry Leon Wilson whose *Merton of the Movies* I ranked as the first and best of novels about Hollywood. Other writers left to the last were Aldous Huxley and Raymond Chandler. My earlier work on the latter preceded the attention given to him after he became a critical cult figure.

At this time I was interviewed by James Mink, head of the UCLA oral history project who went on to national recognition in this area of history. Like Andrew Horn and John Finzi of the Library of Congress, Jim came to library work from the UCLA history department. His dedication to oral history was owed to Allen Nevins, the father of the movement.

The year 1970 was also the one when my compass began to swing strongly east-southeast. It was my last full period of California residency. The next three years, as had been the previous four, were partly spent elsewhere. By 1974 I had done in the Golden State all I was capable of doing as librarian, educator, and writer.

The year 1970 which now appears so important in the

direction my life was to take also held two fruitful experiences with old California colleagues. The first was a request to speak in San Diego at a civic lunch marking the retirement of City Librarian Clara Breed. That southernmost city had long been in my life from when I first went there as a boy of ten to the Panama Pacific Fair. Then in 1928 we musicians on the *S.S. Yale* harbored there three nights a week while four were spent at sea between San Diego, San Pedro, and San Francisco.

During my UCLA years, as I scoured the towns and the hinterland for materials relating to California history and literature, I met the writers Judy Van der Veer and George de Clyver Curtis whose books I wrote about in *Westways*. Both lived in the deep back country, keeping animals and bees and writing in praise of pastoral ways. In the 1890s Curtis had been a cataloger in the NYPL. Through them I met Wilmer Shields, a travelling salesman for an old San Diego wholesale grocery and whose passion was collecting San Diego city and county imprints. I persuaded him to pass his duplicates along to our local history collection at UCLA.

All of this was background in my spoken tribute to Clara Breed. She was one, like Margaret Girdner, with whom I had shared a belief that librarians should be identified with more than library housekeeping and always be in the cultural center of whatever their jurisdiction. That she was indeed such a person was evident in the affection which characterized that civic luncheon. Fourteen years later I paid tribute to her again in a preface to her history of the San Diego Public Library, a book designed by Ward Ritchie.

As a result of that day I had a call from the head of the San Diego civil service commission, asking me to help interview candidates to succeed Miss Breed. By then I was an old hand at drawing people out. I liked to inquire into the background, motivations, and qualifications of the candidates and to lead them to assess and reveal themselves.

An even greater challenge followed when I served on a similar committee to recommend a successor to Harold Hamill as city librarian of Los Angeles. My special interest in that institution came from its librarian, Althea Warren, having been the one who sent me off to library school, almost against my own will, and then after graduation gave me my first job. The beginning salary was then $1620.

Ours was a blue-ribbon committee of three librarians and three civic leaders. My colleagues were the Los Angeles county librarian William Geller, and Edwin Castagna, then at Baltimore's Enoch Pratt after leaving a long career at the Long Beach library in southern California. Ed was well on the way to being one of my library saints. He had lectured for us at UCLA and I for him in Long Beach and Baltimore, and also as his keynote speaker in Detroit to inaugurate his presidency of the ALA. Fay asked him to be our house guest in Malibu while he came for the interviewing.

Interest in the LAPL job was nationwide. The commission eliminated scores of unqualified applicants and then gave us the remaining résumés of about twenty-five bona fides which we narrowed to six finalists for interview. It was a grueling process for all concerned, occupying two eight-hour days. I found it especially taxing. The damp coastal air, plus several years of eating away from home, had congested my bronchials. I went to bed each night after the interviews, leaving Ed and Fay to watch the fire of chaparral roots turn to coals.

One of the civic leaders was Stephen Billheimer, an old schoolmate from South Pasadena. He and his two fellows and we three librarians fired some broadsides and also did some sharpshooting at the candidates. We knew we were determining the next generation of that great city library and we wanted the strongest possible person to head it. The candidates were given at least an hour apiece before us inquisitors. We were both merciless and kindly.

Our final rating placed Wyman Jones, city librarian of Fort Worth, at the top of the list. He had good non-library managerial experience with Sears Roebuck, cultural sophistication, and also an able record as librarian of the Texas capital of the cattle empire. He broke all rules of interviewing etiquette observed by the other candidates: he chain-smoked throughout the hour;

he got carried away by his own responses so that he walked back and forth along the long table that seated us. He gave the impression of enormous energy, drive, motivation, and ambition. The civic leaders were a bit nervous as was Bill Geller. Ed and I finally carried the day, persuading them that L.A. needed that kind of a guy, a supercharger to follow the mild-mannered Hamill, someone to fire up staff and city and lead that great library into the Brave New World of God knows what marvels.

I also liked Jones' having been a jazz pianist. Library staffs always need entertaining—and distracting. He got the job and now in 1986 he is still there. Alas, Castagna and Geller are dead. I haven't checked on the civic leaders.

In addition to Castagna, many of my associates in the book world were our house guests at one time or another. Fay was a perfect hostess, never seeking to be other than herself, thoughtful, humorous, relaxed, and wise in matters of head, heart, and hands. All living things, vegetable and animal, interest her more than the inanimate world of books that occupy the rest of us, although her learning and taste in literature and history are exceptional. I have never forgotten that her I.Q. was at the top of the incoming class at Occidental in 1928 and is certainly higher than mine, then and now.

American guests included Don Coney, Ray Swank, Andy Horn, Bob Vosper, Keyes Metcalf, Jim Babb, Jack Dalton, Fred Adams, Fred Wagman, Ralph Ellsworth, Rudy Gjelsness, Don Powell, Don Dickinson, and Malcolm Glenn Wyer. Foreign librarians who came overnight or longer were Sir Frank Francis, Preben Kierkegaard, Roy Stokes, and Ken Harrison. Our semi-annual open houses to library staff and later library school faculty and students also included Japanese and Indian librarians. Among bookseller house guests were Winnie Myers, Alan Thomas, Stanley Smith, John Carter, David Magee, Harold and Olive Edwards, and Menno Hertzberger.

VI

EVER SINCE AN ARIZONA history conference speech of 1960, "Fountains in the Sands," led to my U. of A. commencement address the following year, President Richard Harvill had continued to express interest in my coming to Tucson without specific assignment. In 1964 my seminar on the literature and libraries of the Southwest included a student-shared project to report on library service to Arizona Indians. During the spring break while Grady Zimmerman went to the Navajo tribal seat at Window Rock, I travelled to the San Carlos Apache reservation with a letter to the tribal chairman from President Harvill. Clarence Wesley, a graduate of the university, received me cordially, but I soon learned that his interests did not include books and reading, at least not for his tribe. The only service the San Carlos children were receiving was from the Gila County library in nearby Globe where the children came once a week by bus, bringing with them, according to the Anglo librarian, their own fleas.

Upon invitation from the Harvills I returned via Tucson to be their overnight guest. He and I drove the next day to the Kitt Peak National Observatory, under construction on the Papago reservation sixty miles west of the city. I liked Harvill even more from seeing him up close. He was a Southern liberal whose education was from Mississippi, Duke, and Northwestern. His special field was Economics. Now in his second decade as president, he had risen from the teaching ranks and deanship to his present dominant position. His statewide strength came from wartime contacts as the Arizona administrator of the OPA. Arizona was still an agricultural state and as a native of rural Tennessee who had chopped cotton as a boy, he could meet rancher legislators at the crossroads whatever their wealth and power. He pressed me with a grave courtesy unusual in university administrators. I said that I might be interested in joining him after I retired two years hence, plus a bit of breathing time. He did not urge me for any kind of commitment, nor did we discuss what I might do at the university. I made clear that I intended to devote my strength mostly to writing of one kind or another.

Five years passed before President Harvill grew specific. At the end of 1969, after first expressing regret at having missed my visit the year before, he wrote that he had succeeded in persuading the Regents to establish Arizona's first graduate library school and that he hoped I would come on whatever basis to help fire up the new school. It was an artful letter that did not call for an answer. I saw that he had outsmarted his counterpart at Arizona State University which had openly sought the library school to be located on the Tempe campus. In founding it at Tucson, the Regents ruled that there would not be another school in the foreseeable future.

Then I heard again from Harry Ransom, as usual in a hurried phone call from Austin. The Texas Regents were giving him trouble, he said, for what they believed were his prodigal ways in stocking the Humanities Research Center with millions of dollars worth of prime Anglo-American literary and iconographical source material. Would I run over for a few days and help him set those old boys right? All he wanted was something over my signature as to the importance of the HRC in the national scene. It would be a confidential document solely for him and the Regents. He offered a thousand dollars and expenses. I agreed to come the following week.

Apart from the interesting proposal, I wanted to look at the Center's holdings of the Oliver La Farge papers, originally offered to me at UCLA and declined as being out of scope. A publisher had asked me to write a life of La Farge for young people and I had made a trip to Santa Fe to meet La Farge's widow, Consuelo. That project aborted when the writer's agent expected me to pay for any and all quotations from La Farge's work. I also wanted to see the manuscript of *The Loved One* in the Evelyn Waugh papers to determine if he had actually written it during his brief visit to L.A. I found that he had.

I flew into Austin via Dallas with my trusty Scripto and notebook. We landed in a rainstorm and as the whistling engines of the Viscount turboprop were shut down and the stairs lowered a far piece from the terminal, there came running a small figure under a big red umbrella. It was Harry giving me the next thing to a red carpet welcome.

Back into the terminal he rushed us under the one umbrella, both getting damp at the edges, and on to campus where we holed up in his office for the rest of the afternoon. He talked and I listened and made an occasional note. It was only our third meeting. The first was in 1954 when he was dean of the graduate school and I was on my way home from Columbia, stopping over for my first meeting with J. Frank Dobie, the greatest Texan of them all, then and still. The rising star of Ransom was lighting up the book world and scaring the wits out of booksellers and librarians alike—all but Bertram Rota and Lew David Feldman (El Dieff) who were Ransom's agents abroad and at home.

In 1954 I thought I'd better meet the man whose hot breath was being felt even in Westwood. His opening remarks then were, "Larry, we need a librarian like you in Texas. Have you got a longtime contract at UCLA?" My answer was we need a dean like you in California and yes, I have a deep devotion to UCLA. I also told him that earlier offers of a tenured professorship at Columbia and the librarianship at Princeton had not lured me away.

After that monologue briefing I spent the next day at the Center with director Warren Roberts and librarian Mary Hirth, testing their processing and service procedures and the depth of the collections. I found to be false the gossip that the HRC had amassed vaults of unprocessed books and manuscripts that would not be available to scholars for twenty years or more. It was better prepared for service than my own library at UCLA.

Then I holed up in the Forty Acre Club and wrote up my notes of interviews, samplings, impressions, and comparisons with other national research libraries used in my own work. I concluded that Texas was to be praised and thanked for its service to scholarship now and for generations to come. What Ransom had wrought was in the same princely vein worked by Henry E. Huntington. Don't buy books, buy libraries and bookstores and even authors themselves. Not since HEH had there been such a fabulous collector.

On my last day in Austin at a farewell meeting with Ransom he again proposed an appointment as visiting professor in the English department and library school. I knew the head of the former and in the latter only Warren Roberts who held a professorship as well as the directorship of the Center. I gathered from him that Ransom made what appointments suited him regardless of academic protocol. Later I learned that a former member of the English department had satirized Ransom in a novel with the Blakean title, *The Horses of Instruction*.

Still the prospect of being swept up in the Ransom hurricane was a heady one. Upon submitting my report I told him that I would consider an appointment in the spring of 1971. No details were ever discussed nor did I ever have a written offer. Two more unalike university administrators than Harry Ransom and Richard Harvill were not even to be imagined.

The next development in my gypsy saga came later in 1970 with an invitation to speak in Colorado at the university campus in Boulder and in downtown Denver to alumni. In a talk called "Shoe on Other Foot" I spoke now as a library user, no longer a manager. I deplored librarians' growing self-preoccupation in the proliferation of committees and conferences whereby the welfare of the user was lost. I also enlarged on the theme of my Coulter lecture that academic librarians would gain true faculty status only by doing what the faculty did, e.g., teach, research and publish and that self-granted rank was rank indeed. As published by Editor Eshelman in the *Wilson Library Bulletin* the talk put me squarely at odds (not for the first time) with many former library colleagues. Faculty status and participative management have yet to be recognized by me as desiderata of good librarianship. Only when librarians achieve intellectual camaraderie with the faculty will they be accorded equal status.

I was the house guest of the Ralph Ellsworths. He was the former librarian of the university and one of the maverick members of the ARL with whom I had made common cause, although not in the matter of faculty status. Richard Dougherty the present librarian turned me over to his deputy, Leo Cobell, who with Marilyn Shuman, one of my former students now on the Colorado staff and who had inspired the invitation to me, made me at ease throughout my stay. A final bonus was a visit to Fred Rosenstock, leading Rocky Mountain bookseller-publisher.

Earlier in the Denver area, I had spoken to a joint meeting of the PNLA-MPLA, also talking with Alan Swallow, Robert Perkin, and Malcolm Glenn Wyer, the latter the only person ever to have been successively university librarian, Denver city librarian, and dean of the Denver library school—not to mention his having founded the Rocky Mountain Bibliographical Center and been president of a bank.

With the closing in 1984 of the University of Denver library school we have lost the school that did the most to encourage rapport between librarians and booksellers. "In it Together" was a theme sounded by me throughout my career in the United States and Great Britain. The Depression years spent in Zeitlin's antiquarian bookshop have never stopped serving me, even as my friendship with Jake has been richly enduring. To be present with Ward Ritchie when Tyrus Harmsen, the college librarian, presented Jacob Israel Zeitlin for an honorary doctorate of humane letters from Occidental College, was immensely gratifying.

On a hunch I telephoned President Harvill that if he were able to see me I would fly back to L.A. via Tucson. Although he was not in his office, his secretary assured me of a welcome and so I changed my flight. What was due to be an early evening non-stop was delayed by a faulty tachometer and an unscheduled stop in Colorado Springs with a change of planes. My nourishment en route was a ham sandwich and coffee. It was long after midnight when I reached Tucson and fell into bed at Ghost Ranch Lodge.

The next morning his secretary admitted that she had expected me a week later. The president had gone for the weekend to the university's Coronado Ranch in the Chiricahuas, 150 miles southeast of Tucson. She put me on the phone to him. He was distressed and said he would drive right down to the city. No, I insisted, I'll drive up to you. I had always wanted to see the legendary mountains of Cochise and his tribe of Apaches. When I insisted, Harvill gave me directions and I took off in a Hertz car, excited by the prospect of a long drive into an unknown mountain range and my own future.

By going east to the crossing of the San Pedro and up Texas Canyon between the Dragoons and Little Dragoons, past the Amerind Foundation and its dazzling display of Apache baskets, thence across the Willcox playa and southward in the Sulphur Spring valley beyond Elfrida nearly to Douglas on the border, and finally up Turkey Creek deep into the Chiricahuas, I came at last to the remote ranch, a former resort and boys' school now used by the university as a retreat and conference center.

We were in the high conifers, the weather was cold, and the huge living room in which the Harvills received me was warmed by massive stone fireplaces at each end. On a table to match the room George Harvill had spread out the colorful makings of the cascarones she was already making for a Christmas party for foreign students' wives. There we were served by the caretaker's wife T-bones in proportion to the room, with baked potatoes and a huge bowl of ranch-grown red tomatoes. I fell to without urging, having had nothing since early coffee and toast.

After we had cleared the dishes from the table, Mrs. Harvill withdrew for her nap and President Harvill began with gentle earnestness. "Dr. Powell," he said, "I believe by now you have some idea of what has long been my hope, that you, sir, are prepared to relinquish your wandering ways and join us for a semester or more. Only Mrs. Harvill knows what I am now about to tell you. After twenty years, this coming one will be my last as president of the university. Both it and I need a change. If you are still of a mind to come, and I sincerely hope you are, I am selfish enough to want you to come while I am still in office."

I was touched by his quiet seriousness, lightened by a humorous, self-deprecatory tone. I liked him more each time we met. I began by telling him so and of my feeling of honor, and yet also of my connection with Harry Ransom and the excitement at the prospect of working with him.

Harvill admitted to only slight knowledge of the Texan and was interested to hear of what Ransom had done to put Austin in library orbit, then asked softly, "Has Dr. Ransom made you a formal offer?" I said that he had not, nor had we gone beyond talk, adding for good measure that I had also had expressions of interest from President Popejoy of the University of New Mexico.

"Well," Harvill said, "I can tell you that old Tom Popejoy and Dick Harvill have never been able to compete with all that Texas oil money, and what I am now going to offer you, Dr. Powell, may seem paltry, and yet I am ready to propose a salary of $30,000 for the year 1970/71, with whatever rank and duties you desire. In short, sir, the ticket is yours to write."

All of this was said in the president's soft southern speech without any pressure. I asked for time to discuss it with Fay and also with Harry Ransom. We talked more about the new library school now nearing the end of its first year, of living costs in Tucson and so forth. I explained our attachment, especially Fay's, to the seacoast and that she never wanted to be away for more than a few months at a time. To that, Harvill suggested the possibility if she did not wish to move, of his providing additional funds for me to fly home weekends. He suggested further that I could come for only the spring semester for half that salary.

Whereupon after a walk around the grounds, I said goodbye

to Mrs. Harvill and headed back to Tucson and a flight to the coast.

A week later I had a letter from Harvill, recapping our conversation and after recognizing Fay's concern, formalizing his offer and inviting her to accompany me on an early visit to Tucson to see for herself what living there would involve.

Accordingly a trip was arranged for early June when the semester and commencement were over and the president had free time. He met us at the airport and with Fay in the front seat he drove us to our lodging at Ghost Ranch Lodge. For the next two days he and George Harvill paid us full attention. One day while the ladies were at Nogales for shopping across the border, I met with Donald Dickinson, director of the library school and his small faculty. At lunch with them and Dean Robert Paulsen of the College of Education, wherein the school was administratively placed, I spoke on what I perceived as the role of libraries and library education in Arizona and the wider Southwest.

The next day the president drove Fay and me to Kitt Peak to see the changes since our last visit in 1961. After viewing the solar and stellar telescopes we lunched with the astronomers in the observatory cafeteria which served food every eight hours around the clock.

Later that day the Harvills gave a reception for us at the Lodge on the Desert at which we met some distinguished members of the faculty. The next morning he drove us to the airport and pressed into my hand a generous check "for consulting services."

That was all it took to persuade Fay to leave seacoast for desert in the spring of 1971. Looking back, fifteen years later, and as permanent residents in Tucson, it now seems inevitable.

We planned to return in October to arrange for a place to live when my appointment began on February first. The Ghost Ranch Lodge was attractive. We could have a housekeeping cottage with a walled patio for our poodle Barlow, Besa's successor. Besa had lived to fourteen and Barlow was destined to live to twelve. Only those who have had small poodles know how dear they grow to be. Our puli Emily, long haired and rambunctious, would have to be boarded in Malibu. Brother Norman was now happily remarried and the house would be shut up and the garden left to languish. (That was before the house plant craze.)

On a return visit we looked at Tucson House, a high-rise apartment building, and found it cold and sterile. The Lodge was set amidst orange and eucalyptus trees with wide lawns, a pool and restaurant, and also one of the most celebrated cactus gardens in Tucson. It was owned by Arthur and Phoebe Pack, dedicated conservationists, who also owned the original Ghost Ranch church retreat near Abiquiu, New Mexico. The manager, Ken Tulloch and wife Gert, and Cottage G's maid Gretchen assured us of cordial care if we decided to reserve the cottage, as we did. We returned to Malibu with the future set and our minds at rest.

The rest of 1970 was spent on winding up the California book and getting ahead on chapters for *Westways*. On my last trip to Texas I had dug out what I needed from the Dobie archives and was ready to inaugurate the new series of Southwest classics with a chapter on his *Coronado's Children*.

I also brought to consummation a commission given to Gordon Newell, old classmate of Ritchie and me, to carve a granite hawk for the entrance of the new addition to the Occidental library. It was to cost $2500, and when I had succeeded in raising only half from friends and classmates, Fay and I gave the rest. I met Newell at the college the day he brought the finished sculpture in a pickup truck from his stoneyard in Monterey. I had not seen it since it was a great block of rough carnelian granite. Now as he stripped away the tarpaulin I saw the polished semi-abstract bird of reddish-brown-black stone and heard Newell's exultant shout when I laid my hands on the stone and said Yes! A love of Jeffers of forty years' standing was one of the bonds between us.

The formal unveiling and library dedication was held the last week before we were to leave for Tucson. I had come down with my old bronchial nemesis and hoped for enough strength to get me through the dedicatory speech and the drive to Tucson. The ceremony was held in the glowing Herrick Chapel next to the library. Fay and Gordon and Ward were there, and President Gilman, Dean Ryf, Librarian Harmsen and an overflow of students and faculty. The hawk was in place on a proper pedestal, its great weight making it an enduring addition to the library. I was happy looking back and looking ahead, grateful for what had been and eager for what was to come, as we approached a new land and life for us both.

VII

WRITING TWENTY YEARS after leaving UCLA and fifteen years since coming to Arizona for what was intended to be a one-semester appointment, I find it hard to sort out the motivations of these two decades, more varied and rewarding than any previous time of my life. I have learned that age increases sensitivity and appreciation at the same time that it takes away stamina and recuperative power.

Was the move as unexpected as it struck many to be? Since 1934 when I wrote my first Southwest book reviews and then twenty years later when I first saw the University of Arizona up close, followed by the Arizona history conference of 1960 and my commencement address a year later, I had felt the magnetism of the lands beyond the river. In 1962 I took the entire library school class and faculty to attend the Arizona State Library Association's conference in Tucson. Even before meeting President Harvill, I had been asked by President J. Lawrence Walkup of Northern Arizona University for library advice. That was in 1957 at a writer's conference in Flagstaff.

During that same decade while in Phoenix to address the Executives' Club at the invitation of City Librarian Jane Hudgins, I met President Grady Gammage of Arizona State University who also was seeking help for the library. My advice led to an ALA survey by Richard Harwell and Everett Moore. Nothing came of it because of the sudden death of the president. When his successor, G. Homer Durham, a UCLA Ph.D. in Political Science whom I had known as a graduate student, sought recommendation of a new librarian who could plan a new building and program, I suggested Everett Moore who declined the offer, preferring to remain at UCLA in charge of library public services. I then recommended Alan Covey of Sacramento State College, an expert library building planner, who carried out the program with distinction.

Such was the longstanding Arizona connection now getting stronger. Actually it began as far back as 1927 when I accompanied the Occidental Tigers on a field trip to play the Wildcats. We split the double-header and after a night on the cowtown, we headed home on the fifteen-hour Pickwick Stages' ride over gravelled roads.

A footnote to that trip came in 1971 when during an address to the University of Arizona Foundation, a support group headed by Leicester Sherrill, I reminisced about those games of the 1920s. I was approached afterward by alumnus Lawson Smith, president of Mountain Bell, who said that he had covered the games as sports editor of the student *Wildcat*.

To prove it not only did he recall the scores of both games, but also the complete Oxy roster—Solly Mishkin at first, Cliff Morse at second, Les Haserot at short, and on third one Tanaka whose first name eluded him. Shigeo, I promptly supplied, whereupon Smith went on to name the Oxy batteries: Teachout and Brobst, Gregory and Condé. He even remembered the nickname "Tiny" of that big Basque who bore the name of the Prince of Chantilly. I had to stop Smith from giving the batting averages of both teams. When I marvelled at his memory, he allowed that a flair for numbers had served him well in the telephone business.

Another way the threads of destiny are woven was illustrated that spring of 1971 when walking across campus to my first class, I encountered Frances Gillmor, the university's distinguished folklorist, whom I had met years before at a Huntington Library conference. I reminded her that it was her book, *Traders to the Navajos*, an account of the Wetherills of Kayenta, that had been the lead book in my debut as a *Westways* reviewer in June 1934.

That first spring of 1971 at the Ghost Ranch Lodge proved ideal for us both. As she had been during our stays at Dolphin Square, Fay was free of house and garden chores. Queenie in London and Gretchen in Tucson were maids to whose problems she could relate. My freedom was from administration and personnel matters, and also from demands as a speaker, writer, judge of contests, etc. which were now more frequent as I found myself a semi-public figure in California.

Although southern Arizona did not offer the remoteness I sensed awaited me in the west of England or the south of Portugal, it was far from the L.A. vortex. The University of Arizona in its organization and direct lines of communication and authority recalled UCLA of the 1930s.

Although the invitation to return on an open-ended appointment did not come until the end of the semester, we realized that a change of life was imminent. We began to think about a winter home in Tucson and a summer home in Malibu. As my juices rose I outlined a book about Arizona similar to the one written after our move to Malibu in 1955. The latter had begun with an essay on the seacoast written for Glen Dawson's miniature book series printed by Will Cheney. Now he suggested one on the desert, illustrated with botanical drawings by Don Perceval. It was reprinted in *Arizona Highways*, edited by Joseph Stacey, successor to Raymond Carlson, the magazine's founding genius for whom I had written many articles yet never met. My new Southwest series in *Westways* was benefiting from source material in the university library. In retrospect that first spring seems like a dream of good fortune after years of routine and responsibility. I have never stopped thanking Richard Harvill for perceiving my potential usefulness. When he said to write my own ticket, he meant it.

Together we chose the title, Professor in Residence, because jokingly no one would know what it meant nor what I did. I insisted that I report only to him. I responded to the unpretentious straightforward authority with which for twenty years he had run the university, steadily raising the standards of admission and recruitment of staff. When he offered me a full-time secretary, I declined as being someone I'd have to keep busy. Mine too was the choice to teach one seminar in the library school. Typing help would come from the president's secretarial pool. He walked me around campus to find a suitable office, finally choosing one in the building housing the History department. I went back to it only once before I decided that I needed to be where the action was, which was on the fourth floor of the Education building where the library school's offices and classrooms were—such as they were. It was makeshift and akin to the school's quarters at UCLA. Library schools are traditionally orphans when it comes to facilities.

Nevertheless I liked the feel of things with faculty, staff and students all crowded together. Director Don Dickinson and Dean Bob Paulsen gave me another warm welcome, although my first recommendation to them and to the president was that the school be taken out of the College of Education and given autonomy under the president or vice president, as well as quarters of its own. I also recommended more money to expand the school's library and was promptly given $10,000 by the president.

Useful early planning was done by University Librarian Robert K. Johnson, Assistant Librarian Donald M. Powell, former university librarian Rudolph Gjelsness who had returned as head of Special Collections after a long career as dean of the University of Michigan's library school. They were aided by Professor Arnulfo Trejo who had worked at UCLA in both library and library school and had returned to the city where he had grown up after his birth in Mexico. The new school had been placed in the College of Education, the president and the dean explained, for want of a better umbrella in its first vulnerable years.

The school had been in existence only a year and a half and it was not yet accredited by the American Library Association. I pointed out that autonomy might prove a factor in accreditation. The invitation to me was another of Harvill's moves toward gaining that cachet essential to its graduates' future placement. He knew that I had successfully been through the procedure twice at UCLA.

We arrived in Tucson the night before I was due to begin teaching. My bronchitis had worsened and after the 525-mile drive from Malibu, I had to lie down at the Lodge and let Fay do the unpacking. My recuperative power did not fail me and I met my first students the next afternoon at two o'clock. The class was again in Research Library Resources. The twenty-five students did not all have the advantage of previous library experience which meant a lot of basics had to be covered.

They were a diverse group, two thirds women, and from all parts of Arizona and the nation. They were assured that if accreditation did not occur until after they had graduated, they would nonetheless be blanketed in as graduates of an accredited school. It was good to be teaching again, using what I had learned at Columbia, UCLA, Wesleyan, Simmons, and Loughborough. Staff and library and administrative support was unfailing. The student morale was high with the excitement of a new venture we had known a decade earlier at UCLA. Mine was an anomalous position with no responsibility to either director or dean. If they were uncertain and even suspicious of my role, they did not show it.

I took to Dickinson from our first meeting. He was open and cordial with a sense of humor and a fair share of political savvy. He was popular with students and faculty from his open door policy. In fact we all had open doors, most of the offices were mere cubicles. The stalwarts were Elinor Saltus who had headed the original undergraduate program and now taught cataloging. Back in the 1950s I had sent over two of my staff, Gladys Coryell and Tatiana Keatinge, to teach in summer session. The other strong teacher was Helen Renthal who was responsible for school library work.

I made several field trips to ASU with Dickinson to see what they were up to in Tempe, and another into the Papago reservation to the village of Santa Cruz, a hundred miles west of Tucson. There Frances Deas Campbell, the first graduate of the school, was living with her husband John, a classical languages student, as librarian to the tribe. She and a driver gave bookmobile service to the remote villages. We lunched with the young couple in their trailer on ham, beans and rice and talked about my friendship with Henry Miller. Alas, no cole slaw in the Papaguería.

Although the Campbells are now separated, I have since joined up with them, in Austin where Deas is a college librarian, and on the western slope of the Rockies where John heads a tricounty consortium of Colorado libraries. For fifty years I have been forming such bonds that stretch and do not break. From them I draw renewed life.

The University of Arizona Foundation (which paid my salary that first year) called on me twice to speak at their monthly luncheon, once on Arizona's literary trails and then on research libraries. My message was that no great university exists which does not have a correspondingly great library. Years before I had said the same thing at a Carleton College convocation when Laurence M. Gould was the president. He was now in residence at the U. of A. since his retirement. He was the world famous Arctic geologist who had been second in command to Byrd at the South Pole. He was at that Foundation lunch when I made a plea for a major library development, and upon greeting me afterward, he warned President Harvill that my presence on campus was going to cost him money. My talk at Carleton, he joked, had resulted in just short of a student riot when they demanded more library support which indeed he gave them. We were delighted to be colleagues now, although our nicknames made for confusion in the president's office, as he was never sure which Larry it was who was calling. Gould and I agreed henceforth to be known by our Social Security numbers. The dedicated president of the Foundation, Leicester Sherrill, became one of my strongest advocates.

At that same luncheon when I repeated Benjamin Ide Wheeler's call in 1899 after he came from Johns Hopkins to the presidency of the University of California, "Give me a library and I will build a university around it," a tall rangy member of the audience strode up afterward, held out his hand and said,

"I'm Jack Schaefer and I agree with all you said."

"I've always wanted to meet the author of *Shane*," I replied.

He looked puzzled. "What do you mean?"

"You mean you're not the Jack Schaefer who wrote *Shane*?"

At that point President Harvill explained. "Dr. Schaefer is the dean of Liberal Arts and the former chairman of the Chemistry department."

Schaefer grinned. "I guess I'd better read *Shane*. Do you have a copy you'll lend me?"

The Dean of Liberal Arts, I soon found out, was next to the president in authority and power. It had been the position held by Harvill before he assumed the presidency and before the year was out, the same thing happened to Schaefer.

As the dark horse in the contest to name a successor to Harvill, Schaefer electrified the campus when he became the next president at age thirty-six. The process was long drawn out, as the candidates rose and fell. I was told later that when Schaefer faced his final interview, he remarked to the committee "If you took any longer, I'd be old enough to hold the job!" I also learned that beneath a brusque exterior and with no gift for small talk, was a warm and witty man with an intelligence both analytical and philosophical. We were destined to become friends and remain so to this day.

That initial encounter at which Schaefer applauded my belief that university and library excellence were inseparable, determined my role at Arizona for the next decade and a half. When I called on him at the end of the semester to congratulate him on his promotion and to give him a copy of the newly published *California Classics*, he said "I hope you will come back next year. You'll always have a friend in this office."

He went on to question me about the need for a new library. Students were increasingly unhappy with the old building's lack of features and services now found in university library buildings throughout the country. In the course of my class in research libraries there was mounting concern by the members over the inadequacy of the library building which was first opened in 1923. One member served as the graduate students' representative on the campus-wide library council, and knowing of my closeness to the president she asked if I could persuade Harvill to meet with the committee to discuss the need for a new building. His reply to me was blunt: "I have never met with them because they have never asked me."

A meeting was arranged at which he asked me to sit in with him. The university librarian explained that an out of town trip would prevent him from attending; he sent his associate librarian Donald Powell in his stead. In the Librarian's absence and Don Powell's diffidence, the meeting proved a waste of the president's time.

In my first meeting with Schaefer he asked if the present building could be added to. No, I said, it has already been enlarged more than once and any future articulation of the units would be impractical if not impossible. I also told him of the student unhappiness. What's to be done? he asked. Authorize an objective survey by an outside team, I replied, and recalled the one carried out earlier at ASU. He concluded by telling me that Harvill had put me in the 71/72 budget as Professor in Residence and Consultant to the President on Libraries and Library Education. A pretty fancy title for a little guy like you, he grinned as I took my leave.

I reported to Fay that everything pointed to our return for the spring semester 1972.

I had made good progress that first spring on the new series in *Westways* and yet much remained to be written. I had originally expected to take up Ransom's deferred proposal in that spring of '72. In the absence of any word from him, I let the Arizona connection strengthen. Then I heard that he had relinquished the chancellorship in one of the periodic shakeups that have occurred in Texas.

That meant the end of the Texas connection. Fay and I have regretted not having experienced Austin, although the leap of that once quiet capital and university town into the high tech age makes it a less attractive place to live. Harry Ransom died in 1976. In a review of his posthumous book on education in Texas, I paid tribute to that brilliant star.

In Tucson we had been paying $30 a day for the cottage at Ghost Ranch Lodge and when we agreed to return for another year it seemed better to own a place of our own. Fay took the initiative. After some talk of building our own house, she arranged for us to go exploring with an agent. She was Ann Frey, wife of Judge William Frey of the Superior Court, and she took us to an attractive area in the Catalina foothills almost to Skyline Drive. We had told her that we wanted a separate house. She proved an artful salesperson for what she showed us was a condominium, although so designed that it first appeared to be a separate dwelling.

We took to it almost on sight as we had to the Malibu property in 1955. Although we looked at one other possibility in the foothills, we knew we had come without knowing it to our inevitable place, to echo Jeffers' words on first seeing Carmel. We bought 6288 North Campbell Avenue in May 1971, paying the price in cash. I have always regarded it as my Uncle Harold's gift to us, as the money was part of a legacy upon his death in 1964.

The semester ended with a party given by my students at which they presented me with a monk's cloth missionary robe and a pair of Mexican sandals, with the stern injunction to go forth and carry the light and the life into the darkest corners of the land.

At commencement my Arizona fate was sealed by the award of an honorary Doctorate of Humane Letters. As I was presented by Dean Paulsen and President Harvill conferred the degree, he clasped my hand and said softly, "This is my last official act."

Before returning to California we closed the unfurnished condo and headed for Malibu. We returned briefly in October to buy basic household furnishings. The weather had turned cold. Rain was falling. Rats had chewed the wiring of the rooftop furnace-cooler unit. We "heated" with a fireplace gas log and wore our English woolens. There are only thirteen other one-story adobe units in Catalina Townhouses, all artfully designed by Juan Werner-Bas, a Mexican architect. The three-acre grounds are planted mostly with Sonoran natives. There is also a swimming pool, a godsend in the summer.

When we returned to Tucson, Dickinson and I staged a regional conference on library education which I had persuaded the Foundation to fund. From UCLA came Andy Horn who was appalled by our school's meager facilities. As a member of the ALA Accreditation committee he was in a strong position to advise Dean Paulsen and President Schaefer on the school's needs.

In Malibu for the rest of the year I was kept informed of the increasing student and staff unrest with the library and its administration, and then in December John Schaefer urgently called to ask if I would come over at once. He went on to say that he was prepared to implement a library survey.

I flew over the next day. We lunched at the downtown Old Pueblo Club where privacy was ensured. Schaefer said that he intended to begin a campus-wide overhaul by assigning the university librarian to the library school where he already had tenure as a full professor, an act which had Richard Harvill's approval. It was agreed that Don Powell could act as head librarian until a replacement were found.

The other startling thing he said was that he and Harvill had agreed before the transfer of power to change the library building priority from 14TH to first place, thus dropping the College of Law back to second place. When he asked what steps should be taken to implement the survey, I produced an outline, complete with recommended personnel, costs of fees, travel, lodging and also publication for limited distribution. I had thus used my time on the hour-long flight from L.A.

We agreed that implementation would wait upon my return a month hence. I flew back the same day with Schaefer's thanks for keeping pace with him. Despite the thirty years between us it was not hard to do. We were the same kind of administrators with the decisiveness that had marked our careers, mine of a much smaller nature.

Changing presidential bosses only meant shifting gears to a higher ratio. Their characters were the same: intelligence, energy, integrity, and devotion to the university. Both were naturally authoritative and ready to act with a minimum of advice. Harvill had come in 1934 as an assistant professor of Economics, Schaefer in 1961 with the same rank in Chemistry. Each rose through department chairmanship and deanship to the presidency. I responded to both as I added them to the pantheon of super bosses I had admired and served: Sproul, Dykstra, and Murphy.

Before returning to Tucson I lined up the survey team: Ray Swank, former Stanford librarian and now dean of the Berkeley library school, as leader, aided by Mel Voigt, librarian of the university's San Diego campus, and Page Ackerman, UCLA's associate librarian—a blue-ribbon group. It took some persuasion as they were all deeply involved in their jobs. I emphasized that theirs was an unusual opportunity: their recommendations would not be filed and forgotten; a new young president and a new librarian and library building in the offing meant an opportunity to set the U. of A. on a new track.

That is what happened in the spring semester of 1972. The team divided up with Swank taking general management, collection development and a look at library education; Voigt technical processes and building planning, Ackerman personnel. These were fields in which all three had achieved notable success on their home campuses and beyond. They worked with intensity and sensitivity to staff morale. Their report was edited by Swank. I made a résumé for the Regents which the president distributed at their earliest meeting. When I laid it on Schaefer's desk he said only, "Larry, you're a prince." In its new president the university had a leader who promised to be fully as strong as his predecessor.

My next assignment was to advise Schaefer on the search for a new librarian. A committee was appointed under the chairmanship of Albert Weaver, a physicist and the new executive vice president. It included Hermann Bleibtreu, an anthropologist and the new dean of Liberal Arts; Jimmye Hillman, professor of Agricultural Economics; Albert Gegenheimer, professor of English and chairman of the Faculty; Don Dickinson, director of the library school, and Patricia Turner, chair of the library staff association. My role was to assist Weaver in the paperwork and procedure.

Two strong administrative assistants helped: Helen Sigmund who had moved from Liberal Arts with the president and Nita Haddock, Weaver's aide. The paper flew back and forth as the position was nationally advertised and résumés snowed in. The job was a plum and many hopefuls applied. One application came from a librarian I had fired at UCLA, another from one who after speaking to the UCLA students had been judged by them as the worst of the year. Neither knew of my presence at Arizona.

I favored no candidate, although I did have knowledge and impressions of many of them from earlier work in the ARL and ALA. A dark horse emerged near the closing date with a telephone call from David Laird, associate director of the University of Utah library. Among other duties he had planned a new building for the Salt Lake school, and as the director was a professor, Laird was actually running the library.

I had not seen him since 1966 when he was the president of my last class at UCLA. He had enrolled after service in the Navy and as an undergraduate he had worked in the music library and as the Clark Library's "Saturday boy." As class president he had represented the students with tact in a matter critical of my administration. In his last semester he had been an outstanding member of my seminar in Southwest studies and had also excelled as a member of Andy Horn's printing chapell.

At his UCLA graduation Laird had told me that his ultimate hope was to head a library somewhere in Utah, New Mexico or Arizona. He then went off to the university's Davis campus as a reference assistant, and later almost emigrated to Australia with wife and children as head of the Richard Abel company, before Utah changed his direction.

When he called to ask if it were too late to apply, I admitted that it was not, then added, "Aren't you at thirty-five a bit young for the job?" His reply was to the point: "No more than you were in 1944 when you became librarian of UCLA." He had me there, although the fact is I had reached the advanced age of thirty-seven. That I had had no administrative experience when President Sproul, acceding to faculty requests, appointed me, Laird was smart enough not to recall.

"All I ask is to be interviewed," he asked, "and the rest is up to me."

That seemed reasonable. I liked his confidence, and yet I was not convinced that he could compete with the two seasoned applicants that had been chosen to come for interview. They were Eldred Smith, formerly at Berkeley and now librarian of SUNY Buffalo (who later went to Minnesota), and David Heron, librarian of the University of Kansas. In 1948 I had given Heron his first job out of library school and then watched him go on to Stanford, the Embassy in Tokyo, Nevada, and now Kansas (who later went to the Hoover Institution and has finally retired).

I made arrangements for the three interviews, including the campus rounds and dinner with the search committee either at the Old Pueblo Club or the Arizona Inn, and a final interview with Schaefer. At his meeting with the president, Heron, aged 57, withdrew, saying that as a young president, Schaefer deserved a librarian of his own generation. When the committee finally recommended Laird, Schaefer recognized the soundness of Heron's advice and offered the job to a man even younger than he was. The ensuing eleven years of the Schaefer-Laird administration confirmed the wisdom of his choice.

That Laird had been engaged since library school on an annotated bibliography of the Hopi tribe was not lost on Anthropologist Bleibtreu. The bibliography was published by the University of Arizona Press in 1977 to excellent reviews.

Schaefer had obtained planning money for a new library providing he would submit schematics to the legislature by July 15. Laird was not due to take up his appointment until July 1. While still in Utah he was given six weeks to prepare the detailed information on the new library's character and needs. When he demurred at what appeared to be an impossible request, Schaefer said bluntly, "If you can't do it, I'll get someone who can."

Whereupon Laird commuted weekends from Salt Lake to Tucson with a change of plane in Phoenix, to work with Don Powell and his staff committee. Somehow the deadline was met and the legislative appropriation secured.

My second spring was even busier than the first. This time my seminar was in Southwest studies to which I brought as guest speakers such notables as Alfred Knopf, Mrs. Joseph Wood Krutch, writer William Eastlake, and the now internationally known UCLA biomedical librarian, Louise Darling.

When I needed to rest my voice I played for the class a recording made at UCLA in 1950 of Dylan Thomas reading his own and the poetry of Hardy, Yeats, and Auden. We made it on his last fatal American tour and it never failed to move hearers by the poet's controlled passion and power. Another special event was a showing of the video recording of "And Now Miguel," the Joseph Krumgold documentary of sheepherding in the Sangre de Cristos of northern New Mexico. At the end of spring 1972 I had the satisfaction of seeing two of our graduates become Tucson's first professional newspaper librarians, Charlotte Kenan at the *Citizen* and Sandy Hall at the *Star*. I also succeeded in steering several other new librarians toward permanent work in Arizona and New Mexico.

One of the most unusual students was a middle-aged ranchwoman named Winogene Bundy. She and her husband Bob, a Hughes aircraft engineer, had also come from Malibu to take up a 500-acre spread 50 miles east of Tucson on the San Pedro river. From there he carpooled to Hughes and she to campus where over two years' time she was concurrently taking an M.A. in History and a Master's degree in Library Science.

Win enrolled in my seminars of 1971 and 1972 and like Roger Mortimer at Loughborough she decided to become a bookseller, and to open a shop at their Singing Wind Ranch. When I sought to discourage her choice of the remote location, she smiled and quoted Emerson on mouse traps.

Now going on fifteen years later she has indeed proved me

wrong. The world has beaten a path of sorts (Please Close the Cattle Gate!) to her door. Despite the tragic loss of Bob to cancer, Win has persisted in selling books and riding herd on her registered Charolais. She also sells a goodly number of my books.

A neat coup was scored by Dickinson in bringing Larry Powell and Jesse Shera to his faculty in the same year. Shera was one of my two favorite library "enemies"; the other was Ralph Shaw. Although I recognized their creative minds, I found Shera's theoretical, Shaw's technical, the one interested in ideas more than practice, the other in process more than people. Yet both proved valuable in what had too long been trade school librarianship. Neither did I care to be with for long. Such were my limitations.

When Shera and I found ourselves on the same campus at the same time, neither expressed any astonishment. Dickinson grinned, rightfully pleased with himself. I attended Jesse's lecture on how foolish it was for a library to own an original Gutenberg Bible and didn't have what once would have been a rise in blood pressure. We shared mesquite-broiled steaks and beans at the desert camp of Jessica and Jim Perry. Both of us had aged, even mellowed.

Shera was one of our few distinguished contributors to library literature, using his pen like a scalpel to dissect our follies. I am grateful to have survived him. I once woke in a cold sweat, having dreamed that he had written my obituary and I was condemned to read it.

Ralph Shaw was a different kind of hombre, using a machete on our sentimentality and needless routines. I felt it first after my ALA keynote speech, "The Alchemy of Books," given at the Waldorf in 1952. When I finished speaking to my largest audience up to then, relieved and reasonably pleased with myself, there came Shaw down the aisle holding out his hand. I extended mine, expecting congratulations such as I was receiving from all sides (the most moving of all from Anne Carroll Moore, retired head of children's work in the NYPL). Instead he slipped me a printed card which read WHAT A LOAD OF BULLSHIT. Whereupon he vanished in the crowd with a hyena laugh.

I also remember our last meeting. We were fellow speakers in 1965 at a UCLA Institute for Indonesian librarians held at Lake Arrowhead. My assignment was to meet him at the L.A. airport and fetch him to the resort high in the San Bernardino mountains. I was driving a Jaguar then, one of the first 3.4 models that would really move. Ralph remained calm as I took the mountain curves at what I regarded as a reasonable speed. We talked all the way up, during the institute (being paid for that), and back down at the end of the next day. I learned a lot about his origins. When I told him that we had a golden puli and a miniature poodle, he was delighted. He proceeded to tell me about the USDA's cross-breeding kennel in Maryland. He also said that the puli and the poodle are the smartest of all dogs.

I have a hunch that if I had spent that much time alone with Shera I would have come to like him. Which proves that I *have* mellowed or does it?

In 1977 we flew to Honolulu with the U. of A. football team as the guests of President Schaefer. By then Shaw had died as the emeritus dean of the University of Hawaii's new library school. I phoned his second wife, Mary Andrews, who had been on the UCLA Biomedical library staff, to ask about a biography of Ralph. "He didn't want one," she said. "His work was all that mattered to him."

Would that he could know that the press he founded is the publisher of this book. Thanks, Ralph, and no b.s.

Waikiki was nearly unrecognizable from what I remembered from my first sight in 1925 when I was on the Dollar liner *President Harrison* en route around the world. Except for the Moana Hotel the beach was now monstrous with highrise hotels and apartments. I strolled over to the old Moana from where we were staying at the Sheraton Waikiki, took a seat in a corner of the lobby of that beautiful lowrise building and remembered that it was here that our ensemble had played for tea dancing the two days we were in port. Nothing is ever really lost. What once was mine still was and would always be.

I resumed writing for *Arizona Highways* and *New Mexico* magazine in addition to the monthly feature in *Westways*. Trips were made to speak to the New Mexico Library Association and to UCLA to join Lawrence Durrell in a tribute to Henry Miller on his 80TH birthday. Assignments carried out for Schaefer included a reorganization of the library's Special Collections, traditionally a troubled area. It was only natural that some longtime members of the staff had come to regard the library as their own sacred province not subject to growth and change.

Both Schaefer and Laird inherited problems Harvill had to leave unsolved. Both had the toughness to tackle them and the stamina to survive attacks, disloyalty, and worse. The university art museum was another troubled area. The president appointed me to an inquiry committee under a new dean of Liberal Arts, Paul Rosenblatt, and then to a search committee with him and Professor Howard Conant of the Art department to seek a new director of the museum. Our choice was Dr. Peter Bermingham of the Smithsonian Museum.

Another committee served on was to select a new director of the University Press. Our choice of Stephen Cox from Nebraska has been richly justified.

I continued to press the dean and the president for more space for the library school, now urgent because of the impending Accreditation visit. During my third year of appointment in the spring of 1973, I persuaded Schaefer to come to the Education building and see for himself how congested our quarters were. The students were working at packing case desks in the corridors. The small library was filled to the walls and ceiling with books and readers. The president walked through with poker face, then offered the choice of three locations, two within a year or more, one within months—a former resort and fraternity house built around a large patio and a block from campus. It was occupied by Education people which meant relocating fifty or more live bodies, and then remodelling the veritable warren of rooms and bathrooms.

How much would it cost? Schaefer asked. $50,000, I ventured. We got the go-ahead, thanks to Dean Paulsen's acquiescence—the dean had to face the evictees—the cost only $100,000 more than my horseback estimate. However we were able to show the remodelling plans to the Accrediting team's visit. The fact that its chairman Allen Veaner and I both drove Citroëns might have helped in our getting the necessary credential.

In that summer of '73 Fay and I lived in Santa Fe for six weeks in an adobe house over the wall from the State Library and the Capitol. I worked every morning in the library on the final chapters of *Southwest Classics* and also visited Frank Waters near Taos. The state library staff took me in as a colleague and gave an example of unprecedented service: their reference librarian commuted every day the hundred and twenty mile roundtrip from Albuquerque; and when I reported needing a reference found only in the University of New Mexico Library, she volunteered to Xerox it that night after she got home and bring it with her the next morning. In my book Margaret Kutcher thus moved another step toward sainthood.

The new library building went forward as planned with $13,000,000 provided by the legislature. Laird's new associate librarian, J. Robert Adams, now the librarian of Wesleyan University, was the chief planning officer. The final result which achieved many awards is one of the most beautiful and functional of modern university libraries.

Meanwhile the president was having problems. Because of a dispute within the university when he relieved the head of surgery in the College of Medicine from his administrative though not professorial appointment, all hell broke loose. Schaefer stood firm and time has vindicated his strength and wisdom.

His stroke of genius in persuading Ansel Adams, his photographic mentor, to donate his lifetime archives to a new Center for Creative Photography, although it was funded by the Foundation from private sources, annoyed the legislature. They vented their displeasure by denying the new library furnishings such as tables and chairs. Whereupon the Foundation staged a luncheon for four hundred in the empty building at which I spoke on the joys of reading while standing. When the legislators began to feel heat from the students who were being denied their new facility, they caved in.

Earlier acquaintance through speaking and writing with former governors, legislators, and regents made me useful to the university on various occasions. Several times during the year when I was writing the Bicentennial history of the state for the National Endowment for the Humanities, I spoke to legislative meetings in Phoenix on the need for research collections on the three campuses. I became persona grata at NAU and ASU when they realized that my devotion to Arizona was not limited to Pima County. It was a role I had played in California in becoming accepted on all of the campuses as a friend of the statewide university. UCLA had long suffered from the parochialism of the old-timers at Berkeley, and in Arizona there was the same feeling on the Tempe campus toward what some regarded as Tucson's dog-in-the-manger attitude. It seemed inevitable—I said so more than once—that the Phoenix area was destined to have a university commensurate with the one at Tucson. In my years in Arizona I watched ASU moving in that direction.

I came to the university at the close of a dominant administrator's twenty-year tenure in which the faculty played a lesser role. This was different from what I had been accustomed in California where the administrators and the faculty were more or less co-equal. In his time Richard Harvill brought the university to the threshold of major rank. Although he served only a little more than half as long, John Schaefer led the university to make a leap forward. He too was a strong man although he increasingly respected the faculty's rising desire for more participation in their governance.

I did not play a strong faculty role. Even while teaching in the library school, I was only marginally concerned with faculty matters and committees nor did I attend the campus-wide faculty senate's meetings. I had been through it all in California. My usefulness now lay elsewhere. That few on campus knew who I was or what I did left me content.

I found the university faculty at large lacking in cohesion and a sense of its potential power. There was no faculty clubhouse like the UCLA Faculty Center or the clubs at Berkeley and Columbia which served as nerve centers for thought and action. A dining room in the Arizona Student Union was a poor substitute. Another lack was of a publication to provide an independent medium for faculty expression and concern. *Arizona and the West* and the *Arizona Quarterly*, devoted to publication in history and literature, both written mostly by scholars elsewhere, did nothing to give the Arizona faculty a sense of itself.

One of the library school's most successful programs and in which I had no part, was carried out by Dickinson, Trejo and staff. With federal funding this was meant to train Spanish speaking librarians. It was repeated for several years with impressive results in training and placement. A memorable feature was the Christmas posada held by the Hispanic students and their families. Now on our visits to Santa Fe I visit with Orlando Romero, history librarian of the Museum of New Mexico, as we recall those joyous GLISA years in Tucson.

When I say I had no part in the program, I must add that I did speak each year to those special students and at the end of the final year, when Don Dickinson had a piano moved into the patio, I sat down at the bench and more than paid my dues.

Several times when I gave the orientation lecture to new faculty at the beginning of the academic year, I referred to myself as the president's biblio-therapist, and on less formal occasions as the court jester. "Like hell he is," Schaefer once interrupted, "he's the palace dwarf!" I remember his once telling me that he didn't care what I did just as long as I was around. I was helpful at times in advising him not to accept gifts with strings attached. A bronze statue of a flute player in front of the university library was acquired from sculptor John Waddell with private funds as a result of my urging. Together Schaefer and I made an unsuccessful one-day flying trip to Southern

California to seek the fabulous Honeyman collection on the history of science.

As a chemist educated at Brooklyn Polytechnic and Illinois and seasoned at Berkeley and Caltech, it was natural that Schaefer would interest himself in seeing the library develop strong holdings in the history of science, and this he did. Unforeseen was his equally strong interest in the Humanities and Fine Arts. Working with Laird he infused the library budget with massive appropriations which gave the U. of A. one of the country's fastest growing research libraries.

During the eleven years I worked with him, my greatest satisfaction came from seeing John Schaefer grow in knowledge and sophistication. I saw him take in stride such diverse authors as Melville, Mark Twain, Lawrence, Jeffers, and Zane Grey. He went beyond me to an appreciation of Virginia Woolf and read an essay on her work to the Tucson Literary Club. Even more extraordinary were the photographs he made in the field with Bernard "Bunny" Fontana for their books about the Tarahumara and Papago Indians. I was proud to dedicate my rivers book to him. To him and Richard Harvill I owe an unexpected new life and career.

JPS and I grew to like each other, offering mutual support and encouragement in different ways. As he was younger than our older son, I sometimes assumed a fatherly role when I saw the pressure he was under from faculty, students, regents, legislators, and citizens suspicious of what was going on behind the ivied walls.

I was glad to be a free agent, home at last from the academic wars and beholden only to one boss. The original appeal of university librarianship had been an escape from a single departmental discipline. Now as I aged, my patience lessened, thus unfitting me for most committee work.

I continued to be an occasional spokesman for the U of A Foundation. Fay and I made annual gifts which brought us membership in the President's Club of donors. Our gifts were used on a matching basis for grants to faculty research projects, publications, and conferences. I kept up a steady schedule of speaking to support groups at ASU and NAU. On campus I gave the annual address to Phi Beta Kappa and Sigma Xi, to the Honors Convocation, and when at the last minute in 1976 a commencement speaker cancelled, I filled in with "A Hunger for Heroes," a roll call of some of the state's greats. I'm probably the only speaker to have given two commencement addresses, fifteen years apart, at the same university. How could I refuse if they should ask me in 1991 when I'll be only 85?

When Bruce Babbitt was elected Attorney General he wrote me that my *Southwestern Book Trails* (1963) had been influential in persuading him to return to Arizona after leaving geology for the practice of law in Austin for President Johnson's End Poverty program. We became friends and after he was twice elected governor, he suggested me as a member of the university board of regents, an honorary and yet demanding post. As much as I appreciated the recognition and the need for an academic voice on the board, I knew it would be the end of me as a writer and I respectfully said no.

I did accept the governor's appointment to a committee to reorganize the troubled *Arizona Highways*. This took me repeatedly to Phoenix for meetings of the statewide blue ribbon committee and to interview candidates for the editorship. I found Bruce Babbitt akin to John Schaefer in youthful idealism and vigor, although more politically oriented.

As the library school moved toward its second accreditation visit, it was apparent that its administration had gone slack. Dickinson had been unable to secure an assistant director or an administrative assistant and the necessary routine and planning work was being neglected as his interest in teaching and research took precedence. He was an increasingly effective teacher and correspondingly ineffective manager.

When the school's faculty split for and against the way the school was being administered, the dean and the president invited Tom Galvin, dean of the University of Pittsburgh's library school and now the executive director of the ALA, to come as a consultant. His recommendation led to the search for a new director.

Chaired by the assistant dean of Education, Mark Smith, and including Lee Jones, dean of the Graduate College, Professor Margaret Maxwell of the library school, David Laird, and myself, the committee chose Ellen Altman, formerly of the Rutgers and Indiana library schools as the new director. Dickinson was thenceforth able to give full time to teaching and research and with outstanding results.

My body was beginning to feel the effects of the demands made on it as I continued the pace I had led since leaving UCLA for what had been meant to be my "sunset years." The university hospital proved a sanctuary as I went "into the pit for repairs,"— in 1972 a long deferred hernia operation and in 1974 relief from bronchial pneumonia. The latter coincided with our leasing our furnished Malibu house to a young couple from New York.

Taxes had kept rising and it also proved increasingly hard to manage two homes as I became more involved the year round in Arizona, although I consistently refused appointment for the full academic year. What they got was full-time work for half-time pay, which is the way I wanted it to be.

Readying the Malibu house for the new occupants proved exhausting for us both, and as we returned to Tucson in the fall of 1974 I was coughing incessantly. Whereupon Fay hustled me to Emergency where for five hours the doctors worked unavailingly to free the impacted bronchials. Finally with the help of tetracycline I yielded up matter the size of a walnut, fell back and craved nothing but ripe canteloupe.

It was the sickest and thinnest I've ever been. Fay nursed me through a few weeks of what passed for idleness. The Lairds came by. The Schaefers sent a terrarium. I made notes on the Bicentennial history due in a year's time, and also met my *Westways* deadline on a new series of Southwest personalities. *Southwest Classics* had appeared in book form that spring, dedicated to Richard Harvill, and a party for the book and him was given at the Overland Bookshop. Alas, Dorothy McNamee was dead of cancer not long after. Tucson has yet to have another bookish rendezvous like her Overland shop.

With the 1974 move we took up legal residence in Arizona.

Although Fay has never stopped missing it, I had had enough of seacoast living. No longer was Malibu the idyllic place of the 1950s. The beach was crowded with litterers. The highway which once took 45 minutes to reach UCLA now took an hour and a half. Then in the fall of 1978 fire meant that our house was no longer there.

Among the answers given when asked why I retired early from UCLA was that I intended to devote more time to writing. Most of what I wrote during my years on the Westwood campus was on the margin of a full-time, often overtime job. While in the library my time was for people and paperwork, never for my own writing. Writing early or late, I became an essayist, bibliographer and book reviewer, with energy for only those shorter forms.

And yet there was always the desire to dig deeper. Long buried and still there is the manuscript of a novel written during student years in Europe. In 1941–43 before administrative responsibility absorbed me, I wrote still another short novel and a long half of a much longer one. Then for more than twenty years I became another kind of a writer.

The dam broke on June 30, 1966 and new work came with a rush and is still coming, although at a slower flow. Since then I have had the freedom and the strength, and most important, the belief to write what demanded to be written. The Arizona years have been the richest yet. I have been able to give my work breathing space in which it could find form for richer substance. I remember coming upon the doctor-poet William Carlos Williams' autobiography when browsing in the London Library and reading these words: "Concentration is what a man needs to bring his mind to harvest. To drain off the good we must find quietude."

This I have found in Arizona, with great freedom to make my own schedule and was why I insisted upon only one-semester appointments.

My last class was met in 1975. For my 70TH birthday the next year a Festschrift, *Voices from the Southwest*, was compiled by Dickinson, Laird, and Maxwell and printed by Paul

Weaver at his Northland Press in Flagstaff. In 1979 I retired to emeritus status although the president assured me I could remain on appointment as long as I wished. We did not need the salary and I wanted the sense of absolute freedom.

As I continued to travel on field work and to speak in different parts of the country, I found that airplanes gave privacy. Even as John Schaefer used his hours aloft for reading, so did I profit as a writer. Now I was able to give form to works of fiction, biography, history, geography, and music. The fruits of fortune also needed friendship to bring them into print. To the *Westways* editors, Larry Meyer, Dave Dutton and Frances Ring, and to publishers Ward Ritchie, Paul Weaver and Mark Sanders, the *Classics* books and two further volumes on the Southwest, owed their being; and it was Ward Ritchie who republished in paperback the Malibu book written in the 1950s with Will Robinson.

A long and fruitful relationship with *Westways*, going back to 1934, came to an end when the publisher, a huge insurance company misleadingly named the Automobile Club of Southern California, decided that the magazine should be ended as the diversified cultural medium it had become beginning in the 1920s with Phil Townsend Hanna, and be made more of a house organ.

With the abrupt dismissal of Editor Frances Ring, I took my leave with a final contribution in the issue of November 1978 on my old sculptor friend Gordon Newell. I am still receiving letters from former *Westways* readers wondering what happened. Frances Ring went on to another career in the School of Journalism at USC and has recently published her reminiscences of F. Scott Fitzgerald whose secretary she was during the last year of his life.

The short novel proved the form most natural for me. In *The Blue Train*, *The River Between*, *El Morro*, and *Portrait of My Father*, I was unconsciously realizing Willa Cather's wish to throw all the furniture out the window and leave the stage bare for essential description and action. I was also seeking essence and meaning, to give form to what had been disordered, and to resolve harmonic discords. To Noel Young and his Capra Press in Santa Barbara are owed those novels and the translation of two of them into French. Henceforth he was to serve as my publisher, as Ward Ritchie and William Targ had done earlier.

The Blue Train was particularly well received in France. In a review in *Les Nouvelles Litteraires*, François Nourissier wrote "Ah! Quel livre seduisante! Un chef d'oeuvre enigmatique et narquois du style rétro."

A review by Robert Kirsch, literary editor of the *Los Angeles Times*, saved the book from the critical neglect it faced because of local publication. It also led to its being optioned several times for films, the latest by Cynthia Cherbak, a Hollywood writer who has written the screenplay. All's lacking now is a producer with big bucks and a couple of trains.

As a graduate student Bob Kirsch had worked in the UCLA library. We first met in the men's washroom where he had gone for a smoke. There we began to talk about literature. Years later in 1980 at a service at the University of Judaism in Los Angeles, I was one of several, including his son Jonathan, who spoke in his memory and also one of the few men present not wearing the traditional skullcap.

I had seen Kirsch not long before he was carried off by cancer. Ours was a chance encounter on State street in Santa Barbara. I was en route to the airport carrying a copy just given me by Noel Young of Kirsch's latest book of collected essays. When I asked him to autograph it, he wrote on the title-page, while resting the book on my shoulder, "For Larry, wise teacher, good friend, the man who proved to me that getting older meant getting better, even younger."

Here also is a paragraph from his review of *The Blue Train*: "The poignance and power, tenderness and excitement Powell was always quick to recognize in others, comes out of the material of his own experience. It is the work of a journeyman novelist and one of the best pieces of fiction I have read in a long time."

The book also found readers after Kevin Starr's review in the *San Francisco Examiner*. His was the most perceptive of all looks at a writer long distinguished as a librarian. "What a wonderful paradox," Starr exclaimed, "The library administrator contains within himself a dialectical opposite—a passionately sensuous literary artist, capable of capturing the incandescence of awakened flesh. The bookman, responsible for the growth of an institution, holds in delicate tension the free-and-easy bohemian, capable of throwing it all over for love or for art. Did Powell not publish this novel some 30 years ago because to publish his alter ego would in some way kill him off?"

These not uncritical publishers and editors did not try to make me write only what they believed the public would buy. Also my not requiring academic advancement or substantial royalties meant that I could be my own kind of writer. Except for Bill Targ and Elizabeth Riley at Crowell, for whom I edited a *Leaves of Grass* for young people (which has continued to sell for more than 25 years), I have had no relations with eastern publishers. I am content to be published in the West.

Paul Weaver and then Mark Sanders of the Northland Press in Flagstaff encouraged and published *From the Heartland* and *Where Water Flows: the Rivers of Arizona*.

The latter which also first appeared as installments in *Westways*, was the most unusual and enjoyable of all my writing projects. It was a collaboration with two young graduate geologists, one a photographer, the other the owner-pilot of a Cessna 180. Michael Collier was tall and rangy, Christopher Condit short and stocky. While Chris flew and Mike shot, I held down the plane's back seat with maps, tools, fig bars and a thermos of tea, and sought to tell them above the roar what I wanted to see. In the course of two years' flying, ground work, and reading, the book boiled down to personal essays illustrated with Collier's color shots. A grant from the University of Arizona Foundation and cooperation with Mark Sanders made a beautiful book to which Governor Bruce Babbitt wrote the Foreword.

The culmination was Babbitt's flying down from Phoenix in his Queenaire, bringing Chris, Michael and Mark to a publication party given by Win and Bob Bundy at the ranch on the San Pedro. Since then Chris has gone on to gain his Geology

Ph.D. from the University of New Mexico and, utterly unlikely, Michael has earned an M.D. from the University of Arizona and is now doing his residency at a Family Clinic in Grand Junction on the Colorado, together with his beauteous wife Rose and their assortment of cameras, rafts, and kayaks. As long as young ones like these keep coming, our future looks good.

When Ansel Adams asked me to write the introductory essay for his *Photographs of the Southwest*, I was inspired to one of my best efforts. My relationship with President Schaefer at the time he and Adams were establishing the Center for Creative Photography had renewed my contact with Adams which first occurred before I left UCLA. As a member of the statewide university committee to plan for the U.C. centennial in 1968, I had proposed that Adams be commissioned to make a photographic record of the several campuses. This was done and published as *Fiat Lux*. When in 1976 Adams wanted my essay for his book, I came back into a memorable association with him and his wife Virginia. This led to another reunion, with Adams' fellow photographer Wynn Bullock, known to me in high school years as a champion tennis player and light opera tenor. One night years later at the Big Sur Hot Springs with Henry Miller, I accompanied Bullock on the piano while his voice soared again in *Harvest Moon*. Now when his archives came to join Adams' and others at the Center in Tucson, Bullock and I met for the last time. His fiery red hair had grayed.

In addition to the encouragement of magazine editors at *Westways* and the *New York Times*, there have been others at *Arizona Highways*, *New Mexico* magazine, *Southwest Review* and the *Los Angeles Times* who welcomed me to their pages. Robert Kirsch of the *L.A. Times* and Margaret Hartley of the *Southwest Review* were other great encouragers.

The Bicentennial history of Arizona, published in 1976, came from a recommendation by A. R. Mortensen of the Utah Historical Society I had served on his doctoral program in History at UCLA. Through writing it I came to know Gerald George, editor of the entire NEH series and profited from his skill with a blue pencil. Two local historians also made it possible: Bernard

"Bunny" Fontana, the anthropologist whom I had persuaded Schaefer and Laird to appoint as the library's Field Historian; and Bert Fireman, head of the Arizona Historical Foundation founded by Senator Barry Goldwater. Many a trip was made to Tempe to check my work with Fireman. "You should be writing it," I said. "You are a better historian." "True," he admitted, "but you are a better writer." Bert died in 1979 and mine was the sad task of writing the introduction to his posthumous Arizona history.

I managed to make the deadline for my Bicentennial book, but know now that I should have had more time and even more knowledge.

While at Wesleyan in 1968 I "discovered" Edward Abbey's *Desert Solitaire* and after coming to Tucson learned that he lived not far away in Aravaipa Canyon as a Nature Conservancy ranger. After obtaining his willingness for me to write about his work, I set out with Dave Laird and Larry Gould to visit Abbey. The reason for including Gould was that it was his doctoral field work years ago in Utah that led him to recommend to the Park Service that the Arches National Monument be created. That was where Abbey had been the ranger of *Desert Solitaire*.

Whereas I hoped to talk literature with Abbey, he and Gould talked geology and wildlife. Dave's job was to open and close gates while Ed gave us a tour in his big Chevy. Now that Abbey lives in Tucson and lectures on writing at the university, we meet occasionally in the library. He is a strong, sensitive, and eloquent man and writer.

Another "discovery" occurred when Bunny Fontana brought by a young writer named Charles Bowden whose manuscript on what is happening to Southwest ground water was in need of a publisher. I urged Alfred Knopf to take it. Although he didn't, he sent it to the University of Texas Press which did, and to critical acclaim.

Friendship with Chuck Bowden led to my introducing him to Kathy Dannreuther and her NEH-funded Sonoran heritage program sponsored by the Tucson Public Library, which promptly took off from their union. Fay and I stood up with them at their Pima County Courthouse wedding. Each has gone on to high achievements as writer and librarian.

Because of a long-standing Guggenheim connection I helped Abbey and Bowden and then Marc Simmons and John Kessell of New Mexico to fellowships. When the Guggenheim's president, Gordon Ray, came to speak at the university, I had the pleasure of taking him to see the Kitt Peak National Observatory. After a tour of the telescopes we lunched in the astronomers' mess on Papago submarine sandwiches. Guggenheim fellowships in 1950 and 1967 were crucial in my growth as a writer.

As I reach eighty and with the publication last year of John David Marshall's *Books Are Basic*, a selection of quotations from my writings about books and libraries and writing, and now this year of *Portrait of My Father* and this further autobiography, I have pretty much had my say. Perhaps I shall henceforth only commission more books from my printer friends, or take excerpts from my journals as I did in *Winter Crossing, 1952*, printed by Ward Ritchie for the Biennial Reunion of the Zamorano and Roxburghe clubs; or select from my journals passages from other writers that were meaningful for me at different times in my life. If one should examine my published writings, he would find that most of it is about writers other than myself, which is not to deny a healthy ego.

I have come to regret that I did not take my mother's advice when a boy and master Greek and Latin as she did. I would have been a better writer.

Another regret is not maintaining more personal contacts with England and what out here on the Apache frontier we call Back East. So many old friends in both places have died: Peter Murray Hill, John Carter, Tim Munby, Winifred Myers, Bill Jackson, Jim Babb, Dave Randall, Don Hyde, and Curt Buhler. Freddie Adams went off to live in France, and though we write letters, it is not like seeing him as we used to do, at the Morgan Library or in Princeton, Great Barrington, or Malibu.

Not since 1969 have I been in New York to attend the annual meeting of the Bibliographical Society of America over which I once presided, or the annual dinner meeting of the Grolier Club. New York in January? Why don't they meet in June?

We do not lack visitors, especially in winter. One of the most recent was Nicolas Barker, editor of *The Book Collector*, who came from London to speak to our Friends group, then climbed in the Catalinas for his morning constitutional and returned home bearing gifts of turquoise and silver for his large family. He plans to return next year for a semester at UCLA, based at the Clark Library.

VIII

I LEARNED EARLY that public speaking has its price as well as its rewards. Giving a good talk to a service club leads to calls for more. Visiting members return home and soon the phone rings and one is asked to repeat that talk in Ogden, Cheyenne, or Wenatchee. Upon arriving in Tucson I made a rule not to speak off campus unless it were to library, literary, or historical groups. I no longer intended to be merely an entertaining luncheon or dinner speaker.

More and more I accepted only invitations which called for breaking new ground or visiting new places and which required thoughtful preparation. I responded to requests from former students or staff, and thus went to Colorado when John Campbell was president of the state library association and wanted me to speak at their annual conference. The same held true when I went to South Carolina, changing planes in Dallas and Atlanta to reach the university at Columbia where Roger Mortimer had asked me to dedicate the new rare book room over which he presided. When the ALA met in Los Angeles in 1983 the program chairman was a UCLA librarian whose invitation I accepted to speak to the Junior Members group. In doing so I recalled my first ALA conference at San Francisco in 1939 when Jens Nyholm and I were among the few who spoke at a general session in favor of F.D.R's nomination of Archibald MacLeish to be Librarian of Congress, despite the ALA's effort to block his nomination.

That Junior Members talk published in *Library Journal*

as "Connecting Up," came only the day after I had taken part in a memorial service for Andy Horn at which I introduced a dozen other speakers. I was relieved to know that I still had the stamina to do both. A year later I shared the podium with the Librarian of Congress in celebrating the 25TH anniversary of the UCLA library school.

My remarks were published a year later by the library school Andy and I had brought into being, I as the spirit, he as the form. No one was closer to me as colleague and friend. Each had what the other lacked, each shared without stint, up to the time of his death in May 1983 from the threefold scourge of leukemia, lung cancer, and emphysema, the result of an unbreakable addiction to tobacco. On the wall of the school is a memorial slate we had cut by David Kindersley.

It has been my lot to deliver eulogies for printer Saul Marks, historian W. W. Robinson, and writer Robert Kirsch. I prepared memorials printed by Richard Hoffman after the double suicides of the Duncan Brents and the Edwin Castagnas. The death of Luther Evans came before we were able to visit him and his wife in San Antonio. He was the nearest to a role model of any of my contemporaries.

I first became acquainted with Luther Evans in the *L.C. Information Bulletin* in whose pages he accounted for his world-wide travels and activities as Librarian of Congress, the head of the greatest of all libraries. His example led me to report with equal fulness in the *UCLA Librarian*, edited by Everett Moore. Such enthusiasm on my part caused that slyest of critics Don Coney, my equivalent on the Berkeley campus, to describe me as the "Little Luther of the Far West."

I first met Evans at a meeting of the ARL advisory committee at the Library of Congress. He asked me to a private lunch in his office with his chief deputy, Verner Clapp, that genial, informed and articulate librarian, and Lewis Hanke, head of the Hispanic Foundation. Earlier I had ridden in the elevator with Evans and had been impressed by his ability to address the other rank and file passengers by name. The staff then probably numbered a couple of thousand.

During lunch served on trays on our laps, as I listened to the others talking more than shop, I realized that Luther Evans was more like my father, as I remembered him, in appearance, nature, and radiant vitality, than any man I had ever met. It was a strange and comforting restoration of the man lost when I was only fifteen, and it was confirmed each time I met Evans, in Washington, London, Los Angeles and on various campuses where the ARL met. After Julian Boyd's departure Evans approached me on behalf of Princeton to learn if I would consider leaving UCLA. I thanked him and said no.

I don't believe I saw him during his five-year tenure as secretary-general of Unesco. Then when he became Columbia's Law Librarian and after his final retirement to his native state of Texas, we corresponded and met again. He wrote to correct a bit of legal Latin I had misread in transcribing some unpublished letters in my 1942 book *Philosopher Pickett*.

As dean at UCLA I invited Evans to come on our Distinguished Speakers program which had brought Sir Frank Francis, Jack Dalton, and Roy Stokes to spend a few days with students and faculty. When Evans said that he wanted to look up one of his former Stanford professors in Political Science, now in retirement on the edge of the UCLA campus, we set out on foot. We stopped en route for coffee and I told him for the first time of how I had come to hold him in fatherly affection. He chuckled and seemed pleased, then said, "When I get back to New York, I'm going to send you something for the school."

Fifteen years passed. We did not meet again and nothing came from him. Then at last a letter from San Antonio to where he had retired. He had read my bicentennial history of Arizona and found it good, and also *The Blue Train* which pleased him even more. "You probably think I've forgotten that I was going to send you something. I haven't. You'll be getting it in a few days."

What came was the second carbon copy of his daily reports on the state of the library to the Librarian of Congress, written when Evans was MacLeish's chief deputy. The ribbon copy is in the library archives, he kept the first carbon, the second was for UCLA where it is now in the archives—several bound volumes of rapid fire typewritten notes by a great administrator reporting to his chief.

There followed an invitation for us to come to San Antonio and occupy their guest bedroom in the condominium of their final home. Alas, he died before we could go. I had a note from Helen Evans saying how much he had cherished our friendship. I only wish he could have lived to read *Portrait of My Father*. He was in my thoughts as I wrote it.

Did I have a comparable woman role model? Two of them, Althea Warren, the ginger-haired city librarian of Los Angeles, who persuaded me to become a librarian, and Frances Clarke Sayers, one of the greatest children's librarians and story tellers of our time. What did they have that I admired and envied? Vitality, certainty, organizational leadership, and most of all, joyousness. In them as in Luther Evans the tides of life ran strong and high.

The death of Dr. Hal Bieler in 1975 also cost me one of my oldest friends and believers. I had the melancholy task of helping his son Barry sort his father's books and papers. We found that he had squirreled away behind his many books virtually all of my letters written to him during the half century he was my doctor and friend. To rules of living he laid down for me I owe my long life.

At a deeply moving service for Win Bundy's husband, I joined the Benson minister and the Bundy sons and daughter and children in paying tribute to that strong, gentle man. The only music was provided by Jerry and Willy, two powerfully built local Hispanos who sang to their own guitar accompaniment Bob's favorite "The San Pedro Valley." Jerry was the Southern Pacific's wrecking crew foreman, on call day and night, to clear the main line after a derailment. The church was full of mourners from up and down the river, Cascabel to St. David, who admired and loved that man who went bravely to his death. I am beginning to be reconciled to more frequent losses as I age and my contemporaries die.

Several talks in Texas were high points of the Arizona

At Lycoming College, 1968

With William Everson (Brother Antoninus) at Middletown, 1968. Photo by Fay Powell

Facing page: Fay with the first Citroën, Middletown, 1968. Fay, Barlow, and LCP, UCLA, July 1970.

With Lawrence Durrell and Henry Miller at UCLA for Henry's 80th, 1972. Photo by David James

D

Lawrence Durrell, holding a copy of *Bookman's Progress,* preparing to introduce LCP as the speaker at Henry Miller's 80th birthday celebration, UCLA, 1972. Photo by David James

E

With Jack Dalton and Ken Toombs, University of South Carolina Library Dedication, 1976.

Age 70, 1976

Photo by John P. Schaefer

A pause for Arizona's most precious commodity.

With President John P. Schaefer

The University of Arizona

H

With Governor Castro and President Schaefer.

Commencement ceremonies, 1976. Photos by George Kew

I

With Grant Dahlstrom, Jake Zeitlin, and Ward Ritchie, 1980

Photo by Marilyn Sanders

Receiving honorary Life Membership in ALA; E.J. Josey and ALA President Peggy Sullivan, 1981

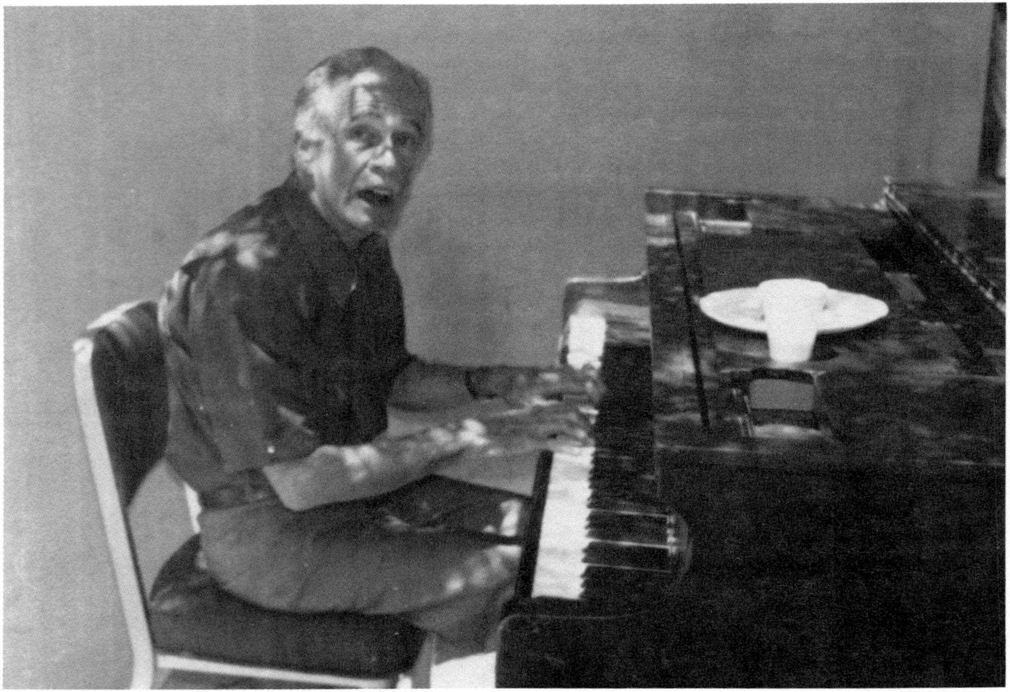

Moonlighting at a Graduate Library School party, Tucson

Photo by Don Dickinson

Michael Collier, photographer and Christopher Condit, pilot

Photo by Dr. Collier's tripod camera

With Ward Ritchie and James D. Hart at Zamorano-Roxburghe dinner, Pasadena, 1982. Photo by Donald Fleming

Addressing ALA's Junior Members Round Table, Los Angeles, 1983: "I don't think I'll ever speak to an ALA group again . . . unless you ask me."
Photo by *Library Journal*

Golden Gate Park,
San Francisco, 1984

Photo by Norman Powell

We have been friends for
75 years—on Ward Ritchie's
80th birthday, June 15, 1985.
Photo by Laurie Dietrich

O

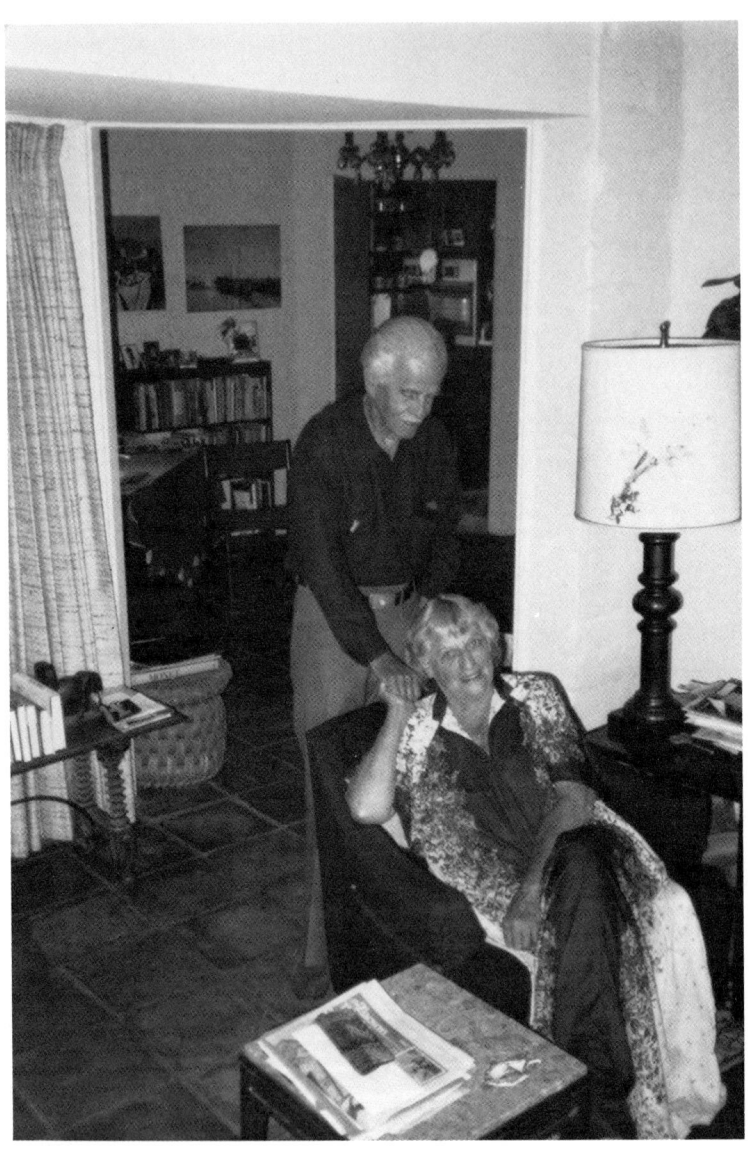

With Fay—sail and anchor.

Photo by Dr. Peter Olch

years—in Fort Worth at the Amon Carter Museum to open an exhibition of Paul Horgan's watercolors made in the field during his research on books of history and biography; and then in El Paso at the request of Mary Sarber, a former Arizona student now head of the Southwest Room in the public library. This occurred at a joint meeting of the Texas and New Mexico library associations to honor artists Tom Lea, Carl Hertzog, Jose Cisneros, and Peter Hurd, who formed in the region what I called a Great Constellation.

In New Mexico, old speaking ground, I addressed the New Mexico Historical Society in Albuquerque, Santa Fe, and Las Vegas, as I had earlier in Las Cruces. Also in Santa Fe I spoke at the annual Book Arts Festival and to the Friends of the St. John's College Library presided over by Saul Cohen, known to me since his undergraduate days at UCLA when he won the student book collecting contest.

Harry Ransom had died by the time I returned to speak to the library school students at the Humanities Research Center which now bore his name. I was introduced by Will Goodwin, another young library bookman I count on one day to lead the return to our origins. The wheel had come full circle.

Back in Los Angeles I gave the centennial address, "A Sense of the Future," to the Historical Society of Southern California, as I had given it at the 75TH anniversary with "The Sense of the Past." This was held at the Los Angeles Biltmore where Fay and I had danced as college sweethearts. We were given a red-carpeted suite overlooking Pershing Square. On another corner of that downtown park stood the building which housed the Sunkist cooperative headed by my father until his untimely death in 1922. From his high office window on Saturday mornings I used to launch paper airplanes until the traffic cop below gestured threateningly. After my talk, at which I was introduced by Franklin Murphy, Fay and I stood at the window of our sitting room and looked down on a gathering of the destitute, rummaging in trash barrels across from the hotel.

Another encore talk was given in Tucson at the 25TH anniversary of the Arizona History Conference. My talk at the first conference in 1960 was what first brought me to the attention of President Harvill. Still another centennial occasion was at the Southwest Museum when I keynoted a day-long commemoration of Lummis's first arrival in Los Angeles on November 1, 1884.

At the Palm Springs Public Library I led a two-day seminar for townspeople on the desert writers who had centered on that now overgrown oasis. There in 1920 my father recuperated from the pressures of war work as Hoover's second in command in the Food Administration only to die two years later.

One of the rewards of my long life is to witness the recognition earned by early colleagues. Such an achiever is Johanna Tallman, classmate in library school at Berkeley fifty years ago. In 1945 she left the Lockheed Corporation to join my growing UCLA staff to establish a library for the newly founded School of Engineering, pioneering to rank with Louise Darling's a year later for the School of Medicine. In 1973 Mrs. Tallman was called by Caltech to be director of libraries, and upon her retirement in 1981 I spoke there in her honor—and slept that night at the Athenaeum in the bed once occupied by Albert Einstein. Together with Page Ackerman these creative librarians were more responsible for UCLA's wide library reputation than any other three.

Wider travels took me to the University of Kentucky for a conference on academic library administration. At Lexington I was the guest of library school professor-historian Wayne A. Wiegand who had come to Tucson to interview me for a book he was editing on leading American academic administrators of our time. In two days of give-and-take with him I profited from what I had learned from Jim Mink on how to behave during an oral history seance. I did object to being typed, insisting to small avail that what influence I have had has been wider than academic.

In 1975 I was invited by Chico State University as one of their Bicentennial speakers to spend several days on campus. I drove down each morning from where we were staying with Fay's parents at Los Molinos 25 miles up the Sacramento River, and gave them a mixed bag: a discussion on D. H. Lawrence with faculty and students from the English department; a conversation on western history with W. H. Hutchinson, the California equivalent of J. Frank Dobie; and finally the dedicatory address for the new university library. The latter was held outdoors, the time was November; and when a cold wind kept blowing the leaves and my pages, I made it short. We drove home via Death Valley and stayed overnight at Darwin in the Panamints with Gordon and Eleanor Newell.

I also kept on the move in Arizona, speaking in Flagstaff at a writer's conference at Northern Arizona University and in Phoenix to a conference on the history of that city. Kathy Dannreuther enlisted me to speak during the remarkable projects on local culture she and the Tucson Public Library persuaded the NEH to fund year after year. She, Mary Sarber of the El Paso Public Library, and Sarah McGarry of the Phoenix Public Library, are among the most creative students I have been blessed with.

Was all this talking worth it? A thousand times Yes! When my subject was fresh and I had worked hard on it and the audience responded, my batteries were recharged. I'd do it all over again only better, and probably in the public library field. The niceties of academia sometimes drove me over the wall to the wider open spaces.

Honors that came were gratefully accepted. Among the most meaningful was the ALA's first Clarence Day award in 1960 for the encouragement of books and reading, although I also cherish honorary life memberships in the ALA and Arizona library association, as well as the Rosenzweig award for service to Arizona libraries. The award of the Sir Thomas More Medal for book collecting by the University of San Francisco was acknowledged in a talk on "Daphnis and Chloe in Literature and Art." This was hand-printed by Andrew Horn in a small edition called "The Enchanted Couple." Memberships not lapsed include the Grolier Club, the Zamorano and Rounce and Coffin clubs, and the Tucson Literary Club.

As our means increased we gave more to charitable and

philanthropic groups or causes. We also added steadily to the Occidental library endowment for the book arts, confident in the college's stewardship now and beyond our time. President Schaefer and then the Foundation continued to match our annual gifts to the library school to provide scholarships for out-of-state students to help meet the rising cost of their tuition. When Mrs. Joseph Wood Krutch gave the university library her husband's collection of his own writings, we commissioned my friend George Pilling to build a massive oak bookcase to house it. Since joining the board of the Tucson Zoological Society, Fay has been a devoted and generous worker for better habitats for the denizens of the Reid Park Zoo. The Salvation Army, Community Food Bank, Humane Society, and Nature Conservancy are our chosen local beneficiaries. All of these gifts were made less for tax relief than from a desire to share what we no longer need.

Our late in life affluence has also enabled me to commission printing from Paul Weaver and Mark Sanders of Flagstaff, Carl Hertzog of El Paso, David Holman of Austin, and in Southern California from Ward Ritchie, Will Cheney, Andrew Horn, and Richard Hoffman, some of them friends back to the Depression years.

We brought Ritchie to speak in Tucson about his French printing mentor, François-Louis Schmied. The library and library school published the talk as later they did Mary Sarber's bibliography of Lummis.

Each year during the 1970s Hoffman printed a keepsake for our fellow members of the Zamorano and Rounce and Coffin clubs and friends beyond. Commonplace books on Mozart and Haydn, a play about Mozart in which he does not appear, or an essay on our Occidental mentors, MacIntyre and Stelter; a book which reproduced my family's bookplates—all were given varying formats by Hoffman. He like Ritchie kept active in retirement with commissions that threatened to swamp him it if were not for the support of his wife Ruth and former L.A. State University printing students.

By an unexpected series of events both Hoffman and Ritchie unwittingly produced for me an Archibald MacLeish keepsake which brought me into correspondence again with the poet-statesman-librarian whose work and person I had admired for fifty years. I have already written about my first ALA conference at San Francisco in 1939 when only a few of us spoke in favor of F.D.R.'s nomination of MacLeish as Librarian of Congress. Not long afterward when MacLeish came to UCLA, I arranged an exhibit of his books together with those of Yeats and Rilke. When he saw it, he said only "You do me great honor."

Among the books taken with me to France in 1930 was one which included a poem by MacLeish giving the sense of a moon-dweller's view of earth. Years later when our men landed there and sent back pictures of the earth and a commemorative stamp was issued, that poem rose to the top of my mind.

Before asking Hoffman to make a keepsake of it, I wrote to MacLeish for permission, enclosing a copy of the poem. He replied: "This is astonishing. I have no memory of the poem and, like the listeners you speak of (I used to read it to students and ask them to identify the author—none ever could), I do not recognize the rhythms as mine. But now, fifty years later, the image that dominates the poem (the image of the earth in the sky of the moon) reappears in a poem when it exists not only in the imagination but in fact—in photographic fact—in the great photograph of the earth in the sky of the moon taken by Apollo VIII. (Only there the earth is blue, not white.) By all means print it privately if you wish. And explain to me where the ghost image came from fifty years ago."

Time passed and nothing came from Hoffman. When I queried him he confessed that he had misplaced what I had sent him, adding that he was overloaded with work. Whereupon I sent it to Ward Ritchie who proceeded to print it, with Rex Brandt decorations, on his Laguna Verde Albion handpress. It was a sentimental job for Ritchie; one of his first printing ventures in 1929 was a poem by MacLeish.

Then out of the blue came word from Hoffman that he had found the missing manuscript and hoped I'd like what he had done with it. I did indeed. It was a broadside in two colors, utterly different from Ritchie's booklet, with my note and MacLeish's set in small type in the margin, as bold and beautiful in its way as Ritchie's was in his.

MacLeish died not long after at the age of eighty-nine.

Of all my printer friends Ward Ritchie came first, and as we venture into our 80s he bids fair to outlast them all and me as well. From when we were in grammar school and as editor of the *Marengo Literary Leader* he published my first lurid prose, "The Purple Dragon" and the prophetic "Desert Sunset," he has believed in my work to the extent of printing and publishing it. His view of my ambiguous nature is the same as Fay's: objective, tolerant and, lucky for me, affectionate. His talent for design is so varied and original that now with more than five hundred books behind him it is impossible to select any one as characteristic. Ritchie is also an inveterate playboy with type, using ornaments, devices and cuts in the witty manner of W. A. Dwiggins and Jane Grabhorn. On the wall of Imprenta Laguna Verde hangs his favorite motto: *This body is much too fragile for the life I lead.* In 1985 he summed up his lifetime of printing in which he achieved an international reputation with a lecture at the Library of Congress on the Southern California Tradition.

My turn came a year later when I presented a lecture on books and reading in the same Engelhard series sponsored by the Center for the Book, directed by John Cole. As Librarian of Congress the distinguished historian Daniel Boorstin has reasserted the Library's responsibility in our book-oriented culture which reaches from Jefferson through MacLeish.

IX

IT IS NOT MINE to say what these years have meant for the University of Arizona. I know what they have done for me—given me a new life in which for a brief time I played a small part in the growth of the institution, seeing it gather momentum similar to what I saw happen when I came to UCLA in 1938. I felt a renewed sense of community, of being part of something beyond myself. My life has been committed to education, to the simultaneous act of learning and teaching on whatever campus I found myself, at home and abroad. Now I was free to choose my associates among old and young, all drawn by the university's magnetism, deriving strength and belief from what we shared. Particular pride was taken in seeing younger faculty colleagues become outstanding teachers and researchers in their fields. Such are Margaret Maxwell, Donald Dickinson, and Charles Scruggs.

The most extraordinary of these colleagues in the breadth and depth of his interests was the oldest. Now nearly ninety, Watson Smith, one of the most distinguished Southwestern archaeologists, came like Larry Gould to an active haven at the university from a long career of noted digs in Zuni and Hopi country. Quizzical, shrewd, tolerant, Wat Smith kept morning hours at the State Museum on campus and was also to be found on almost any level in the Main Library stacks, seeking to extend or confirm his reading interests. I gave up trying to top his knowledge of whatever esoteric subject, and when he gave me a thousand-page Xeroxed autobiography, written in his mid-80s, I capitulated completely to that *parfait gentilhomme*.

In the fallout of a long life with books, people, and ideas, I am now having an added bonus of working with the recently founded Friends of the UA Library. During the last three years as chairman I have helped plan programs and speakers, foster publications and recommend acquisitions. Thus I have helped pay my rent for the small yet adequate office I occupy in the library. With Bunny Fontana on the Friends board and editor of the Newsletter, I benefited once again from association with that generous, learned, and loving man.

One program brought James Laughlin of New Directions to speak about authors and to read his own poetry. We had met only once before, forty years ago, when he came to UCLA to thank us for having placed the first standing order for his publications. He and Alfred Knopf should have shared the nonexistent Nobel Prize for publishing. Until eye trouble grounded him, "Alfred the Great" spent winter months in Tucson where we renewed an old friendship. He also delighted my seminar with vintage crustiness. My profile of him in *Westways* did *not* delight him for the way I wrote of him as a mortal man as well as an olympian publisher among pygmies. In fact he threatened to sue me if I ever reprinted it. I never have, although I stand by it. We were soon friends again.

When Laughlin was reluctant to stand before an audience and give a formal talk, I suggested that we sit together on stage and hold a conversation. To the delight of the audience I drew him out on authors he had published, including Ezra Pound, William Carlos Williams, and Henry Miller.

It was Henry Miller who in 1941 suggested that Laughlin include me in his L.A. itinerary. He found me, still an unknown junior librarian, typing order cards and dreaming of what I would do when I became head librarian. He was tall, slim, sunburned from skiing in Idaho, and wearing sandals on his bare feet—a most unlikely eastern publisher.

Laughlin's use of his own fortune—Jones and Laughlin Steel—to serve literature is unique in American publishing. His help to Miller, Patchen, and Rexroth, as well as to Pound and Williams, made possible their creative survival. When near the end of his life Kenneth Rexroth lay paralyzed in Santa Barbara, J. L. provided round-the-clock nursing to that gifted man of letters.

Throughout these years my closest associates have been the President and the Librarian. I watched John Schaefer grow into a strong administrator and become a supporter of my work. David Laird led the Library to wider usefulness and higher ranking, as at the same time he attained national stature. In an age when managers have temporarily triumphed over bookmen, Laird remains both, taking the Library into the computer age while he edits *Books of the Southwest*, a monthly critical checklist begun at UCLA in 1957, then given to Don Powell in 1966 who at his retirement passed it along to Laird. Together with Mark Sanders, Dave also operates a small publishing press.

My role with Schaefer and Laird was no more than that of a consultant, visiting over early coffee and taking trips with the Librarian to conferences and with the President as he made photographs to accompany my work on Arizona history and geography. Schaefer's relinquishing the presidency in 1982 for that of the Research Foundation did not end our friendship. With him, Laird, Fontana, and others I continue to share the fellowship of the Tucson Literary Club.

Whatever influence I had on the president and the librarian was indirect. Only if asked did I offer comment on organization and operation, although I did complain to John Schaefer when the price of coffee in the Student Union was raised from ten to fifteen cents. Now it is thirty cents and I long since became reconciled.

I have always recognized that my mind is neither analytical nor philosophical, that is not to say that it is not pragmatic. For 20 years I have been a user not a manager, regarding universities and their libraries as institutions to serve me among others. Library resources not library housekeeping are what interests me. I expect the techniques of acquisition, cataloging, and housing of library materials to be efficiently managed by those appointed to do so. I observed that Schaefer and Laird knew what they were supposed to do and were doing it well. Whatever counsel I gave them was directed toward the increase of university and library resources, usually of materials, sometimes of people. They left me mostly to my own devices, including writing books and giving talks to enhance the university's and the library's image.

Pain from the loss of our coastal sanctuary is mostly gone, although twinges recur when we realize that we can no longer eat our peasant supper at the table by the sea-window. The view was toward the flashing Anacapa Light. The table was a gate-leg of an unknown age, discovered by my father in his furniture-conscious years being used by his mother as a kitchen table painted white and bearing the scars of long use. He had it finished with high varnish and it came down to me through my mother.

During her last summer in Malibu, Fay and her sister-in-law tediously took the cherry wood down to its original grain, then waxed it satin smooth. Two months later it was reduced to ash in the fiery furnace that fused metal and glass.

Now in old age with all classes met, most lectures given, and a few books yet to be written, I am drawing rich returns from the time and strength given to a lifelong commitment through myself to others. Letters come from men and women I have reached, telling them that life can be good if learning remains constant and self discipline is practiced. Only in those we reach, influence, and change do we go beyond self interest. Only thus is gained immortality. What recognition I have known, and never of a kind or amount to change my direction or goals, has been enough to satisfy my ego. Success is a poison to be taken late in life, Trollope warned, and then only in small doses. Jeffers declared that the only fame worth having is posthumous fame.

Although twenty years have passed since I left UCLA, the bond of April 16, 1936, has never broken. It was to there in the rotunda of what is now the Powell Library that I returned after forty-five years to celebrate my 75TH birthday. Two members of my former staff, James Cox and James Davis, with the support of University Librarian Russell Shank, hosted a gathering of colleagues and friends, capped by a cook-out supper with Dean Hayes and his faculty. Not long after that Jim Cox began a new midlife career as Librarian of the University of Melbourne. No frontier has ever been too far for that kind-hearted iron man who followed me into librarianship from the antiquarian booktrade.

Again in 1981 the rotunda was the setting for the GSLIS' commencement at which I spoke. In the presence of Andy and Mary Horn I recalled that it was there in 1938 that he and I first became aware of one another. Only to Fay do I owe more than I do to him.

I concluded my brief address with these gospel words:

> What is it that affects those who come to study and work here? There seems to be a magnetic power that imbues this young university and younger library school—a power that engenders affection and commands loyalty. There is not room enough for all of us to spend our lives here. Most of you will have to leave. If you are fortunate, as I have been, you will find your place on earth where you will put down roots and grow and become a member of the honorable company of librarians.
>
> Yet wherever it is the world around, a part of you will remain here and will call you back from time to time, who knows, perhaps to stay, as Dean Horn and then Dean Hayes were called. You will be proud to be known as one of our graduates. If I am known today in Arizona and elsewhere, it is always as one who came from UCLA. Wherever you go, you will find our degree a good passport.
>
> And so in closing I wish you good going and may you always come back. I'll be here.

My wheel came full circle in the spring of 1986 when I returned for the first time in many years to the city of my birth to speak at the Library of Congress. Seventy-six years earlier one night in May my mother wakened me to see the comet in the sky. Now once again Halley's punctual traveller was passing overhead.

I have come to realize that where we now are is the Shangri-la I once sought in foreign lands. My restlessness has subsided, although I shall never attain Fay's natural tranquility. Writing remains the best way to subdue the demons that more than once threatened to disrupt our life.

Although we are sometimes attacked by "condo fever" and talk of building a house of our own, we subside with the realization that living in a mostly congenial small group is the best life for us at our age.

Now when the wind blows from the east it means rain not fire. The city is coming closer, invading the foothills, shattering the quiet while "development" devours the arboreal bajada, an alluvial slope of rock, sand, and gravel which supports the native vegetation of palo verde, saguaro, ocotillo, and whitethorn acacia. What continues to draw settlers, as we were drawn fifteen years ago, leads to the destruction of what drew all of us. Coyotes wisely seek sanctuary in the canyons. The foothills seem doomed, as the seacoast was blighted by highrise buildings, each striving for a better view. The Santa Cruz valley's water table keeps dropping. When the water is gone or too deep for pumping, the people will go, as desert dwellers have always gone when their resources were exhausted. In Arizona they are called the Hohokam or the People Who Went Away. What will we be called when our time comes to go?

Now I intend to do what Candide did: cultivate my garden. Mine is out back looking up at the Santa Catalinas, Fay's is out front where it overlooks the valley to the Santa Ritas and the mountains of Sonora. Hers has flowers, mine cactus.

There is much to be grateful for. College baseball comes every spring. We have seen our Wildcats win two national championships in 1976 and 1980. Our friend Charlie Scruggs' International Film Festival which runs throughout the year showed our first Truffauts and my first John Wayne. I hadn't had so much enjoyment since seeing William S. Hart in my movie heyday at age 12.

Unlike Fay who likes the shade as she takes siesta, I walk when the sun is high, exulting in the heat on my body. In summer we swim in the pool after sundown when coolness descends on the land and Vega is overhead. Or we picnic in the oak grove on Kitt Peak as bluejays swoop for crumbs. The summer monsoons from the Gulf bring half our annual rainfall. Then everything comes to a stop or is swept away. In autumn we take the Scout to Sasabe on the border for a load of mesquite firewood. That fragrance is as characteristic of southern Arizona as piñon is of northern New Mexico. Miles of open space surround us, easily gained when the city becomes oppressive.

My body's failures seem arrested, although stamina and recuperative power are waning. In nearby barrancas I watch the flowering in springtime of yellow palo verde and mesquite and in autumn the golden chamisal and desert marigold. An early homesteader built small rock dams to prevent erosion. Now only I know where they are. Dove, quail, and rabbits do not fear me. Alas, I no longer have little Barlow to walk with me.

I rise with the morning star and watch the day come. Fay joins me for coffee, then feeds her wild birds. A pair of cardinals come to her call. We make our own breakfast and I go off early to campus, six miles distant, while she has the morning for her own apartness. Family and friends are in our thoughts if not our lives. Now is the time of winding down after years of winding up.

Fifty-eight years have passed since we first met. Fay was then a wild and lovely seventeen. Now at seventy-five she is not quite as wild though even more beautiful in my eyes. Most all of these years we have shared, at home and abroad, in agreement and disagreement, learning to communicate in quietness and with never a dull moment. We are closer to a final acceptance of our profoundly different natures and needs, as we reach toward reconciliation—"Reconciliation, word over all, beautiful as the sky."

Photo by Cynthia Farah.

Checklist of Publications

by

Robert Mitchell and Betty Rosenberg

Introduction to the Checklist

THIS CHECKLIST was begun in 1958 by Betty Rosenberg. Undaunted by the task of imposing bibliographic order on a diverse body of literature dating back to 1919, she ultimately produced the *Checklist of the Published Writings of Lawrence Clark Powell*. It was published in 1966, on the occasion of LCP's retirement from UCLA's Graduate School of Library Service.

I met LCP in 1974, when, as an impressionable young library school student at the University of Arizona, I began updating the Rosenberg checklist. I soon discovered that, although he was gradually relinquishing his professorial duties, LCP was just hitting his stride as a writer. Indeed, his published output in the nearly twenty years since his "retirement" may well exceed that of his first sixty years. Fortunately for me, no bibliographer ever had a more cooperative subject. LCP is scrupulous about keeping me posted on newly published Powelliana.

An early version of my bibliography was published in 1976, in *Voices From the Southwest: A Gathering in Honor of Lawrence Clark Powell*. For this second volume of his autobiography, the Rosenberg *Checklist*, the *Voices* bibliography, and my collection of citations from 1976 through 1985 have been incorporated into a single checklist. I have followed Betty Rosenberg's example throughout: citations are grouped chronologically by broad subject categories, with added sections covering epigraphs and fiction.

Since this checklist covers only the years 1919 through mid-1986, it is, of necessity, incomplete. I look forward to publishing an expanded version at a later time—perhaps as a part of the third volume of LCP's autobiography twenty years hence.

Robert Mitchell

Essays

Islands of Books. Los Angeles, The Ward Ritchie Press, 1951.
The Alchemy of Books. Los Angeles, The Ward Ritchie Press, 1954.
Books West Southwest: Essays on Writers, Their Books, and Their Land. Los Angeles, The Ward Ritchie Press, 1957. Reprinted, Westport, Greenwood Press, 1974.
A Passion for Books. Cleveland and New York, World Publishing Company, 1958. Also: London, Constable, 1959. Reprinted, Westport, Greenwood Press, 1973.
The Malibu. [With W. W. Robinson] Los Angeles, Dawson's Bookshop, 1958. Reprinted, Los Angeles, Ward Ritchie Press, 1970.
Books in My Baggage: Adventures in Reading and Collecting. Cleveland and New York, World Publishing Company, 1960. Also: London, Constable, 1960. And as Talking Books for the Blind. Reprinted, Westport, Greenwood Press, 1973.
Southwestern Book Trails: a Reader's Guide to the Heartland of New Mexico & Arizona. Albuquerque, Horn and Wallace, 1963; 2nd corrected ed., 1964. Reprinted, Santa Fe, William Gannon, 1982.
The Little Package: Pages on Literature and Landscape from a Traveling Bookman's Life. Cleveland and New York, World Publishing Company, 1964. Reprinted, Freeport, Books for Libraries, 1971.
Oak-wooded Malibu. In *Zamorano Choice: Selections from the Zamorano Club's Hoja Volante 1943–1966,* compiled by W. W. Robinson. Los Angeles, The Zamorano Club, 1966.
Bookman's Progress: The Selected Writings of Lawrence Clark Powell. Los Angeles, Ward Ritchie Press, 1968.
Fortune & Friendship: An Autobiography. New York, R. R. Bowker Company, 1968.

Librarianship, Books, & the Booktrade

Academic Library Notes. *California Library Association Bulletin,* 1939–1949. (Contributed quarterly.)
Problem of Rare Books in the College and University Library. *Library Journal,* April 1, 1939.
The Function of Rare Books. *College and Research Libraries,* December 1939. And in *Books, Libraries, Librarians,* by John David Marshall and others. Hamden, Connecticut, 1955.
Librarians and War, an Editorial. *California Library Association Bulletin,* December 1940.
Book Exhibits at the UCLA Library. *UCLA Magazine,* December 1941.

I Read What I Like. *Wilson Library Bulletin*, October 1943.
Travel Notes from the Shipping Room. *Wilson Library Bulletin*, May 1944.
The Library and the Alumni. *UCLA Magazine*, December 1944.
An Almanac for Librarians. *Wilson Library Bulletin*, June 1945.
We Moderns. *SCOP*, Summer, 1945. And *Wilson Library Bulletin*, November 1945. And Ben Abramson's *Argus Book Shop Catalog*, No. 20 1945. [Excerpts]
Wanted: Aids in Research. *Hollywood Quarterly*, October 1945.
A University Librarian Takes Pen in Hand. *Library Journal*, April 1, 1946.
We Scrutinize; Report of the Activities Committee on the CLA Bulletin. *California Library Bulletin*, September 1947.
Librarians as Readers of Books. *Pacific Northwest Library Association Quarterly*, September 1947. And *Wilson Library Bulletin*, February 1948. And [pamphlet] Seattle, The Dogwood Press, 1949.
San Joaquin Vision. *California Library Bulletin*, June 1948. And *Wilson Library Bulletin*, October 1948.
Islands of Books. *Hoja Volante*, August 1948.
The Chief Librarian: Bookman or Administrator? *Stechert–Hafner Book News*, October 1948. And *Antiquarian Bookman*, January 8, 1949. And *Publishers' Circular and Bookseller's Record* [London] March 26, 1949.
Education for Academic Librarianship. *Papers of the Institute on Education for Librarianship*, Chicago University Graduate Library School. Chicago, American Library Association, 1949.
The UCLA Library. Age: Thirty Years. *UCLA Magazine*, January 1949.
Nine by Nine. *Hoja Volante*, May 1949.
The William Andrews Clark Memorial Library. [With H. R. Archer] *Antiquarian Bookman*, July 9, 1949.
In It Together. *Antiquarian Bookman*, July 9, 1949. *AB: Bookman's Yearbook*, 1958. *Bookseller*, September 12, 1959. And in *A Passion for Books*.
Rare Books in the University Library: Policy and Administration. *College and Research Libraries*, July 1949.
Books and People and the Earth on Which We Live. *Pacific Northwest Library Association Quarterly*, October 1949. And *Wilson Library Bulletin*, February 1950.
The Time and the Place and the Book. *Hoja Volante*, November 1949.
Recollections of an Ex-Bookseller. Los Angeles, Zeitlin & Ver Brugge, 1950.
Books on the Land. *California Library Bulletin*, March 1950. And *Hoja Volante*, May 1950.
From Private Collection to Public Institution: The William Andrews Clark Memorial Library. *Library Quarterly*, April 1950.
Bookseller and Librarian. An Address Given Before the Southern California Chapter of the Antiquarian Booksellers' Association of America, May 11th, 1949. *Antiquarian Booksellers' Association News Letter* [London], Spring 1950.
Invitation from CLA. *Bulletin of the School Library Association of California*, May 1950.
A Source of Power and Beauty. [Remarks at the Dedication of the Montana State College Library, Bozeman, May 10, 1950] *Montana Collegian*, June 1950. And *PNLA Quarterly*, July 1950.
Book Collectors and California Libraries. *California Library Bulletin*, June 1950. And *Antiquarian Bookman*, June 30, 1951.
The President Says—"Meet Me in Sacramento!" *California Library Bulletin*, June 1950.
Librarianship in California. *California Librarian*, September 1950.
Bookman in Britain. *Hoja Volante*, November 1950.
A California Bookman Abroad. *California Librarian*, December 1950.
A Rare Book Code. *Antiquarian Bookman*, January 6, 1951.
A Librarian Takes Stock. *Antiquarian Booksellers' Association News Letter* [London], January 1951.
Book Hunter in Britain. *California Librarian*, March 1951.
Address [at a meeting of the National Book League, London, November 1950]. *Antiquarian Bookman*, March 3, 1951.

Book Thoughts from Abroad. *California Librarian,* June 1951.
The Association. *Antiquarian Booksellers' Association News Letter* [London], July 1951.
Bookhunting in Britain. *Westways,* October 1951. And *National League for Women's Service Magazine,* February 1955.
The Free Flow of Books. *Library Journal,* October 15, 1951.
Book Thoughts from Oxford. *Book Club of California Quarterly News Letter,* Winter 1951.
Bruin Librarian Brings Home the Books. *UCLA Alumni Magazine,* December 1951.
Multum in Parvo. *California Librarian,* December 1951.
Librarian-on-Leave, Letters . . . to His Staff at UCLA. . . . Los Angeles [Printed at Los Angeles City College], 1952.
The College in My Life. *Occidental Alumnus,* March 1952.
Two Small Books. *Hoja Volante,* May 1952.
The Alchemy of Books. *Antiquarian Bookman,* July 19, 1952. And *ALA Bulletin,* September 1952. And in *Books, Libraries, Librarians,* by John David Marshall and others. Hamden, Connecticut, 1955.
Bookshops and Cathedrals. *Hoja Volante,* August 1952.
(Once Upon a Time . . .). *Antiquarian Bookman,* August 2, 1952.
A Summer Miscellany. *California Librarian,* September 1952.
In Praise of English Books. *Books of the Month* [London], October 1952.
On the Virtues of Smallness. *Hoja Volante,* November 1952.
The Folklore of Books. *Journal of the National Book League* [London], November 1952.
Vroman's of Pasadena. Pasadena, California, Vroman's Bookstore, 1953.
Books to Keep Me Warm. *Hoja Volante,* February 1953.
A Smoke-Filled Room. *California Librarian,* March 1953.
An American Library Reports. *Journal of the National Book League* [London], March-April 1953.
Clark Collection of Oscar Wilde. In Campus Theater 170, UCLA, *Program:* "An Ideal Husband," April 1953.
Greetings to A.L.A. *California Librarian,* June 1953.
Bookshops in the Los Angeles Area. *ALA Bulletin,* June 1953.
The Power to Evoke. *Manuscripts,* Summer 1953.
This Dry and Wrinkled Land. *Arizona Librarian,* July 1953. And *Hoja Volante,* May and August 1953.
Resources Unlimited: Special Collections at UCLA. *California Librarian,* September 1953.
Librarian Powell Takes to the Air. *Los Angeles Daily News,* Christmas Book Section, December 7, 1953.
On Being up in the Air. *California Librarian,* December 1953.
Stop Thief! A Nocturnal Episode in Library History. *Wilson Library Bulletin,* December 1953. In *American Library History Reader,* edited by J. D. Marshall. Hamden, Connecticut, Shoe String Press, 1961.
To Newbury to Buy an Old Book. London, Curwen Press, 1954.
Nothing Else Matters. *Hoja Volante,* May 1954.
The Excitement of Administration. *College and Research Libraries,* July 1954.
Learning to Teach, Teaching to Learn. *California Librarian,* October 1954.
The Magnetic Field. In *University of Tennessee Library Lectures.* Knoxville, 1954. *UCLA Alumni Magazine,* February 1959. And in *A Passion for Books.*
Ten Books. In *The Books of Bookmen,* edited by Page Gilman. Ojai, 1955.
Three Loves Have I [Randolph G. Adams Memorial Lecture]. *Michigan Alumnus Quarterly Review,* February 1955.
Trailing Books. *Los Angeles Times,* March 15, 1955.
A Leisurely Stroll Back to the Street of Second Hand Books. *Los Angeles Times,* June 22, 1955.
West Southeast, Impressions of Southern Libraries. *Southeastern Librarian,* Summer 1955.
Books Determine. In *Papers and Proceedings of the Southwestern Library Association,* Fifteenth Biennial Conference, November 3, 4, and 5, 1954. Albuquerque, N.M. And *Wilson Library Bulletin,* September 1955.

Reading on the Malibu. *California Librarian,* October 1955.
Eucalyptus Trees and Lost Manuscripts. *California Librarian,* January 1956.
One Book in a Million. *Los Angeles County Public Library News Letter,* May 1956 and January 1957. *News Notes of California Libraries,* January 1957.
The Power and the Glory. [Address at a banquet honoring Doris Hoit, City Librarian of Pasadena, on her retirement] *California Librarian,* July 1956.
My Favorite Four-Letter Word. *AB: Bookman's Yearbook, 1956.* And *Southern Observer,* August 1956. And *California Librarian,* July 1957. In *Of, By and For Librarians,* selected by John David Marshall. Hamden, Conn., Shoe String Press, 1960. And in *A Passion for Books.*
Books, Piñon Nuts, and Shadows. *Arizona Highways,* August 1956.
Trouble With Titles. *Los Angeles Times,* November 26, 1956.
Book Collecting and Libraries. *AB: Bookman's Yearbook,* 1957.
At the Heart of the Matter. Los Angeles, Friends of the UCLA Library, 1957. And *Hoja Volante,* February 1957. And *UCLA Alumni Magazine,* February 1957.
The Gift to be Simple. *Library Journal,* February 1, 1957. And *South Carolina Librarian,* April 1957. In *Of, By and For Librarians,* selected by John David Marshall. Hamden, Conn., Shoe String Press, 1960.
The Heart of a University: Its Library. *University Bulletin* [University of California], February 11, 1957.
Catalysts of Knowledge. *Library Journal,* December 15, 1957.
Through the Burning Glass. *Bulletin of the Louisiana Library Association,* Spring 1957. And *Alabama Librarian,* 1957. And *Wilson Library Bulletin,* September 1957. And *The New Mexican,* June 15, 1958. [excerpts] And *Books and Libraries at Emory University,* April 1, 1959. Special issue title: Books for the general reader, a symposium, edited by Guy R. Lyle.
My Biggest Flop. *Hoja Volante,* August 1957.
The Elements of Fruitfulness. *Bulletin of the Southern California Chapter, Antiquarian Booksellers' Association of America,* November 1957.
Care and Feeding of the Bookish Administrator. *Library Journal,* December 15, 1957.
Living Hand to Book. *Westways,* December 1957.
A Little Sermon on Binding. *The Rub-Off,* January-February 1958.
Books Will Be Read. In *Papers and Summaries of Discussions* at the Harrogate Conference of the Library Association, September 1957. And *Library Journal,* February 1, 1958. And *Montana Library Quarterly,* April 1958.
Book Time. *Washington Education,* March 1958.
Bookman in Seven-League Boots. *Southwest Review,* Summer 1958.
To Touch or Not to Touch. *ALA Bulletin,* September 1958.
Rendezvous in Cadogan Square. *Manuscripts,* Fall 1958. And *Antiquarian Booksellers' Association (International) News Letter,* March 1959.
Dr. Powell on "the Special Librarian." *Sci-Tech News,* Winter 1958. [Replies to this article in the Spring 1959 issue.]
Administration in One Easy Lesson. *Wilson Library Bulletin,* February 1959.
". . . And Brown": A chronicle of B. F. Stevens & Brown, Ltd., Library and Fine Arts Agents of London, with emphasis on the years since 1902. London, Privately Printed, 1959.
Librarians and Their Books. *Saturday Review,* April 11, 1959.
The Library in the Expanding University. A Discussion of its research need and services with reference to book substitutes and rapid transmittal devices, plus a footnote on the old fashioned art of Reading. *University Bulletin* [University of California], April 27, 1959. [excerpts]
With Books in My Baggage, or, A Bookman Traveler in Arizona. *Arizona Highways,* April 1959.
More Precious Than Oil. *The Long Beach Public Library Courier,* April 21, 1959. [excerpts from the Bertrand Smith Lecture]
Return to the Heartland. *ALA Bulletin,* June 1959.
The Elements of a Good Librarian. *Wilson Library Bulletin,* September 1959. Reprinted in *Of, By, and For Librarians.* Second Series. Compiled by J.D. Marshall. Hamden, Shoestring Press, 1974.

A Time to Join. *UCLA Librarian,* January 8, 1960.
Speaking of Books. *New York Times Book Review,* February 7, 1960. Reprinted by the Dallas Public Library; at head of title: Lawrence Clark Powell . . . while in Texas.
From Librarian-on-Leave. [Visit to Hawaii, Japan, Paris] *UCLA Librarian,* April 15, 1960 –May 27, 1960.
[Speech to Antiquarian Booksellers Association.] *The Clique,* June 18, 1960.
Opinion. [reply to article by D. M. Broderick] *Library Journal,* August 1960.
Oasis of Books. *Arizona Highways,* August 1960.
Man With a Long Purse. *Hoja Volante,* August 1960.
The Library School at U.C.L.A. *California Librarian,* October 1960.
Golden Apples and Cherry Blossoms. *Library Journal,* October 1, 1960.
The UCLA School of Library Service. *Bulletin School Library Association of California,* November 1960.
Reading in Orbit: "Global" Books. *Los Angeles Examiner Highlight,* November 13, 1960.
The Book Barons. [Originally a radio script in University Explorer Series based on interview material.] *Antiquarian Bookman,* May 15, 1961. And *UCLA Alumni Magazine,* October 1961.
The Little Package. *Arizona Librarian,* Fall 1961. And *Southwest Review,* Spring 1962. In *Challenge to American Youth,* edited by Phillip Angeles. Philadelphia, Macrae Smith, 1963. [Title: The Value of Reading]
A Library is a Library is a Library. *Montana Libraries,* July 1961. [Excerpt from *A Passion for Books.*]
Notes from Dean's Desk; Dean Powell Reports. *CALibrarian,* Fall 1961, Spring 1962, Summer 1962, Winter 1963, Summer and Fall 1963, Winter 1964, Spring and Summer 1964, Fall 1964, Winter 1965, Spring and Summer 1965, Fall 1965.
Into the Mainstream. *Special Libraries,* July-August 1961. And *Library Journal,* October 1, 1961.
Building with Books. In *Dedication Exercises,* the Hunt Library and the Rachel McMasters Miller Hunt Botanical Library, Pittsburgh, October 10, 1961.
Act of Enchantment. Santa Fe, Designed and printed at the Stagecoach Press for the Historical Society of New Mexico, 1961. Also in hard cover: Houston, Stagecoach Press, 1961.
William Andrews Clark Memorial Library. In *A Bookman's View of Los Angeles.* Los Angeles, Zamorano Club, 1961.
The Reader, the Book and Christmas. *New York Times Book Review,* December 3, 1961.
On the Grindstone. *Library Journal,* January 1, 1962; February 1, 1962 (Let Librarians Specialize); March 1, 1962 (Farewell, L'Image); April 1, 1962; May 1, 1962; June 1, 1962 (Suffer Little Children); July 1, 1962; August 1, 1962 (Go Forth and Be Useful); September 1, 1962 (Find Them and Fund Them); October 1, 1962 (Of Those Who Were Truly Great); November 1, 1962; December 1, 1962 (Time to Go).
On Getting and Giving Books. *The Rub-Off,* January-February 1962. And *Library Information Bulletin,* Auburn University, February 1962.
Go Forth and Be Useful: Valedictory Address of the Dean to the Class of 1962. UCLA School of Library Service, 1962. And *Library Journal,* August 1, 1962.
Paperback Rack: Some Hints on Book Buying. *Los Angeles Herald Examiner,* July 28, 1962.
The Southwest: Proving Ground for Librarians. *New Mexico Library Bulletin,* Summer 1962.
Up Near the Source. *Minnesota Libraries,* December 1962.
The Prospect Before Us. San Francisco, The Grabhorn Press, 1963. And *Quarterly News Letter,* Book Club of California, Spring 1963. [Reprinted in *Second Reading.* Selections from the *Quarterly News Letter,* 1933 1968. San Francisco, Book Club of California 1965]
Shake Well and Speak *The Clique,* June 1, 1963. And *Antiquarian Bookman,* July 15, 1963.
Books That Weren't in My Baggage. *New York Times Book Review,* June 9, 1963. And *New York Times Western Edition,* June 12, 1963 [abridgement]. [Reprinted in *Opinions and Perspectives from the New York Times Book review,* edited by Francis Brown. Boston, Houghton, 1964]

Book Hunter in Britain. *Westways*, August 1963.
Northland Press. *Arizona Highways*, September 1963.
A World That's Wide and Wonderful. *New York Times Book Review*, January 5, 1964. [Also in supplement to Western Edition, January 6, 1964]
Happiness is a Stall in Zurich. *Los Angeles Herald-Examiner*, January 12, 1964.
The Education of an Educator. *Library Journal*, February 1, 1964.
Henry Stevens, Bookman. *New York Times Book Review*, April 12, 1964.
The Lure of Californiana. *California Librarian*, July 1964. And *Quarterly News-Letter*, Book Club of California, Fall 1964.
Speaking of Books: In the Words of Kenneth Rexroth. *New York Times Book Review*, November 22, 1964.
Make Mine a Small One. *New York Times Book Review*, December 6, 1964. [Reprinted as a pamphlet, Berkeley, Peacock Press, 1965]
Speaking of Books: Yeats-Wellesley Letters. *New York Times Book Review*, March 28, 1965.
The Three L's. *California School Libraries*, May 1965. [Reprinted as a pamphlet, Los Angeles, The Press in the Gatehouse. 1964; and *in Collectors' Institute Commemorative Brochure*. Austin, Collectors' Institute, 1968.]
Great Land of Libraries. *ALA Bulletin*, July-August 1965. [Reprinted in *Of, By, and For Librarians*. Second Series. Compiled by J.S. Marshall. Hamden, Shoestring Press, 1974.]
Trikrát Tri. ["Nine by Nine" from *Books in My Baggage*] Translated by Kamil Bednár. *Ucitelské Noviny*, 1965.
Book Shops. Los Angeles, 1965. [Reprinted in *Antiquarian Bookman*, December 6, 1965] Second edition, with portrait. Los Angeles, Dawson & Boswell, 1966.
The Elements of a Good Librarian. *Occidental College Alumnus*, Winter 1967.
Epilogue. *Arizona Librarian*, Fall 1968.
Northland Press in the Pinewood. *Arizona Librarian*, Fall 1968.
Ole Olin. *Wesleyan Library Notes*, Autumn 1968.
To D.C. Subject: The L.C. From L.C.P. Los Angeles, The Gatehouse Press, 1968.
The Ella Strong Denison Library. *Scripps College Bulletin*, October 1968.
The Example of Miss Edith Coulter. (Keepsake Number 8.) Sacramento, California Library Association, 1969.
Shoe on the Other Foot: From Library Administrator to User. *Wilson Library Bulletin*, December 1970.
Talk at Antiquarian Booksellers Banquet, Ambassador Hotel, Los Angeles, October 14, 1970. *AB: Bookman's Weekly*, November 2, 1970.
Library Addition Dedicated. *Occidental College Alumnus*, February 1971.
LCP Raps with RAP. *The Bookworm's Digest* [University of Arizona Library Staff Association], 1971.
Remarks on the Occasion of the Dedication of Addition to the Mary Norton Clapp Library. Los Angeles, Occidental College, 1971.
The Three H's. Los Angeles, Press in the Gatehouse, 1971.
Three Loves Have I. *The 1971 AB: Bookman's Yearbook*, Part 1. 1971.
California Fried Franchise. *American Libraries*, October 1972.
Graduate School of Library Science, The University of Arizona. In *Fifth Annual Report*. Tucson, The President's Club of the University of Arizona, 1972.
A Cold Look at a Hot Subject; Or Whose Library Is It? In *University of Arizona Library Occasional Papers Number 1: Service or Organization; Two Views—Three Responses*. Tucson, University of Arizona Library, 1973.
To Newbury to Buy an Old Book. Edinburgh, The Tragara Press, 1973. Booklet reprinted from *Books in My Baggage*.
A Backward Look Ahead. *The UCLA Monthly*, November 1973.
Westview. *Los Angeles Times Book Review*, April 20, 1975.
Bookman's Credo. In *American Library Philosophy*, compiled by Barbara McCrimmon. Hamden, Shoestring Press, 1975.

The Extra Dimension [library dedication speech]. *The University Journal* (California State University, Chico), Spring 1976.
A Librarian's Holiday. *Westways*, November 1976.
Books and Edwin Corle. In *Edwin Corle Memorial Undergraduate 1977 Book Collection Contests*. Santa Barbara, The Library, University of California, Santa Barbara, 1977.
Reminiscences on Books and Booksellers. *AB: Bookman's Weekly*, January 10, 1977.
Well Stacked [UCLA Library]. *Westways*, May 1977.
Letter to Claire Morrill. In *A Keepsake Presented in Honor of Claire Morrill, Octogenarian, August 11, 1978*. Wichita, Hal Ottaway, 1978.
Seed Money. *Arizona Report*, May 1979.
A Remembrance for the 50th Anniversary Meeting of the Rounce & Coffin Club Held at Occidental College, Los Angeles. Los Angeles, Rounce & Coffin Club, 1981.
Ten Years (Almost) of Rounce & Coffin-ism. In *R & C Golden Jubilee 1931–1981: An Historical Effusion by Lawrence Clark Powell, Jake Zeitlin, Ward Ritchie, Tyrus G. Harmsen*. Los Angeles, Rounce & Coffin Club, 1981.
The Library as Sanctuary. In *The South Pasadena Public Library: A History, 1895 to 1982*. South Pasadena, South Pasadena Public Library, 1982.
Connecting Up. *Library Journal*, August 1983.
Books of the Southwest Celebrates Its 300th Issue Quietly. [co-authored with W. David Laird] *Book Talk* [New Mexico Book League], January 1984.
The Chairman Wishes to Say. *Anchor & Bull*, November 1984.
Ex Libris: Notes on My Family's Bookplates. Tucson, Press on the Bajada, 1984.
The Long Commitment. *Colorado Libraries*, March 1984.
Printer at the Pass. *Anchor & Bull*, November 1984.
Books Are Basic: The Essential Lawrence Clark Powell, edited by John David Marshall. Tucson, University of Arizona Press, 1985.
On the Typographical Taos Trail. *Hoja Volante*, August 1985.
Friend-ship. *Lo Que Pasa*, October 1985.
The UCLA Graduate School of Library and Information Science, Its Origins and Founding: A 25th Anniversary Address on May 2, 1984. Los Angeles, UCLA Graduate School of Library and Information Science, 1985.
Navigating Academic Waters. *The Journal of Academic Librarianship*, March 1986.

Bibliography

Robinson Jeffers, 1905–1935; an Exhibition Commemorating the Thirtieth Anniversary of his Graduation from Occidental College, Los Angeles, California, April 11 to 18. Los Angeles, Ward Ritchie, 1936.
Ward Ritchie: Printer. In *Occidental College Founder's Day Exhibition*, 1936. Los Angeles, The Ward Ritchie Press, 1936. And *Book Collector's Packet 4*, number 9–10.
The Manuscripts of D. H. Lawrence, a Descriptive Catalog. Los Angeles Public Library, 1937. [Reprinted, New York, Gordon Press, 1972.]
John Ernst Steinbeck. *Publishers' Weekly*, April 17, 1957.
Toward a Bibliography of John Steinbeck. *Colophon*, Autumn 1938.
Tom Wolfe's First Opus. *Publisher's Weekly*, November 25, 1939.
Ten Years (almost) of Rounce & Coffin-ism. Los Angeles, Rounce & Coffin Club, 1941.
[Editor] Rounce & Coffin Club. *Exhibition of Western Books, 1941*. Stanford University Press, 1941.
The Writings of Aldous Huxley, 1916–1943; an Exhibition of the Collection of Jacob I. Zeitlin at

the Library of the University of California, July 1 to August 15, 1943.   Edited and with an Introduction by Lawrence Clark Powell.   Los Angeles, 1943.
Bibliography of Gregg Anderson, 1926–1942.   In *To Remember Gregg Anderson.*   Los Angeles, 1949.
Land of Fiction; Thirty-two Novels and Stories about Southern California from Ramona to The Loved One: a Bibliographical Essay. Los Angeles, Glen Dawson, 1952.   And *California Librarian,* June 1953.
Heart of the Southwest; a Selective Bibliography of Novels, Stories and Tales Laid in Arizona and New Mexico & Adjacent Lands. Los Angeles, Dawson's Book Shop, 1955.   And *Arizona Highways,* February 1957.   [Revised & Enlarged]
The First Book Printed in Guatemala, in the Year 1663.   Treasures of California Collections: Keepsakes for 1956, for members of the Book Club of California.
A Southwestern Century, a Bibliography of One Hundred Books of Non Fiction about the Southwest.   Van Nuys, California, J. E. Reynolds, 1958.   And *Arizona Highways,* March 1958.
The Twenty-Five Most Important Works of Californiana Published in the Twenty-Five Years 1932–1957.   In *Libros Californianos, or Five Feet of California Books,* by Phil Townsend Hanna.   Revised and Enlarged by Lawrence Clark Powell.   Los Angeles, Zeitlin & Ver Brugge, 1958.
The Southwest Broadsides printed for the Friends of Lawrence Clark Powell 1953–1958.   Los Angeles, 1958.   [Comment on twelve Southwest broadsides]
Fifty Books of the Half Century.   *Westways,* February 1959.
50 Good Books About New Mexico.   *New Mexico Magazine,* January 1960.
One Hundred Titles for the Library of a Sophisticated Family.   *New York Times Book Review,* January 14, 1962.   And *UCLA Alumni Magazine,* March 1962.   And *College Store Journal,* August-September 1962 under the title: One Hundred Paperbacks for the Sophisticated Family.
Reading to Increase your Travel Pleasure; 52 Vacations a Year.   In *A Ford Times Pocket Guide to America's Western Southland.* Ford Motor Company, 1962.
A Basic Home Reference Library for the College Graduate.   *Dartmouth Alumni Magazine,* December 1962; *Notre Dame Alumnus,* Year End 1962; *Johns Hopkins Magazine,* January 1963; *UCLA Alumni Magazine,* Winter 1963; *California Monthly,* March 1963; and *Arizona Alumnus,* 1963 Commencement Issue.   [This syndicated article has also appeared in other alumni magazines]
Supplementary Reading List   In *Mexico: a Sunset Discovery Book.* Menlo Park, Calif., Lane Book Co., 1963.
Good Reading about the Desert.   *Westways,* October 1963.
A Backward Look by the Retiring Editor.   *Books of the Southwest,* June 1966.
Books for Your Baggage.   *Westways,* April 1968.
Los Angeles Bibliography.   In *Los Angeles: Portrait of an Extraordinary City.*   Edited by Paul C. Johnson. Menlo Park, Land Magazine & Book Company, 1968.
Reading San Diego.   In *San Diego and the Back Country.*   Edited by Davis Dutton.   New York, Ballantine Books, 1972.
An Arizona Reading List.   *Book Talk* [New Mexico Book League], February 1980.   [Reprinted in *In Celebration of the Book: Literary New Mexico.*   Edited by Dwight Myers and Carol Myers. Albuquerque, The New Mexico Book League and The Lightning Tree, 1982.]
Back in the U.S.A.: "The Southwest Classics" and "The California Classics."   In *The Book Book.*   By Steven Gilbar.   New York, St. Martin's Press, 1981.

Literature and Criticism

D. H. Lawrence.   [Letter in controversy with Louis Untermeyer and Arthur Colton]   *Saturday Review of Literature,* April 12, 1930.

Leaves of Grass and Granite Boulders, a Comparison of Whitman and Jeffers. *The Carmelite*, October 22, 1931.
An Introduction to Robinson Jeffers. Dijon, Imprimerie Bernigaud & Privat, 1932.
Robinson Jeffers: the Man and His Work. Los Angeles, the Primavera Press, 1934. And Pasadena, San Pasqual Press, 1940. [Reprinted, New York, Haskell House, 1970.]
Robinson Jeffers on Life and Letters. *Westways*, March 1934.
Carey McWilliams: an Estimate. *Apéritif*, January 1935.
Robinson Jeffers, '05. *Occidental Alumnus*, March 1935.
Robinson Jeffers and His Garden. *Sunset*, May 1935.
The Man at Tor House. *Vo-mag*, March 1936.
On Collecting John Steinbeck. *Book Collectors'* Packet, July 1938.
Who is B. Traven? *New Masses*, August 2, 1938. [Reprinted in *New Masses: An Anthology of the Rebel Thirties*, edited by Joseph North. New York, International Publishers, 1969.]
C. F. MacIntyre. *Wilson Bulletin*, March 1939.
John Steinbeck. *Black and White*, June 1939.
D. H. Lawrence and His Critics. A Chronological Excursion in Bio-bibliography. *Colophon*, new graphic series, February 1940.
An Unpublished Mark Twain Letter. *American Literature*, January 1942.
A Great American Nature Writer: Donald Culross Peattie. *Phi Gamma Delta*, June 1945.
Confessions of a Reconstructed Westerner. *Hoja Volante*, August 1947.
Leaves of Whitman. *Hoja Volante*, November 1947.
Giacomo Giralamo Casanova, Chevalier de Seingalt, 1726–1798. Pasadena, The Ampersand Press, 1948.
Rabelaisian Notes. *Hoja Volante*, February 1948.
The Enjoyment of Joyce. *Hoja Volante*, May 1948.
Lines on Lawrence. *Hoja Volante*, November 1948.
My Melville. *Hoja Volante*, February 1949.
Glory of Life. *Hoja Volante*, August 1949.
Ripeness is All. *Hoja Volante*, February 1950.
Robinson Jeffers. *Montevallo Review*, Summer 1950.
Robinson Jeffers: a Lecture to Professor James L. Wortham's Class in Narrative Poetry given on May 22, 1949. Los Angeles, The Press of Los Angeles City College, 1951.
Homage to Browning. *California Librarian*, December 1952.
D. H. Lawrence. *Books and Libraries at the University of Kansas*, May 1954.
The Novelist's Southwest. *Los Angeles Times*, February 21, 1955.
The Double Marriage of Robinson Jeffers. *Southwest Review*, Summer 1956.
The Islandian World of Austin Wright. An Address to the Zamorano Club. Printed by Merle Armitage, 1957.
All That is Poetic in Life. *Wilson Library Bulletin*, May 1957.
Southwest Broadsides, number 1–12, 1953–1958. Edited by Lawrence Clark Powell. [Various Printers] [A pamphlet of bibliographical descriptions and brief comments on these broadsides is listed under Bibliography]
Landscapes and Bookscapes of California. Berkeley, Friends of the Bancroft Library, 1958.
Landscape with Books. *Hoja Volante*, February 1959. And *Southwest Review*, Summer 1959. Also in *The Southwest of the Bookman*, University of California Library, Los Angeles, 1959.
Reading of a Revolutionary. *UCLA Librarian*, April 3, 1959.
The Roots of Regional Literature. Designed and printed by Carl Hertzog for Rodgers Library, New Mexico Highlands University, 1959. And *New Mexico Magazine*, October 1959.
Homage to Big Sur. *L.A.*, December 1960/January 1961. Also in *Books West Southwest*.
Some Uncollected Authors XXIII: Lawrence Durrell. Recollections of a Durrell Collector, by Alan G. Thomas and Lawrence C. Powell. *Book Collector*, Spring 1960.
Speaking of Books. *New York Times Book Review*, October 16, 1960.
Catching Up with "The Catcher." *ALA Bulletin*, June 1961.

Speaking of Books. [Raymond Chandler]. *New York Times Book Review,* December 22, 1963.
The Writer in an Automated World: a Discussion by Eric Hoffer, Robert Kirsch, and Kenneth Rexroth. Moderator, Lawrence Clark Powell. *California Librarian,* April 1964.
[Chapter in] *Richard Aldington:* an Intimate Portrait, edited by Alister Kershaw and Frédéric-Jacques Temple. Carbondale, Ill., Southern Illinois University Press, 1965.
Letters from the Famous and the Faceless. [*To Henry Miller*]. *New York Times Book Review,* May 9, 1965.
Down Where the Rockies End. *Mountain Plains Library Quarterly,* Fall 1965. And *PNLA Quarterly,* October 1965.
Strictly Local. *Southern California Quarterly,* December 1965.
You, John Milton. Norman, The Library, University of Oklahoma, 1966.
Books of the West. *Westways,* January, February, March, May, June, July, August, September, October 1966; March, April, June, July, August, September, October, November, December 1967; January, February, March 1968.
Books on the Gold Rush. *Westways,* May 1967.
California Classics Reread: *The Land of Little Rain. Westways,* April 1968; *Two Years Before the Mast. Westways,* May 1968; *The Mountains of California. Westways,* June 1968; *Ramona. Westways,* July 1968; *The Silverado Squatters. Westways,* August 1968; *The Splendid Idle Forties. Westways,* October 1968; *Give Your Heart to the Hawks. Westways,* November 1968; *To a God Unknown. Westways,* December 1968.
Landscape With Books. *Arizona Librarian,* Fall 1968.
California Classics Reread: *California Coast Trails. Westways,* January 1969; *Reminiscences of a Ranger. Westways,* February 1969; *Farewell, My Lovely. Westways,* March 1969; *The Cattle on a Thousand Hills. Westways,* April 1969; *McTeague. Westways,* May 1969; *The Luck of Roaring Camp. Westways,* June 1969; *Roughing It. Westways,* July 1969; *Martin Eden. Westways,* September 1969; *Anza's California Expeditions. Westways,* October 1969; *Death Valley in '49. Westways,* November 1969; *The Shirley Letters. Westways,* December 1969.
California Classics Reread: *The Land of Sunshine. Westways,* January 1970; *The Wonders of the Colorado Desert. Westways,* February 1970; *The Vineyard. Westways,* March 1970; *Up and Down California. Westways,* April 1970; *Mountaineering in the Sierra Nevada. Westways,* May 1970; *California and the West. Westways,* June 1970; *The Journey of the Flame. Westways,* July 1970; *Boy on Horseback. Westways,* August 1970;*Oil! Westways,* September 1970; *Merton of the Movies. Westways,* October 1970; *The Day of the Locust. Westways,* November 1970; *After Many a Summer Dies the Swan. Westways,* December 1970.
The Untarnished Gold, the Immutable Treasure: A Report of a Book-in-Progress. (Library Associates of the University Library, Davis, *Keepsake* Number 3.) Davis, University of California, Davis, 1970.
California Classics: The Creative Literature of the Golden State. Los Angeles, Ward Ritchie Press, 1971. Reprinted with new preface, Santa Barbara, Capra Press, 1982.
Classics at Continent's End. *Westways,* August 1971.
Southwest Classics Reread: *Coronado's Children. Westways,* February 1971; *Dancing Gods. Westways,* March 1971; *Interlinear to Cabeza de Vaca. Westways,* April 1971; *Commerce of the Prairies. Westways,* May 1971; *The Desert Year. Westways,* June 1971; *Vanished Arizona. Westways,* July 1971; *Sky Determines. Westways,* September 1971; *Adventures in Apache Country. Westways,* October 1971; *The Plumed Serpent. Westways,* November 1971; *Laughing Boy. Westways,* December 1971.
The Silverado Squatters — Robert Louis Stevenson. St. Helena, Norman and Charlotte Strouse, 1971.
Exploring Arizona's Literary Trails. *Arizona Highways,* September 1972.
Southwest Classics Reread: *Wolf Song. Westways,* January 1972; *Death Comes for the Archbishop. Westways,* February 1972; *The Desert. Westways,* March 1972; *Massacre and Vengeance in Apacheria.* [Will Levington Comfort] *Westways,* May 1972; *The Man Who Ran*

the River. [John Wesley Powell] *Westways,* June 1972; When Teddy Went West. [Theodore Roosevelt] *Westways,* July 1972; Writer of the Purple Page. [Zane Grey] *Westways,* August 1972; Two for the Santa Fe Trail. [Lewis H. Garrard and Susan Magoffin] *Westways,* October 1972; The Fathers of Pimeria Alta. [Kino and Garces] *Westways,* November 1972; A Land to Know, a West to Love. *Westways,* December 1972; Lady of Taos. [Mabel Dodge Luhan] *Westways,* January 1973; A Prophetic Passage. [Mary Austin] *Westways,* February 1973; How He Pictured the West. [Ross Santee] *Westways,* March 1973; From Cattle Kingdom Come. [Eugene Manlove Rhodes] *Westways,* April 1973; Song of the Southwest. [Charles F. Lummis] *Westways,* May 1973. Reprinted as *Song of the Southwest.* Los Angeles, Southern California Historical Society, 1973.

A Valentine to Gertrude Stein. *Westways,* February 1974.

Jeffers. In *Tales of Monterey,* edited by Davis Dutton and Judy Dutton. New York, Ballantine Books, 1974.

Southwest Classics: The Creative Literature of the Arid Lands. Pasadena, Ward Ritchie Press, 1974. 2nd edition, with map, 1974. Reprinted without map, Tucson, University of Arizona Press, 1982.

Letter from the Southwest. *Westways,* January, March, May, July, September 1975; May, September 1976; January, March 1977.

The Enchanted Couple [Longus' *Daphnis and Chloe*]. *Hoja Volante,* May 1977 and August 1977.

Letter from the Southwest. *Westways,* August, October 1977; January 1978.

Letter from a Farther Southwest. [*Hawaii*]. *Westways,* April 1978.

Letter from the Southwest. *Westways,* June, August, November 1978.

Lawrence Clark Powell's Letter from the Southwest. [Rio Verde] In *A Southwest Reader: Selections from the Varied Literature of the Southwest,* edited by Sarah Bouquet. Cottonwood, Cottonwood Public Library, 1978.

Archibald MacLeish: On the Beaches of the Moon. Van Nuys, Richard J. Hoffman, 1978. Broadside of the MacLeish poem flanked by comments by Lawrence Clark Powell. Reprinted with a minor revision in 1982.

Letter from the Southwest. *Westways,* January 1979.

The Editorial Thrust. [50th anniversary of the magazine] *Westways,* February 1979.

Letter from the Southwest. *Westways,* April, June, August, October 1979.

The Enchanted Couple. Glendale, The Battledore Press of Andrew Horn, 1979.

Letter from the Southwest. *Westways,* March, May 1980.

Lawrence on Lawrence. *Westways,* July 1980.

Letter from the Southwest. *Westways,* July, September, November 1980.

Goethe's Dream of Sicily. Van Nuys, Richard J. Hoffman, 1982.

Sex (and Success) in the Southwest Novel. *Book Talk* [New Mexico Book League], June 1982.

Délicieuse Ville, Mélancolique et Douce: Dijon, 1930–32. *Robinson Jeffers Newsletter,* January 1983.

Islandia: The Wisdom of the Heart. *NIEKAS,* Winter 1983.

The Magical Powers of the Written Word. *Los Angeles Herald Examiner,* October 5, 1983.

Robinson Jeffers. *In re Curb Science?* Tucson, Research Corporation, 1983.

Two Diary Vignettes of Jeffers. *Robinson Jeffers Newsletter,* December 1984.

My New Mexico Literary Friends. Santa Fe, Museum of New Mexico, 1986.

History and Travel

The Remarkable Contempt Case of Philosopher Pickett. *Interchange Fortnightly,* June 28, 1940.

Flumgudgeon Gazette in 1845 Antedated *The Spectator. Oregon Historical Quarterly,* June 1940.

The Western American — an Early California Newspaper. *Bibliographical Society of America Papers*, October 1940.
Philosopher Pickett: the Life and Writings of Charles Edward Pickett. Berkeley and Los Angeles, University of California Press, 1942.
Resources of Western Libraries for Research in History. *Pacific Historical Review*, September 1942.
Thomas C. Lancey, Chronicler of '46. *Pacific Historical Review*, February 1947.
Personal Landscape. *Hoja Volante*, August 1950.
Return to France. *Pacific Spectator*, Summer 1951.
Sentimental Journey. *California Librarian*, September 1951.
Manhattan Winter. *Hoja Volante*, February 1952. And *California Librarian*, March 1952. And *The Bridge*, January-February 1954.
Transcontinental. *California Librarian*, June 1952. And *Pi Lambda Theta Journal*, Summer 1953.
Essences of Britain. *ABA Annual*, 1952. And *PNLA Quarterly*, January 1953.
Some Writing About Los Angeles. *Los Angeles Times*, November 12, 1953.
Sky, Sun and Water; the Southwest of Frederick Webb Hodge. Printed for Presentation to Members of the Roxburghe and Zamorano Clubs at their Second Annual Corrida, Los Angeles, September 11–12, 1954. And *Southwest Review*, Spring 1954.
Angels Flight. *Hoja Volante*, November 1954.
Beanfields, Builders and Books. *Historical Society of Southern California Quarterly*, December 1954.
A Poet's Land. In *Monterey Peninsula and Big Sur: a Guide to State Highway 1*. 2nd Edition. Big Sur, E. White, March 1955.
Homage to the Big Sur. *Hoja Volante*, May 1955.
New Mexico North. *Hoja Volante*, August 1955.
We Moved to the Malibu. *Hoja Volante*, February 1956.
Malibu Manna. *Hoja Volante*, May 1956.
Did Drake Duck L.A.? *Hoja Volante*, November 1956.
The Malibu Fire. *Hoja Volante*, May 1957.
Revista Nueva Mexicana. *Southwest Review*, Winter 1957. [Reprinted in *Southwest Review*, Autumn 1974. And *The Southwest Review Reader*, edited by Margaret L. Hartley. Dallas, Southern Methodist University Press, 1974. And *The Spell of New Mexico*, edited by Tony Hillerman. Albuquerque, University of New Mexico Press, 1976.]
Roundup of the Waters. *New Mexico Magazine*, February 1958. Also in *This Is New Mexico*, edited by George Fitzpatrick. Albuquerque, Horn & Wallace, 1962.
Rio Grande del Norte. *Westways*, April 1958.
Photographer of the Southwest. *Westways*, August 1958.
The Sense of the Past. *Quarterly of the Historical Society of Southern California*, December 1958.
Oak Grove Summer. *Hoja Volante*, November 1959.
Oak Grove Winter. *Hoja Volante*, February 1960.
Fountains in the Sand. *Arizona and the West*, Spring 1960.
Winter Days with Martha Summerhayes. *Arizona Highways*, November 1961.
Talismans for Travelers. *Southwest Review*, Autumn 1962.
In Search of Spring. *Hoja Volante*, August-November 1963. [Reprinted in *Southwest Review*, Winter 1964; and as a pamphlet in a student project under Richard Hoffman, Los Angeles State College, 1964]
The Way West. *Rodgers Library Notes*, October 1963/July 1964.
A Place of Intense Radiation. *New Mexico Quarterly*, Winter 1964/65.
South From Lisbon. *Southwest Review*, Spring 1968. Reprinted, Dallas, Southern Methodist University Press, 1968.
Arizona's Dry and Wrinkled Land. *Arizona Librarian*, Fall 1968.
A Tribute to a Mere Magazine by a Great Man. *Arizona Highways*, December 1971.

Some Thoughts on the Republication of Frederick Hastings Rindge's *Happy Days in Southern California (1898)*. Los Angeles, Malibu Historical Society, 1972.
The Desert as Dwelled On. Los Angeles, Dawson's Book Shop, 1973. Reprinted in *Arizona Highways*, March 1974.
The Mystique Endures. [appeared later as the opening chapter of *Southwest Classics*] *Westways*, June 1973.
The Desert. *Arizona Highways*, March 1974.
Land of Many Returns. *New Mexico Magazine*, May–June 1974.
The Southwest of the Travelling Reader. *Hoja Volante*, August 1974. Reprinted in *Occidental*, Summer 1974.
Fifty Years of Treasure: The First Half Century of *Arizona Highways*. *Arizona Highways*, April 1975.
An Introduction to the Arizona Environment. *Arizona Alumnus*, September 1975.
To Visit Monterey. *Westways*, January 1976.
Beyond the Bicentennial. *Westways*, March 1976.
Youthful Sentiments/So. Pasadena. *Westways*, July 1976.
Photographs of the Southwest. Photographs by Ansel Adams with an essay on the land by Lawrence Clark Powell. New York, New York Graphic Society, 1976. Text relating to Arizona reprinted as The Southwest. *Arizona Highways*, October 1976. Excerpts reprinted in *Arizona Highways*, April 1985.
Arizona . . . the Peaceful Land. *Arizona Highways*, December 1976.
Arizona, a Bicentennial History. New York, Norton, 1976.
Desert Splendor. Phoenix, Arizona Highways, 1977.
Great Constellations. [tributes to Jose Cisneros, Paul Horgan, Peter Hurd, Tom Lea, and El Paso] *Texas Library Journal*, Spring 1977. Issued separately by El Paso Public Library Association, 1977.
The Phoenix Has Risen — Now What? *The Journal of Arizona History*, Autumn 1977.
To Visit Monterey. *photo-image*, 1977.
Water: There Oughta Be a Law. *Tucson Weekly News*, April 23–29, 1980.
Where Water Flows: The Rivers of Arizona. With photographs by Michael Collier. Flagstaff, Northland Press, 1980.
The Desert Odyssey of John C. Van Dyke. *Arizona Highways*, October 1982.
Farewell to the Encinal. Van Nuys, Richard J. Hoffman, 1982.
The Museum as Oasis. *Sonorensis*, Summer 1983. Issued separately by the Tucson Audubon Institute of Desert Ecology, 1984.
A Memory of Byways. *California History*, Winter 1984.
A Sense of the Future. [centennial address] *Southern California Quarterly*, Spring 1984.
The Sense of the Past. [reprint of 75th anniversary address] In *A Southern California Historical Anthology*, edited by Doyce B. Nunis, Jr. Los Angeles, Historical Society of Southern California, 1984.
Winter Crossing 1952; Travel Notes from a Bygone Era. Privately printed, 1986, in press.

Music

Music Into Silence. *Pacific Spectator*, Winter 1951. And *Santa Barbara Home Life*, December 1951 and January 1952. [Reprinted in *The Little Package*. Cleveland and New York, World Publishing Company, 1964]
The Way it Sounds to Me. [Based on a talk which is reported in *Proceedings of the Workshop*

for *Educational Secretaries,* July 1956, in Los Angeles. Title: "All That is Poetic in Life"]. *Southwest Review,* Autumn 1957. And *Best Articles & Stories,* January 1959.
Books I've Enjoyed. *Montana Library Quarterly,* January 1960. And in *Books Are Friends.* Bozeman, Montana State Library Association, 1962. [Entitled: Mozart in Midwinter]
A Toast to Wolfgang. *Hoja Volante,* May 1960.
In Quest of Orpheus. *Catholic Library World,* February 1962.
On the Road to Salzburg. *Hoja Volante,* November 1962. And in the "Speaking of Books" column of the *New York Times Book Review,* November 11, 1962.
Musical Blood Brothers: Wolfgang Amadeus Mozart, Franz Josef Haydn. Malibu, Press of the Prevailing Westerly, 1966. And in *The Quest for Truth,* Vol. 2, *The Continuing Quest.* Compiled by Martha Boaz. Metuchen, Scarecrow Press, 1967.
My Mozart Commonplace Book. Van Nuys, Richard J. Hoffman, 1980.
Susanna's Secret or The Lost Mozart Letters. Tucson, Press of the Mesquite Harpsichord, 1981.
My Haydn Commonplace Book. Van Nuys, Richard J. Hoffman, 1983.

UCLA Library Publications

Report of the Librarian to the Chancellor. UCLA Library (1944–1961)
[Contributions to] *Acquisitive Notes,* edited by Robert Vosper. (Nos. 1–9, 1946–1949)
The Librarian's Occasional Letter to the Faculty. No. 1–7, 1945–1950.
[Editor] *William Andrews Clark Memorial Library: Report of the First Decade, 1934–1944.* Berkeley and Los Angeles, University of California Press, 1946.
From the Librarian. *UCLA Librarian,* Bi-weekly Bulletin for the Staff. (October 16, 1947–June 30, 1961)
[Acknowledgments] in *Handlist of an Exhibition of Great Historical Documents, Manuscripts & Books.* Compiled by Andrew Horn and Edwin Carpenter. UCLA Library, 1949.
[Foreword] *Staff Handbook.* (Revised Edition) UCLA Library Staff Association, 1950.
[Editor] *Rare Books and Research.* Los Angeles, University of California Press, 1951.
Mercurius Redivivus; Being an Occasional News-letter from the William Andrews Clark Memorial Library. No. 1, Autumn 1952 to No. 3, Fall 1958.
[Editor] *UCLA Library Occasional Papers,* Numbers one–twelve, 1954–1961.
[Editor] *Acquisitions Policies of the UCLA Library.* UCLA Library, 1954.
The Responsibilities of Southern California in Southwestern Library Development. In *Libraries in the Southwest.* UCLA Library, 1955.
[Foreword] *A Glossary of Russian Terminology used in Bibliographies and Library Service,* compiled by Dimitry M. Krassovsky. UCLA Library, 1955.
William Andrews Clark Memorial Library: Report of the Second Decade, 1945–1955. Los Angeles, 1956.
Libraries and Learning, Outline and Bibliography for English 195. UCLA Library, 1956. Second Revised Edition, 1958.
[Foreword] *The Papers of Cornelius Cole and the Cole Family.* UCLA Library, 1956.
[Foreword] *Oscar Wilde and His Literary Circle;* a Catalog of Manuscripts and Letters in the William Andrews Clark Memorial Library. Compiled by John C. Finzi. Berkeley and Los Angeles, University of California Press, 1957.
[Foreword] *The Merle Armitage Books in the William Andrews Clark Memorial Library,* Program for an Exhibition, 1957.

[Foreword]   *The Last Frontiersman.*   An exhibit at the UCLA Library, June 1957.
[Foreword] *Know Your Library.*   First Edition, 1946–16th Edition, 1960–61.   Foreword to 13th Edition reprinted in *Northwestern Library News,* October 25, 1957, under title: Bull's Eye.   Foreword to 14th Edition reprinted in the Santa Barbara Public Library *Fly-Leaf,* October 1958.
[Foreword]   *Books Are Being Read,* by Norah E. Jones, UCLA Library, 1959.
[Preface; oral reporting; and chapter entitled: On Conspiring to Inspire]   In *Mean What You Say,* edited by Betty Rosenberg. UCLA Library, 1959.
[Compiler] *The Southwest of the Bookman.*   UCLA Library, 1959.
Annual Report.   University of California, Los Angeles, School of Library Service.   No. 1, 1959/60–No. 6, 1964/65.
[Compiler] *Around the World in Sixty Books.*   UCLA Library, 1960.
[Foreword] On Collecting Lawrence Durrell.   In *Lawrence Durrell, a Checklist.*   UCLA Library, 1961.
[Preface] *Good Reading.*   (Los Angeles, 1961)
[Farewell] From the Librarian and Dean.   *UCLA Librarian,* June 30, 1961.
[Oral reporting] Dean Powell: The Background of the School of Library Service   In *The UCLA Library School,* Oral History Project.   UCLA Library, 1963.
Papers of Henry Stevens, Bookseller.   *UCLA Librarian,* April 10, 1964.
[Editor] *William Andrews Clark Memorial Library: Report of the Third Decade, 1956–1966.*   Los Angeles, 1966.

Biography and Memorials

Harry Ward Ritchie: Printer.   *Phi Gamma Delta,* October 1931.
Ward Ritchie: Printer.   *Reading and Collecting,* October 1937.
H. Clark Powell, 1900–1938.   Memoirs of His Life and a Bibliography of His Writings.   Los Angeles, The Ward Ritchie Press, 1939.
John Fiske—Bookman.   *Bibliographical Society of America Papers,* Fourth Quarter, 1941.
William Broadhead Rice, 1915–1942.   *Historical Society of Southern California Quarterly,* September 1942.
Robert Ernest Cowan, 1862–1942.   *California Library Association Bulletin,* September 1942.
A Tribute to Benjamin F. Stelter.   *Occidental Alumnus,* December 1946.
Ward Ritchie, Printer.   *Western Printer & Lithographer,* August 1948.
John E. Goodwin.   *UCLA Librarian,* December 9, 1948.
[In Memoriam] Edward Niles Hooker.   *UCLA Librarian,* January 25, 1951.
Harold L. Leupp.   *UCLA Librarian,* February 29, 1952.
[Biography] Robert Vosper.   *College and Research Libraries,* July 1952.
[In Memoriam] J. Gregg Layne.   *UCLA Librarian,* Supplement, August 29, 1952.
Mitchell of California.   *Wilson Library Bulletin,* May 1954.   In *A Passion for Books.*   Excerpts in *CALibrarian,* Summer 1959.   Also in *American Library History Reader,* edited by J. D. Marshall, Hamden, Conn., Shoe String Press, 1961.
A Man Named Dobie.   Printed by the Bookman Press for the First Joint Meeting of the Zamorano Club and the Los Angeles Westerners, December 1, 1954.
[Biography] Andrew H. Horn.   *College and Research Libraries,* October 1954.   And *University of North Carolina Library School Alumni Association Bulletin,* December 1954.
Inspiration of Dr. Moore to Last Long at UCLA.   *Los Angeles Times,* February 7, 1955.
Provost Recalled as Renowned Scholar.   *UCLA Daily Bruin,* Supplement, February 8, 1955.
[In Memoriam]   In *Memorial Addresses at a Service Honoring Ernest Carroll Moore, 1871–1955,*

Held in Royce Hall Auditorium on the Los Angeles Campus of the University of California, February 15, 1955.
[In Memoriam] Ernest Carroll Moore. *UCLA Librarian*, Supplement, February 25, 1955.
[A Tribute to Ben Abramson] *Antiquarian Bookman*, September 24, 1955.
Faithful, Persistent and Believing. In *Memorial Addresses Honoring Edward Augustus Dickson*. Los Angeles, 1956.
[In Memoriam] Regent Edward A. Dickson. *UCLA Librarian*, Supplement, March 9, 1956.
Late Author Paid Tribute. [Edwin Corle] *Los Angeles Times*, July 25, 1956.
Rose Mitchell. *CALibrarian*, Winter 1956.
Nathan Van Patten. *Libri*, Vol. 7, No. 1, 1956.
His Work. In *In Memoriam, Tributes Paid at the Bier of Henry Raup Wagner*, April 1957. Also printed under title: Henry R. Wagner, 1962–1957, *Antiquarian Bookman*, May 13, 1957.
Mr. Southwest: J. Frank Dobie of Texas. *Arizona Highways*, June 1957.
Farewells to Phil Townsend Hanna. Los Angeles, June 4, 1957.
An American Tribute. [to Peter Murray Hill] *Antiquarian Booksellers' Association News Letter* [London] Spring 1958.
In Memoriam Ralph A. Brown. *UCLA Librarian*, October 10, 1958. And *Antiquarian Bookman*, November 3, 1958.
Tribute to John Anson Ford. *Los Angeles County Public Library News Letter*, November 1958.
[William Andrews Clark, Jr., 1877–1934] In *Grolier 75, a Biographical Retrospective to Celebrate the Seventy-fifth Anniversary of the Grolier Club in New York*. New York, Grolier Club, 1959.
Althea Warren. *UCLA Librarian*, January 9, 1959.
[Biography] Gordon R. Williams. *College and Research Libraries*, May 1959.
Thomas S. Dabagh. *California Librarian*, July 1959.
Roland Dennis Hussey. *UCLA Librarian*, November 13, 1959.
William R. Eshelman. *California Librarian*, July 1960.
In Memoriam [Miss Mattaline G. Crabtree]. *Los Angeles Times*, September 15, 1960.
William Holman. *California Librarian*, July 1961.
Mabel Ray Gillis (1882–1961): A Tribute by her Friends to the California State Librarian, 1930–1951. *California Librarian*, October 1961.
Robert Vosper. *California Librarian*, October 1961.
Speaking of Books. [Robert Payne] *New York Times Book Review*, October 29, 1961.
First Lady of Letters. [Erna Fergusson] *New Mexico Magazine*, March 1962.
Raynard C. Swank. *California Librarian*, July 1962.
Profile: Edwin Castagna. *Library Journal*, October 1, 1962.
New Arizona Librarian: Alan Dale Covey. *Arizona Librarian*, Fall 1962.
[Robinson Jeffers]. In *Ave, Vale, Robinson Jeffers*. (San Francisco, Grabhorn Press, 1962)
Robinson Jeffers, '05. *Impromptu* (Faculty-Alumni Publication of Occidental College) 1963.
A Tribute to Mrs. Dolbee and Mr. Cosacco. *UCLA Librarian*, June 28, 1963.
Mr. Southwest. J. Frank Dobie. [Abridgement of an essay from *Books West Southwest*] In *Texas and the West*, by Price Daniel, Jr. Waco, Texas, 1963. [Bookseller's Catalog]
Books and Edwin Corle. Edwin Corle Memorial, Undergraduate Book Collection Contest, the Library, University of California. Santa Barbara — 1964. Published 1963.
The Miller of Big Sur. In *Henry Miller and the Critics*, edited by George Wickes. Carbondale, Southern Illinois University Press, 1963. [Reprinted from *Books in My Baggage*, and the Foreword to *The Intimate Henry Miller*. New York, A Signet Book Published by New American Library, 1959]
Aldous Huxley, 1894–1963. Addresses at a Memorial Meeting held in the School of Library Service, February 27, 1964, by Lawrence Clark Powell, Robert R. Kirsch, and Jacob Zeitlin. Los Angeles, University of California, 1964.
Harold Haines Clark, 1878–1964. Santa Monica, Printed by William M. Cheney, 1964.
Edna H. Yelland, Secretary-Treasurer (1947–1963): the Presidents Salute Seventeen Years of Devoted Service. *California Librarian*, January 1964.

Viva Wagner! Remarks by Lawrence Clark Powell at the Memorial Award Dinner given by the California Historical Society at San Francisco on September 25, 1964. Los Angeles, The Press in the Gatehouse, 1964.

Charles K. Adams. *Hoja Volante,* November 1964.

William Alexander Jackson, 1905-1964. *Hoja Volante,* November 1964.

Ralph Macknight Smith, 1943-1965. Los Angeles, At the Gatehouse Press, 1965.

Wyer at 88. *Library Journal,* May 15, 1965.

Jack Schurch (1905-1965), Occidental 1930. *Tiger Fiji,* Winter 1966.

Bibliographers of the Golden State. Berkeley, University of California Press, 1967.

Memo to Jake Zeitlin. In *A Garland for Jake Zeitlin on the Occasion of His 65th Birthday & the Anniversary of His 40th Year in the Book Trade,* edited by J. M. Edelstein. Los Angeles, Grant Dahlstrom and Saul Marks, 1967.

Climbing the Ladder. *Library Journal,* January 1, 1968.

Majl Ewing, 1903-1967. *Hoja Volante,* February 1968.

A Dedication to the Memory of Mary Hunter Austin, 1868-1934. *Arizona and the West,* Spring 1968.

Brother Antoninus at Wesleyan. *The Tin Drum,* June 1968.

Melba Berry Bennett. *Robinson Jeffers Newsletter,* April 1969. Reprinted in *Melba Berry Bennett,* by Theodore M. Lilienthal. Pasadena, Ward Ritchie Press, 1969.

Margaret Girdner. *California Librarian,* July 1970.

A Tribute to Bradford Booth. *Modern Fiction Studies,* Summer 1970. Reprinted by Friends of the UCLA Library, 1971.

John E. Goodwin. Founder of the UCLA Library; an Essay Toward a Biography. *Journal of Library History,* July 1971. Reprinted in *Vignettes of Library History,* Number 10. Los Angeles, Friends of the UCLA Library, 1972.

Henry Miller at Eighty. *Westways,* April 1972.

Ralph D. Cornell and UCLA. *California Horticultural Journal,* October 1972.

W. W. Robinson, 1891-1972. *Westways,* October 1972.

W. W. Robinson (1891-1972). *Hoja Volante,* November 1972. Reprinted by Dawson's Book Shop, 1974.

[Theodore M. Lilienthal]. *Roxburghe & Zamorano Clubs,* 1972.

Personalities of the West: A Nice Place to Visit [Alfred A. Knopf]. *Westways,* September 1973; The Adventurous Englishman [George Ruxton]. *Westways,* November 1973; A Writer's Landscape [Frank Waters]. *Westways,* January 1974; A Singular Ranger [Edward Abbey]. *Westways,* March 1974; Maynard Dixon's Painted Desert. *Westways,* May 1974; Mr. Bookseller [Jake Zeitlin]. *Westways,* July 1974; A Yorkshireman Wanders West. [Godfrey Sykes]. *Westways,* September 1974.

To Remember J. Gregg Layne, 1893-1952. Los Angeles, Ward Ritchie Press, 1974. Reprinted from *UCLA Librarian,* Supplement, August 29, 1952.

West View: Dean of Western Letters Pushes His Own Cart. *Los Angeles Times Book Review,* April 20, 1975.

Printing Was His Art. [Saul Marks] *Westways,* November 1975.

Remembering Bob Sproul. *California Monthly,* November 1975.

Vein of Silk, Vein of Steel: Words in Memory of Saul Marks. Los Angeles, Richard J. Hoffman, 1975.

Rivers of Books: A Tribute to Edwin Corle. *Soundings: Collections of the University Library* (University of California, Santa Barbara), June 1977.

Coulter, Edith Margaret. In *Dictionary of American Library Biography,* edited by Bohdan S. Wynar. Littleton, Libraries Unlimited, 1978.

Goodwin, John Edward. In *Dictionary of American Library Biography,* edited by Bohdan S. Wynar. Littleton, Libraries Unlimited, 1978.

Mitchell, Sydney Bancroft. In *Dictionary of American Library Biography,* edited by Bohdan S. Wynar. Littleton, Libraries Unlimited, 1978.

The Professor and the Poet. *Hoja Volante,* February 1979. Reprinted by Library Patrons of Occidental College, 1981.
Edward A. Dickson — 1879 –1956. *UCLA Weekly,* May 7, 1979.
The Centenary of Edward A. Dickson. *UCLA Monthly,* May-June 1979.
A Doff to Don [Don Perceval]. *Westways,* January 1980.
In Memory of Bert Fireman. *Arizona Republic,* January 20, 1980.
Henry Miller (1891–1980). *UCLA Librarian,* June 1980.
I Call Him Richman. In *Ward Ritchie, Printer: A Seventy-Fifth Birthday Salute on June 15, 1980.* Flagstaff, Northland Press, 1980.
No Ordinary Man [Henry Miller]. *Westways,* August 1980.
Remembering Henry Miller. *Southwest Review,* Spring 1981.
James Laughlin. *Conjunctions,* Winter 1981–82.
Jake Zeitlin at Eighty. *The Book Collector,* Autumn 1982.
Le Monde Passe La Figure de ce Monde Passe: A Remembrance of Duncan Brent. In a Memoir and Commentary on His Correspondence with Lawrence Clark Powell. Van Nuys, Richard J. Hoffman, 1983.
Words Spoken by LCP at the Memorial Service for Robert C. Bundy 1921–1983 Held at the Community Presbyterian Church Benson, Arizona 9 February 1983. Tucson, 1983.
Remembering Ed Castagna. Van Nuys, Richard J. Hoffman, 1984.
[Winifred Myers]. *AB: Bookman's Weekly,* April 22, 1985.

Miscellaneous Writings

Desert Sunset. *Marengo Literary Leader,* October 28, 1919.
The Purple Dragon. *Marengo Literary Leader,* December 2, 1919. [Facsimile reprint, 1984]
The Blockade Runner. *Marengo Literary Leader,* March 3, 1920.
Impressions. *Tawney Kat* [Occidental College], November 1928.
March Wind. [poem] *Sabretooth* [Occidental College], April 1929.
Religio Musici. [poem] *Sabretooth,* June 1930.
Memories. *Phi Gamma Delta,* May 1932.
Abandons Bitters for Buskin. *Phi Gamma Delta,* May 1934.
La Machine à Ecrire. *Apéritif,* 1935.
Thomas Beck in Hollywood. *Phi Gamma Delta,* March 1935.
My Neighbor Farber of Kappa Alpha. *Kappa Alpha Journal,* May 1935.
Ex Libris Omega Kappa. *Revista Occidental,* 1936.
Comme-ci, Comme-ca. *Los Angeles Saturday Night,* February 26, 1938.
Oktoberlied: Occidental Acquires a Bas-relief by a Distinguished Son. *Occidental Alumnus,* October 1939.
The Flying Hiatus. No. 1–5, December 1942–January 1948. Los Angeles, Rounce & Coffin Club. Editor-in-Name Only, Larry Powell. [LCP wrote numbers 1 & 2]
I am an Escapist. *Hoja Volante,* May 1947.
On the Poetry of Place. *Journal of the National Book League,* June 1951.
Return of the Native. *Hoja Volante,* August 1954.
The Fate of a Plate. In *The Plate of Pewter.* Los Angeles, Zamorano and Roxburghe Clubs, August 1954.
Three O'Clock Appointment. *Hoja Volante,* February 1955.
Occupation Student. *Hoja Volante,* October 1955.
Ocian in View. *Hoja Volante,* August 1956.

The Language of the Heart. Los Angeles City College, 1957.
The Sea as Seen by El Sea Powell. Malibu, 1962. [Printed by W. M. Cheney, Published by Dawson's Book Shop]
Letter. *American Libraries,* July–August 1971, October 1972.
Looking Back at Sixty: Recollections of L.C.P., Librarian, Writer, Teacher. Interview with James V. Mink. Oral History Program, University of California, Los Angeles. Los Angeles, 1973. (Restricted during Powell's lifetime.)
A Computer Analysis of Library Postcards (CALP). *Journal of the American Society for Information Science,* September–October 1974.
Letter. *AB: Bookman's Weekly,* August 8–15, 1977.
Letter. *The O.P. Bookletter,* January 1978.
Letter. *AB: Bookman's Weekly,* May 8, 1978.
1928 Appeals for Admission. *Occidental College Fifty Year Club News,* Fall 1978.
Editor, *Desert Sky and Clouds,* by John C. Van Dyke. Northland Press Occasional Broadside Number 1. Flagstaff, Northland Press, 1979.
Editor, *Indian Summer,* by Sir William Rothenstein. Austin, Wind River Press, 1980.
Letter. *Los Angeles Times Book Review,* November 2, 1980.
Letter. *Tucson Citizen,* December 17, 1980.
Letter. *Arizona Daily Star,* Decemer 21, 1980, August 2, 1982.
Letter. *Arizona Daily Star,* November 13, 1984.
UA is "the Best Between Austin and L.A.," Powell Says. *Arizona Daily Star,* March 12, 1985.
If I Could Tell You. [commencement address] *St. Gregory High School Annual Report, 1984/ 85.* Addendum. Tucson, St. Gregory High School, 1985.

Forewords and Introductions

The Wrath of John Steinbeck, by Robert Bennett. Los Angeles, Albertson Press, 1939.
San Joaquin, by William Everson. Los Angeles, The Ward Ritchie Press, 1939.
The Ghost in the Underblows, a Fragment, by Alfred Young Fisher. Edited and with an Introduction by Lawrence Clark Powell. Los Angeles, The Ward Ritchie Press, 1940.
Biographical Note on Thomas Perry Stricker. In *Elizabeth's Merlin,* by Anthony Hillyer. Los Angeles, 1947.
A Landmark Gone, by Lawrence Durrell. Los Angeles, 1949.
California Local History: A Centennial Bibliography, compiled by the California Library Association Committee on Local History. Stanford University Press, 1950.
Books on the Wing. In William P. Wreden. *A Catalogue of English Books Printed Prior to 1701* (Catalogue 31). 1951. [Book dealer's catalogue]
An Obstinate Exile, by Laurie Lee. Los Angeles, 1951.
Human Side of Bookplates, by Louise Seymour Jones. Los Angeles, The Ward Ritchie Press, 1951.
Bibliographies, Subject and National, by Robert L. Collison. New York, Hafner, 1951.
A Time to Read. In Harry A. Levinson. *Catalog 44.* 1954. [Book dealer's catalogue]
Robinson Jeffers at Occidental College. A Check List of the Jeffers Collection in the Mary Norton Clapp Library. Published on the Fiftieth Anniversary of his Graduation, June 1955.
The Southwest of Edwin Corle. In *Fig Tree John,* by Edwin Corle. Los Angeles, The Ward Ritchie Press, 1955.
University of California at Los Angeles; Its Origin and Formative Years, by Edward A. Dickson. Los Angeles, Friends of the UCLA Library, 1955.

The Published Writings of Henry R. Wagner. Los Angeles, 1955.
Christmas, the Southwest, and J. Frank Dobie. In J. E. Reynolds. *A Holiday Catalog, Western Americana,* 1956. [Book dealer's catalogue]
The Hand of Zamorano; a Facsimile Reproduction of a Manuscript by Don Agustin Vicente Zamorano. Los Angeles, Zamorano Club, 1956.
Up in Coconino County, Pages from the Journal of the Honorable Henry Fountain Ashurst, United States Senator from Arizona, 1912–1941. Pasadena, The Castle Press, 1957.
The Quiet Side of Europe, by Gertrude Clark Powell. With a Memoir of the Author by her Son Lawrence Clark Powell. Los Angeles, 1959.
The Time, the Place and the Book. In *A Vaquero of the Brush Country,* by J. Frank Dobie. Boston, Little, Brown [1959]. [Reprinted, Austin, University of Texas Press, 1982.]
The Intimate Henry Miller. New York, A Signet Book Published by New American Library, 1959. Also in *Henry Miller and the Critics,* edited by George Wickes. Carbondale, Southern Illinois University Press, 1963.
One of the Quietest Things, by Paul Horgan. Los Angeles, School of Library Service, University of California, 1960. [Dedicatory address at inaugural meeting of UCLA School of Library Service]
The Wrath of John Steinbeck, by Robert Bennett. *The Monthly Record* (Connecticut State Prison) November 1960.
Mitchell of California; the Memoirs of Sydney B. Mitchell, Librarian-Teacher-Gardener. Berkeley, California Library Association, 1960.
The Ward Ritchie Press and Anderson, Ritchie & Simon. [Los Angeles, Anderson, Ritchie & Simon] 1961.
[With LeRoy Charles Merritt] *Bibliography: Some Achievements & Prospects,* by F. N. L. Poynter. Los Angeles and Berkeley, University of California, 1961.
Afterword. In *The Rough Riders,* by Theodore Roosevelt. New York, A Signet Classic Published by the New American Library, 1961.
El Morro; Inscription Rock, New Mexico, by John M. Slater. Los Angeles, Plantin Press, 1961.
Death Valley and the Creek Called Furnace, by Edwin Corle. Los Angeles, The Ward Ritchie Press, 1962.
[With LeRoy Charles Merritt] *Bibliography & Literary Studies,* by William A. Jackson. Los Angeles and Berkeley, University of California, 1962.
Francis Bacon's Intellectual Milieu, by Virgil K. Whitaker. Los Angeles, William Andrews Clark Memorial Library, University of California, 1962.
Methods of Textual Editing, by Vinton Adams Dearing. Los Angeles, William Andrews Clark Memorial Library, University of California [1962].
Maud Durlin Sullivan, 1872–1944: Pioneer Southwestern Librarian. A Tribute by Tom Lea. Printed by Carl Herzog of El Paso for the Class of 1962, School of Library Service, University of California, Los Angeles, 1962.
An Islandian on the Islands: a field report by Austin T. Wright . . . author of *Islandia,* on the Southern Californian Islands of Santa Rosa and Santa Cruz. . . . *The Southern California Quarterly,* March 1963.
A Backward Look at Christmas Time. In J. E. Reynolds. *The West, A Holiday Roundup of Choice Books & Pamphlets,* December 1963. [Book dealer's catalogue]
Bibliographical Resources for the Study of Nineteenth Century English Fiction, by Gordon N. Ray. Los Angeles, School of Library Service, University of California, 1964.
Magpie Press Typographical Cookbook. Santa Monica, 1964.
The Raymond Chandler Omnibus. New York, A. A. Knopf, 1964. [Reprinted, New York, Modern Library, 1980.]
Leaves of Grass, Poems of Walt Whitman. Selected [and with an introduction] by Lawrence Clark Powell. New York, Thomas Y. Crowell Company, 1964. [Reprinted in paperback edition, 1971.]
Thomas Willis as a Physician, by Kenneth Dewhurst. Los Angeles, William Andrews Clark Memorial Library, 1964.

Summoned by Books, by Frances Clarke Sayers. New York, Viking Press, 1965.
The Man Who Killed the Deer, by Frank Waters. Flagstaff, Northland Press, 1965.
History of Botany, by George Lawrence and Kenneth F. Baker. Los Angeles, William Andrews Clark Memorial Library, 1965.
The Stagecoach Press. In Texas and the West, Catalogue no. 32 featuring Books Printed and Designed by Jack D. Rittenhouse of the Stagecoach Press. Waco, Price Daniel Jr., Bookseller, 1965. [Bookseller's catalogue]
The Making of the Cambridge Bibliography, by George Watson. Los Angeles, School of Library Service and the University Library, University of California, 1965.
Milton and Clarendon. Two Papers on 17th Century English Historiography presented at a Seminar held at the Clark Library on December 12, 1964, by French R. Fogle and H. R. Trevor-Roper. Los Angeles, William Andrews Clark Memorial Library, 1965.
Neo-Latin Poetry of the Sixteenth and Seventeenth Centuries. Papers by James E. Phillips and Don Cameron Allen presented at a Seminar held on October 17, 1964 at the Clark Library. Los Angeles, William Andrews Clark Memorial Library, 1965.
Moxon, by Carey S. Bliss. Los Angeles, William Andrews Clark Memorial Library, 1965.
Library Publications, by William R. Holman. San Francisco, Roger Beacham, 1965. [Reprinted in *Antiquarian Bookman*, January 3/10, 1966]
Come Hither! Papers on Children's Literature & Librarianship. Edited [with a Preface] by Lawrence Clark Powell. Los Angeles, The Yeasayers Press, 1966.
The Stone Mason of Tor House; the Life and Work of Robinson Jeffers, by Melba Berry Bennett. Los Angeles, Ward Ritchie Press, 1966.
A Guidebook to the Mojave Desert of California, Including Death Valley, Joshua Tree National Monument, and the Antelope Valley, by Russ Leadabrand. Los Angeles, Ward Ritchie Press, 1966.
Kenneth Rexroth: A Checklist of His Published Writings, compiled by James Hartzell and Richard Zumwinkle. Los Angeles, Friends of the UCLA Library, 1967.
W. W. Robinson; a Biography and a Bibliography, by Jimmie Hicks. Los Angeles, Ward Ritchie Press, 1970.
Dr. Bieler's Natural Way to Sexual Health, by Henry G. Bieler and Sarah Nichols. Los Angeles, Charles Publishing Company, 1972.
Charles F. Lummis: Crusader in Corduroy, by Dudley Gordon. Los Angeles, Cultural Assets Press, 1972.
School Libraries Worth Their Keep: A Philosophy Plus Tricks, by Carolyn Clugston Leopold. Metuchen, Scarecrow Press, 1972.
Books in Our Time: Essays by Lawrence S. Thompson, by Lawrence Sidney Thompson. Washington, Consortium Press, 1972.
The Story of Street Literature: Forerunner of the Popular Press, by Robert Lewis Collison. London, Dent, 1973.
Infinite Riches: The Adventures of a Rare Book Dealer, by David Bickerstith Magee. New York, Paul S. Eriksson, 1973.
Bartok, a Memoir, by Yehudi Menuhin. Los Angeles, Plantin Press, 1973.
Poems and Light Verse, Chittenden Turner. Sherman Oaks, Pen-n-Quill, 1973.
A Conversation on D. H. Lawrence, edited by Haruhide Mori. Los Angeles, Friends of the UCLA Library, 1974.
A Select Bibliography to California Catholic Literature 1856–1974, by Francis J. Weber. Los Angeles, Dawson's Book Shop, 1974.
Quince, etc., by Ward Ritchie. Laguna Beach, Laguna Verde Imprenta, 1976.
Fig Tree John, an Indian in Fact and Fiction, by Peter G. Beidler. Tucson, University of Arizona Press, 1977.
John Muir: A Reading Bibliography, by William F. Kimes and Maymie B. Kimes. Palo Alto, William P. Wreden, 1977.
Charles F. Lummis, a Bibliography, by Mary A. Sarber. Tucson, Graduate Library School, University of Arizona, 1977.

California Heartland: Writing from the Great Central Valley, edited by Gerald W. Haslam and James D. Houston. Santa Barbara, Capra Press, 1978.

The Ripened Fields: Fifteen Sonnets of a Marriage, by Peggy Pond Church. Santa Fe, The Lightning Tree, 1978.

On the Beaches of the Moon, by Archibald MacLeish. Laguna Beach, Laguna Verde Imprenta, 1978.

People of the Sun: Some Out-of-Fashion Southwesterners, by Buddy Mays and Marc Simmons. Albuquerque, University of New Mexico Press, 1979.

Saul Marks and the Plantin Press: The Life & Works of a Singular Man, by Lillian Marks. Los Angeles, The Plantin Press, 1980.

A Unifying Influence: Essays of Raynard Coe Swank, edited by David W. Heron. Metuchen, Scarecrow Press, 1981.

The Alida Roochvarg Collection of Books About Books, by Alida Roochvarg. New Castle, Oak Knoll Books, 1981.

Arizona: Historic Land, by Bert M. Fireman. New York: Knopf, 1982.

October Songs, by Carlyle MacIntyre. Van Nuys, Richard J. Hoffman, 1982.

In Celebration of the Book: Literary New Mexico, edited by Dwight Myers and Carol Myers. Albuquerque, The New Mexico Book League and The Lightning Tree, 1982.

The Mystique of Printing: A Half Century of Books Designed by Ward Ritchie, by Ward Ritchie. San Juan Capistrano, The Library of San Juan Capistrano, 1983. Issued also with imprints of California State Library and Scripps College Library.

Turning the Pages: San Diego Public Library History, 1882–1982, by Clara E. Breed. San Diego, Friends of the San Diego Public Library, 1983.

The Drawings of Maynard Dixon, by Maynard Dixon. San Francisco, Achenbach Foundation for Graphic Arts, The Fine Arts Museums of San Francisco, 1985.

Library Literacy Means Lifelong Learning, by Carolyn Dennette Clugston Leopold Michaels. Metuchen, Scarecrow Press, 1985.

Lecture on Learning, by Charles D. Poston. Tucson, Friends of the University of Arizona Library, 1985.

Raymond Chandler. *The Big Sleep.* San Francisco, Arion Press, 1986, in press.

Jane Apostol. *South Pasadena, a Centennial History, 1888-1988.* South Pasadena, South Pasadena Public Library, 1988, in press.

Book Reviews

A Guide for Beginners. Books. *Tawny Kat* [Occidental College], October 1928.

New Poetry 'The Brimming Cup' [Carlyle MacIntyre]: a former Occidental Professor's First Publication is Reviewed. *Sabretooth* [Occidental College], June 1930.

Robinson Jeffers. *Descent to the Dead.* The Carmelite, July 7, 1932.

Velia Ercole. *Dark Windows. Los Angeles Times,* October 14, 1934.

Robinson Jeffers. *Solstice and Other Poems. Los Angeles Times,* October 13, 1935. And *Los Angeles Saturday Night,* November 30, 1935.

D. H. Lawrence. *Phoenix. Los Angeles Saturday Night,* December 12, 1936.

Rudolph Gilbert. *Shine Perishing Republic. Los Angeles Saturday Night,* January 9, 1937.

C. F. MacIntyre. *Poems. Los Angeles Saturday Night,* February 13, 1937.

Ernest J. Simmons. *Pushkin. Los Angeles Saturday Night,* March 6, 1937.

M. F. K. Fisher. *Serve it Forth. Reading and Collecting,* October 1937.

Goncourt Journals. Los Angeles Times, October 3, 1937.

Knud Merrild. *A Poet and Two Painters. Los Angeles Times,* March 13, 1939.

R. M. Rilke. *Fifty Selected Poems*, Translated by C. F. MacIntyre. *Los Angeles Times*, June 16, 1940.
John W. Caughey. *California*. *Los Angeles Times*, August 4, 1940.
Joseph Noel. *Footloose in Arcadia: a Personal Record of Jack London, George Sterling, Ambrose Bierce*. *Pacific Historical Review*, December 1940.
Thomas Blake Clark. *Omai, the First Polynesian Ambassador to England*. *Pacific Historical Review*, March 1941.
Louis K. Koontz. *Robert Dinwiddie*. *Los Angeles Times*, March 2, 1941.
Dixon Wecter. *The Hero in America*. *Los Angeles Times*, April 27, 1941.
Catalogue of the Estelle Doheny Collection. *Print*, May–June 1941.
Poetry. *On the Record*, June 1941.
The Letters of John Fiske. *Pacific Historical Review*, September 1941.
Writers' Program. *The Monterey Peninsula*. *Pacific Historical Review*, December 1941.
Henry Miller. *The Colossus of Maroussi*. *Los Angeles Times*, December 14, 1941.
Henry Miller and M. Fraenkel. *Hamlet, a Philosophical Correspondence*. *Los Angeles Times*, December 14, 1941.
Henry R. Wagner. *Bullion to Books*. *Bibliographical Society of America Papers*, Third Quarter, 1942.
John Steinbeck. *The Forgotten Village*. *Pacific Historical Review*, June 1942.
John Steinbeck and E. F. Ricketts. *Sea of Cortez*. *Pacific Historical Review*, June 1942.
Ernest Marchand. *Frank Norris: a Study*. *Pacific Historical Review*, September 1943.
D. C. Haskell. *The U.S. Exploring Expedition, 1838–1842, and its Publication, 1844–1874, a Bibliography*. *Bibliographical Society of America Papers*, Second Quarter, 1943.
Edward Rowland Sill. *Around the Horn: a Journal*. *Pacific Historical Review*, September 1944.
Fremont Rider. *The Scholar and the Future of the Research Library*. *Modern Language Forum*, December 1944.
Ulrich and Kup. *Books and Printing, a Selected List of Periodicals, 1800–1942*. *Bibliographical Society of America Papers*, First Quarter, 1945.
Annual Report of the Librarian of Congress for the Fiscal Year Ending June 30, 1945. *Library Quarterly*, January 1947.
G. P. Putnam. *Death Valley and its Country*. *Pacific Historical Review*, February 1947.
Van Wyck Brooks. *The Times of Melville and Whitman*. *Los Angeles Daily News*, Book Section, November 29, 1947.
Robinson Jeffers. *The Double Axe and other Poems*. *Los Angeles Times*. August 1, 1948.
John Carter. *Taste and Technique in Book Collecting*. *College and Research Libraries*, April 1949.
Standards of Bibliographical Description, by Buhler, McManaway, and Wroth. *Library Journal*, October 15, 1949.
Studies in Bibliography: Papers of the Bibliographical Society of the University of Virginia. *College and Research Libraries*, January 1953.
A. N. S. Munby. *The Formation of the Phillipps Library up to the year 1850*. *Library Journal*, May 1, 1955.
Theodore C. Blegen and others. *Book Collecting and Scholarship: Essays*. *Library Quarterly*, July 1955.
Paul G. Morrison. *Index of Printers, Publishers and Booksellers in Donald Wing's Short Title Catalogue of Books*. *Library Journal*, October 1, 1955.
Clifford K. Shipton. *The American Bibliography of Charles Evans*. *Library Journal*, May 15, 1956.
Archer Taylor. *A History of Bibliographies of Bibliographies*. *Library Journal*, August 1956.
S. C. Roberts. *The Evolution of Cambridge Publishing*. *Library Journal*, October 1, 1956.
W. G. Hiscock. *The Christ Church Supplement to Wing's "Short-title Catalog, 1641–1700."* *Library Journal*, June 15, 1957.
Scott O'Dell. *Country of the Sun*. *Los Angeles Mirror-News*, July 22, 1957.

H. P. Kraus. *The Eightieth Catalogue: Remarkable Manuscripts,, Books and Maps from the Ninth to the Eighteenth Century*. Library Quarterly, October 1957.
John Carter. *Books and Book Collectors*. Bibliographical Society of America Papers, 4th Quarter, 1957.
Radcliffe Squires. *The Loyalties of Robinson Jeffers*. Southwest Review, Winter 1957.
Armine D. MacKenzie. *A Fine Contagion*. California Librarian, January 1959.
Paul Jordan-Smith. *The Road I Came*. Historical Society of Southern California Quarterly, June 1960.
Edwin Wolf 2d with John F. Fleming. *Rosenbach, a Biography*. New York Times Book Review, November 20, 1960. [Titled: It Was Fun to Pay Through the Nose]
Van Allen Bradley. *More Gold in Your Attic*. Los Angeles Times, January 22, 1962. [Titled: 'Gold in Attic' Hardly Worth It]
Dwight L. Clarke. *Stephen Watts Kearny, Soldier of the West*. Reprinted from column in *Westways*, January 1962 in *Incidentals* [Occidental Life Insurance Company periodical], February 1962.
Lawrence Durrell. *The Dark Labyrinth*. New York Times Book Review, February 18, 1962. [Titled: A Way of Saying Urgent Things]
Marjorie H. Nicolson. *Voyages to the Moon*. New York Times Book review, August 25, 1963. In "Speaking of Books" column.
Harvey Einbinder. *The Myth of the Britannica*. New York Times Book Review, February 2, 1964.
Library Trends: Education for Librarianship Abroad in Selected Countries. Library Journal, March 15, 1964.
Harvie Branscomb. *Teaching with Books*. Library Journal, July 1964. [Titled: Branscomb's Bible]
Malcolm Glenn Wyer. *Books and People: Short Anecdotes from a Long Experience*. Library Journal, August 1964. [Titled: Bookman and Humanist]
Wilhelm Munthe. *American Librarianship from a European Angle*. Library Journal, September 1, 1964.
Richard Henry Dana. *Two Years Before the Mast*. Southern California Quarterly, March 1965.
Jesse H. Shera. *Foundations of the Public Library*. Library Journal, August 1965.
Frank Waters. *The Man Who Killed the Deer*. Southwest Review, Autumn 1965.
R. L. Duffus. *Queen Calafia's Island*. New York Times Book Review, November 21, 1965. [Titled: A Tale of Two Cities]
Books of the Southwest. A Critical Checklist of Current Southwestern Americana. [with Betty Rosenberg] Published by the Library and later by the School of Library Service of the University of California. Number 1, June 1957–Number 109, June 1966. Monthly.
Western Books and Writers. Monthly Column in *Westways*, occasionally 1934–1942, quarterly 1943–1945, and monthly 1946–to date; title changed to *Books of the West*, 1966.
Speaking of Books: The Horgan File. New York Times Book Review, May 14, 1967.
Things We Need to Know. New York Times Book Review, November 5, 1967.
Charles Colley. *Documents of Southwestern History: A Guide to the Manuscripts Collections of the Arizona Historical Society*. The Papers of the Bibliographical Society of America, 4th Quarter, 1967.
W. A. Jackson. *Records of a Bibliographer: Selected Papers*. Journal of Library History, January 1968.
Speaking of Books: The Grand Obsession. New York Times Book Review, March 10, 1968.
William Targ. *Carrousel for Bibliophiles*. Library Journal, October 1, 1968.
Speaking of Books: Robinson Jeffers. New York Times Book Review, October 6, 1968.
David A. Randall. *Dukedom Large Enough*. Library Journal, September 15, 1969.
Robert B. Downs. *Books That Changed America*. The Library Quarterly, October 1970.
Robinson Jeffers. *Cawdor and Medea*. California Librarian, January 1971.
Al Lowman. *Printer at the Pass: The Work of Carl Hertzog*. Southwestern Historical Quarterly, October 1973.

Josephine DeWitt Rhodehammel and Raymund Francis Wood. *Ina Coolbrith, Librarian and Laureate of California*. California Librarian, January 1974.

Robert J. Brophy. *Robinson Jeffers: Myth, Ritual and Symbol in His Narrative Poems*. Southwest Review, Spring 1974.

Harry Clark. *A Venture in History: the Production, Publication, and Sales of the Works of Hubert Howe Bancroft*. The Library Quarterly, October 1974.

Margaret Maxwell. *Shaping a Library: William L. Clements as Collector*. The Papers of the Bibliographic Society of America, October–December 1975.

Leona Rostenberg and Madeleine B. Stern. *Old and Rare: Thirty Years in the Book Business*. The Library Quarterly, October 1976.

Paul Horgan. *The Thin Mountain Air*. Books of the Southwest, November 1977.

Charles Bowden. *Killing the Hidden Waters*. Books of the Southwest, December 1977.

Joyce Y. Pinney. *A Pasadena Chronology, 1769–1977*. Books of the Southwest, April 1979.

William H. Nolte. *Rock and Hawk: Robinson Jeffers and the Romantic Agony*. The American Spectator, May 1979.

Bruce Babbitt. *Grand Canyon: An Anthology*. The Journal of Arizona History, Spring 1979.

Peter Bermingham. *The New Deal in the Southwest: Arizona and New Mexico*. Books of the Southwest, April 1980.

Jay Martin. *Always Merry and Bright*. Tucson Weekly News, April 2–8, 1980.

Ralph F. Palmer. *Doctor on Horseback: A Collection of Anecdotes Largely But Not Exclusively Medically Oriented*. Books of the Southwest, May 1980.

Laurie Lisle. *Portrait of an Artist: A Biography of Georgia O'Keeffe*. Books of the Southwest, June 1980.

Jean Peters. *Collectible Books: Some New Paths*. The Library Quarterly, October 1980.

John David Marshall. *The Southern Books Competition at Twenty-Five: A Silver Anniversary Tribute*. Southeastern Librarian, Winter 1980.

Gordon Stuart. *Meditations of the Old Mule Skinner*. Books of the Southwest, June 1981.

William G. McGinnies. *Discovering the Desert: Legacy of the Carnegie Desert Botanical Laboratory*. Books of the Southwest, July 1981.

John D. Margolis. *Joseph Wood Krutch: A Writer's Life*. The Journal of Arizona History, Autumn 1981.

Robinson Jeffers. *"What Odd Expedients" and Other Poems*. Arizona Quarterly, Winter 1981.

M. F. K. Fisher. *A Cordiall Water: A Garland of Odd & Old Receipts to Assuage the Ills of Man & Beast*. Books of the Southwest, January 1982.

Ruth Frey Axe. *Henry R. Wagner: An Intimate Profile*. Books of the Southwest, March 1982.

Guy Lyle. *Beyond My Expectation: A Personal Chronicle*. The Library Quarterly, April 1982.

New Mexico Artists and Writers, a Celebration: Special Republication of the June 26, 1940 Artists and Writers Edition of the Santa Fe New Mexican. Books of the Southwest, May 1982.

Evelyn Brack Measeles. *Lee's Ferry: A Crossing on the Colorado*. Arizona Quarterly, Spring 1982.

Bill Jamison. *Santa Fe, An Intimate View*. Books of the Southwest, December 1982.

A. B. Guthrie. *Fair Land, Fair Land*. New Mexico Historical Review, Spring 1983.

Rolly Kent and Susan North. *Willa & Marie: Poems From a Nursing Home*. Books of the Southwest, May 1983.

Harry Huntt Ransom. *The Conscience of the University and Other Essays*. The Journal of Library History, Summer 1983.

Marta Weigle and Kyle Fiore. *Santa Fe and Taos: The Writer's Era, 1916–1941*. The Pacific Historian, Summer 1983.

Amadeo M. Rea. *Once a River: Bird Life and Habitat Changes on the Middle Gila*. Books of the Southwest, August–September 1983.

William B. Ready. *Files on Parade: A Memoir*. The Library Quarterly, January 1984.

Ann Zwinger. *A Desert Country Near the Sea: A Natural History of the Cape Region of Baja California*. Books of the Southwest, March 1984.

Ruth Lilly Westphal. *Plein Air Painters of California: The Southland.* Books of the Southwest, March 1984.

Louis Adamic. *Robinson Jeffers: A Portrait.* Fine Print, April 1984.

Robert Metzger. *My Heart Is the Southwest: Peter Hurd Letters and Journals.* Books of the Southwest, April 1984.

Edward Abbey. *Beyond the Wall: Essays from the Outside.* Books of the Southwest, May 1984.

Marshall Berges. *The Life and Times of Los Angeles: A Newspaper, a Family, and a City.* Books of the Southwest, May 1984.

Catherine Catellani and Marvin Diogenes. *Sonora Review: Number 5.* Books of the Southwest, May 1984.

Augusta Fink. *I — Mary, a Biography of Mary Austin;* and Mary Austin. *The Land of Journeys' Ending. Southern California Quarterly,* Summer 1984.

Ann Woodin. *Home Is the Desert.* Books of the Southwest, August 1984.

Ralph Webster Yarborough at 80: A Gathering of Tributes from Several of His Book-loving Friends. With W. David Laird. Books of the Southwest, August 1984.

Dawn Glanz. *How the West Was Drawn: American Art and the Settling of the Frontier.* Books of the Southwest, October 1984.

Patricia Trenton and Patrick Houlihan. *Native Faces: Indian Cultures in American Art, From the Collections of the Los Angeles Athletic Club and the Southwest Museum.* Books of the Southwest, December 1984.

Michael P. Cohen. *The Pathless Way: John Muir and American Wilderness.* Books of the Southwest, December 1984.

Harriet Rochlin and Fred Rochlin. *Pioneer Jews: A New Life in the Far West.* Books of the Southwest, December 1984.

Candace C. Kant. *Zane Grey's Arizona.* Books of the Southwest, December, 1984. And *The Journal of Arizona History,* Spring 1985.

Ann Hodges Morgan and Rennard Strickland. *Arizona Memories.* Books of the Southwest, January 1985.

John H. Jenkins. *Basic Texas Books: An Annotated Bibliography of Selected Works for a Research Library.* Books of the Southwest, April 1985.

Harry Huntt Ransom. *The Other Texas Frontier.* Books of the Southwest, April 1985.

Edward Abbey. *Slumgullion Stew: An Edward Abbey Reader.* Books of the Southwest, April 1985.

David Gebhard and Robert Winter. *Architecture in Los Angeles: A Compleat Guide.* Books of the Southwest, August–September 1985.

Patricia Nelson Limerick. *Desert Passages: Encounters with the American Deserts.* Books of the Southwest, August–September 1985.

Kevin Starr. *Inventing the Dream: California Through the Progressive Era.* Books of the Southwest, October 1985.

The Drawings of Maynard Dixon. Books of the Southwest, October 1985.

Donald J. Hagerty. *Images of the Southwest, Past and Present.* Books of the Southwest, October 1985.

Robert B. Downs. *Perspectives on the Past: An Autobiography.* The Library Quarterly, April 1986.

Epigraphs

Wise Men Fish Here: The Story of Frances Steloff and the Gotham Book Mart, by W. G. Rogers. New York, Harcourt, Brace & World, 1965.

AB Bookman's Weekly, September 23, 1968.
AB Bookman's Weekly, November 12, 1973.
Special Collections, by UCLA Graduate School of Library Service, Students Association.   Los Angeles, UCLA Graduate School of Library Service Students Association, 1971.
Rare Books, by Betty Smedley.   Austin, Betty Smedley, 1980.
The Writer's Quotation Book: A Literary Companion, edited by James Charlton.   New York, The Pushcart Press, 1980.
The Colorado Plateau, by Parker and Hildegard Hamilton.   Prescott, Classic Printers, 1981.
Catalogue 227A (Summer 1982).   Bertram Rota Ltd. Booksellers
AzU Library Newsletter, November 21, 1984.
Creative Writing Newsletter, November 1985.
Christmas Card, Blackwell North America, Inc., 1985.
AB Bookman's Weekly, January 6, 1986.

Fiction

The Blue Train.   Santa Barbara, Capra Press, 1977.
Le Train Bleu.   Paris, Buchet/Chastel, 1978.   Translated from the American edition by Anne Joba.
On the Main Line at Last; or, the Genesis of *The Blue Train.*   *Hoja Volante,* August 1979.
The River Between.   Santa Barbara, Capra Press, 1979.
De l'autre Cote du Fleuve.   Paris, Editions Buchet/Chastel, 1982.   Translated from the American by Nicole Tisserand.
El Morro.   Santa Barbara, Capra Press, 1984.
Portrait of My Father.   Santa Barbara, Capra Press, 1986, in press.

Selected Biographical Material About LCP

Introduction, by W. W. Robinson.   In *Checklist of the Published Writings of Lawrence Clark Powell,* compiled by Betty Rosenberg.   Los Angeles, School of Library Service, University of California, Los Angeles, 1966.
Introduction, by William Targ.   In *Bookman's Progress,* by Lawrence Clark Powell.   Los Angeles, Ward Ritchie Press, 1968.
Lawrence Clark Powell at 70, by W. David Laird.   *AB Bookman's Weekly,* October 18, 1976.
Commencement Speaker, by [Pendleton Gaines].   In *Eighty-First Annual Commencement Exercises. Program.*   Tucson, University of Arizona, 1976.
Voices From the Southwest: A Gathering in Honor of Lawrence Clark Powell, gathered by Donald C. Dickinson, W. David Laird, and Margaret F. Maxwell.   Flagstaff, Northland Press, 1976.
A Talk Honoring Lawrence Clark Powell on the Occasion of His 70th Birthday, by Bert Fireman.   Tucson, Platyne Press, 1977.
Librarian Powell, by Roy Meador.   *Air California Magazine,* July 1979.
Lawrence Clark Powell — Bookman, by Saul Cohen.   *Book Talk* [New Mexico Book League],

November 1979. Reprinted in *In Celebration of the Book: Literary New Mexico,* edited by Dwight Myers and Carol Myers. Albuquerque, New Mexico Book League and The Lightning Tree Press, 1982.

LCP: A Keepsake from the UCLA Library & Friends of the UCLA Library for the Friends of Lawrence Clark Powell in Celebration of His 75th Birthday September 3, 1981. Los Angeles, Friends of the UCLA Library, 1981. Selected quotations.

Editor's Corner: Lawrence Clark Powell Is Honored by A.L.A. [Story reporting honorary membership in ALA, quoting from the citation written by Wm. R. Eshelman]. *AB Bookman's Weekly,* September 14, 1981.

"Next Time a Public Library," by John Berry. *Library Journal,* October 15, 1982.

Lion in the Desert: An Interview with Lawrence Clark Powell, by Michelle B. Graye. *Footnotes: Newsletter of the Library Students Organization* (Graduate Library School, University of Arizona), December 1982.

Lawrence Clark Powell, by Wayne A. Wiegand. In *Leaders in American Academic Librarianship: 1925–1975,* edited by Wayne A. Wiegand. (Beta Phi Mu Chapbook number 16.) Pittsburgh, Beta Phi Mu, 1983.

Lawrence Clark Powell: A Bookman in the Library, by Jacob Zeitlin. *AB Bookman's Weekly,* June 18, 1984.

Powell, Lawrence Clark, by Wm. R. Eshelman. *ALA World Encyclopedia,* 2nd edition. Chicago, American Library Association, 1986. In press.

Books Dedicated to LCP

Henry Miller. *The Books in My Life.* Norfolk, New Directions Books, 1952.

Robert L. Collison. *Dictionaries of Foreign Languages.* New York, Hafner Publishing Company, 1955. 2d revised edition, 1971.

Donald M. Powell. *An Arizona Gathering: A Bibliography of Arizoniana, 1950–1959.* Tucson, Arizona Pioneers' Historical Society, 1960. Joint dedication to LCP and Patricia Paylore.

Robert Payne. *The Roman Triumph.* London and New York, Abelard–Schuman, 1963.

George Wickes. *Lawrence Durrell. Henry Miller. A Private Correspondence.* New York, E.P. Dutton, 1963. Joint Dedication to LCP and Alan Thomas.

William Everson (Brother Antoninus). *The Poet Is Dead: A Memorial for Robinson Jeffers.* San Francisco: Auerhan Press, 1964.

Fredson Bowers and Lyle H. Wright. *Bibliography. Papers Read at a Clark Library Seminar, May 7, 1966.* With an introduction by Hugh G. Dick. Los Angeles, William Andrews Clark Memorial Library, University of California, Los Angeles, 1966.

Richard H. Dillon. *Fool's Gold: The Decline and Fall of Captain John Sutter of California.* New York, Coward–McCann, 1967.

Earl Roy Miner. *Stuart and Georgian Moments.* (Clark Library Seminar Papers on Seventeenth and Eighteenth Century English Literature.) Berkeley, University of California Press, 1972.

D. H. Lawrence. *The Hopi Snake Dance.* With a foreword by Linda Laird and David Laird. Flagstaff, Peccary Press, 1980.

Margaret F. Maxwell. *A Passion for Freedom: The Life of Sharlot Hall.* Tucson, University of Arizona Press, 1982.

Kevin Starr. *Inventing the Dream: California Through the Progressive Era.* New York, Oxford University Press, 1985. Joint dedication to LCP, Oscar Lewis, and Albert Shumate.

Johanna E. Tallman. *Check Out a Librarian.* Metuchen, Scarecrow Press, 1985.

Index

Capital letters indicate locations in the photographic insert section of the book.

Abbey, Edward 112–113; *Desert Solitaire* 112
Abbey Theatre 8
Abel, Richard, Company 95
Ackerman, Page 3, 94, 120
Adams, Ansel 101, 111; *Fait Lux* 111; *Photographs of the Southwest* 111
Adams, Frederick B. 32, 73, 113
Adams, J. Robert 101
Adams, Virginia 111
"After Long Silence," Yeats 8
Alchemy of Books, The, Powell xii, 98
Aldington, Richard 21
Alioto, Joseph 40
Altman, Ellen 106
American Geographical Society 53
American Library Association (ALA) x, xii, xv, xvi, 29, 39, 42, 72, 84, 87, 93, 95, 98, 115, 121, 123, **N, K**
Amherst College 41
Amon Carter Museum 119
"And Now Miguel," Krumbold (video) 97

Anderson, Emily 8
Apache reservation, San Carlos 74
Apollinaire, Guillaume 44
Archer, Margot 45
Archer, H. Richard 45
Arizona, A Bicentennial History, Powell 102, 106, 111, 112, 117
Arizona and the West 103
Arizona Highways 86, 100, 105, 111
Arizona Historical Foundation 112
Arizona Library Association 84
Arizona Quarterly 103
Arizona State University (ASU) 75, 84, 88, 91, 102, 105
Armies of the Night, Mailer 47
Arrowsmith, William 41
Art Institute of Chicago 13
Aspen Institute 55
Association of Research Libraries (ARL) 53, 78, 95, 116–117
Atherton, Gertrude 50; *The Splendid Idle Forties* 50
Auden, W.H. 10, 50, 97; "Down by the River" 50

165

Austin, Mary 35, 36, 41; *The Land of Little Rain* 36

BBC 5
Babb, Jim 42, 73, 113
Babbitt, Bruce 105, 110
Bancroft, H.H. 32
Bancroft Library 32, 55
Barker, Nicholas 114; *The Book Collector* (ed.) 114
Bartók, Béla 53
Baudelaire, Charles 33
Bay State Librarian 50
Beinecke Library 42, 66
Belloli, Joe 57
Benge, Ronald viii
Berg Collection, New York Public Library 30
Berlioz, Hector 58
Bermingham, Peter 100
Berninghaus, Oscar 58
Bernstein, Leonard 5
Berry, John 7, 29, 43
Bertram Rota, Ltd. 68
Bevan, Aneurin vii
"Bibliographers of the Golden State," Powell 32, 35
Bibliographical Society of America (BSA) 39, 41, 113
Bibliography of American Literature, Blanck 51
Bieler, Barry 118
Bieler, Hall 55, 118
Billheimer, Stephen 72
Bishop Musuem 14
Blanck, Jacob 51; *Bibliography of American Literature* 51
Blasingame, Ralph 43
Bleibtreu, Hermann 94, 96
Blue Train, The, Powell 2, 5, 6, 52, 108, 109, 117
Book Collector, The 114

Book of Kells 10
Bookman's Progress, Powell (Targ, ed.) 44, **E**
Books Are Basic, Powell (Marshall, ed.) 113
Books in My Baggage, Powell 2
Books of the Southwest 127
Boorstin, Daniel 124
Boston Public Library 51
Bowden, Charles 112–113
Bowdoin College 41
Bowers, Fredson 32
Bowker, R.R., Company xi, 43
Boyd, Julian 117
Brandt, Rex 123
Brattle Book Shop 51
Breed, Clara 71
Brent, Duncan 59, 116
Brent, Fredrika 59, 116
British Museum 8
Broadcasting House, London 9
Brodersen, Arvid 41
Brooklyn Polytechnic Institute 104
Brother Antoninus *see* Everson, William
"Brother Antoninus Reads at Wesleyan," Everson (recording) 46
Brown, Andreas 44
Brown, Francis 43–44, 64
Brown, James Duff viii
Brown Library 66
Browning, Robert 21, 25; "Home Thoughts from the Sea" 21
Bryant, Douglas 51
Bryon, F.W. 16, 17
Buhler, Curt 113
Bullock, Wynn 111
Bundy, Bob 97–98, 110, 118
Bundy, Winogene 97–98, 110, 118
Butterfield, Victor 12, 40

Byrd, Richard E. 89

Cabral, Pedro Alvares 25
Cabrilho, João Rodrigues 21, 25
Caedmon 46
Cage, John 41
Cain, Robert 50
Calder and Boyars 19
California Book Trails published as *California Classics*, Powell 12
California Classics, Powell 55, 90, 108
"California Classics Reread," Powell 37–38
California Institute of Technology 35, 104, 120
California Library Association 56–58
California State Library 55
Callahan, James 33
Campbell, Frances Deas 88–89
Campbell, John 88–89, 115
Canadian Library Association 43
Capra Press 6, 109
Carleton College 89
Carlson, Raymond 86
Carlyle, Thomas 62
Carnegie Foundation 14
Carnegie-Mellon University 43
Carter, John 74, 113
Castagna, Edwin 39–40, 72–73, 116
Castagna, Rachel 39–40, 116
Castro, Raul Hector I
Cather, Willa 108
Caughey, John Walton 4
Cave, Roderick 66
Center for Advanced Studies, Wesleyan University 11, 30, 40, 47

Center for the Book, Library of Congress 124
Cerf, Bennet 69
Chandler, Raymond 70
Chase, J. Smeaton 55
Chemical Abstracts (Yugoslav) 13
Cheney, Will 35, 37, 86, 122
Cherbak, Cynthia 109
Chico State University 120
Cisneros, Jose 119
Clapp, Verner 116
Clark, Harold Haines 92
Clark Library *see* University of California at Los Angeles
Clarke, Frances 60–61
Clarke, Stanley 60–61
Clements Library 67
Cobell, Leo 78
Coffin, William Sloan 47
Cohen, Saul 119
Cole, John Y. 124
Collier, Michael 110–111, **M**
Collier, Rose 111
Collis, Ruth 8
Colorado Library Association 115
Columbia University 76, 88, 103, 117
Columbus, Christopher 25
Combs, Adele 48
Combs, Richard 48
Conant, Howard 100
Condit, Christopher 110–111, **M**
Coney, Donald 73, 116
Connecticut College Library 41
Connecticut Library Association 42
"Connecting Up," Powell 116
Connes, Georges 61
Conway, William 3
"Coole Park, 1929," Yeats 11
Coronado's Children, Dobie 82

Corrigan, Philip 17
Coryell, Gladys 88
Coulter, Edith M. 56; Edith M. Coulter Memorial Lecture Lecture 56, 77
Covent Garden 18
Covey, Alan 85
Cowan, Robert Ernest 32
Cox, James 129
Cox, John 66, 67
Cox, Stephen 100
Creager, George 41
Croatian Library Association 12
Crowell, Thomas Y. (publisher) 110
Curtis, George de Clyver 71
Cutter, Charles Ammi viii

Dahlstrom, Grant **J**
Dalton, Jack 74, **F**
Dana, John Cotton viii
Dana, Richard Henry 41, 61; *Two Years Before the Mast* 61
Dannreuther, Kathy 112, 121
"Daphnis and Chloë in Literature and Art," Powell (printed as *The Enchanted Couple*) 121
Darling, Louise 3, 12, 97, 120
Dartmouth College 41, 53
Davis, Edna 3
Davis, James 129
Dawson, Glen 86
Death Valley in '49, Manly 56
Desert Solitaire, Abbey 112
"Desert Sunset," Powell 124
Dewey, Mevil viii
Dickens, Charles 64
Dickinson, Donald 81, 87–88, 93, 95, 98, 103, 105–107, 125, **L**
Dietrich, Laurie **O**

Dobie, Bertha 58
Dobie, J. Frank 58, 76, 82, 121; *Coronado's Children* 82
Dougherty, Richard 78
"Down by the River," Auden 50
Downs, Robert viii
Drexel Institute 42
Duke University 35, 74
Dukedom Large Enough, Randall 64
Durbridge, Leonard 66
Durham, G. Homer 84
Durkan, Michael 41
Durrell, Lawrence 100, **D, E**
Dutton, Davis 37, 108
Dwiggins, W.A. 124
Dworski, David 59
Dworski, Susan 59
Dykstra, Clarence 45, 94
Dykstra, Lillian 45

Eastern New Mexico University 4
Eastlake, William 97
Edel, Leon 41
Edwards, E.I. "Eddie" 55
Edwards, Harold 7, 19, 73
Edwards, Olive 8, 19, 73
Einstein, Albert 12
El Morro, Powell 68, 108
El Paso Public Library, 121
Ellithorpe, Marian 7
Ellsworth, Ralph viii, 73, 78
Emerson, Ralph Waldo 97
Enchanted Couple, The, Powell 121
Enesco, Georges 5
Engley, Donald B. 41
English Poems, Pessoa 21
Enoch Pratt Free Library 40, 72
"Epithalamium," Pessoa 21

Eshelman, William R. ix, xvi, xvii, 78
Esterquest, Ralph 51
Esterquest, Shelley 51
Evans, Helen 118
Evans, Luther x, xii, 43, 116–118
Everson, William (Brother Antoninus) 45–47, 69–70, **B**; *San Joaquin* 45; "Rose of Solitude" 46; "Tendril in the Mesh" 47; "Brother Antoninus Reads at Wesleyan" (recording) 46
Ewing, Majl 11

Farah, Cynthia 132
Farewell to the Encinal, Powell 32
Feldman, Lew David 76
Fiat Lux, Adams 111
Finzi, John 70
Fireman, Bert 112
Fitzgerald, F. Scott 108
Fleming, Donald **N**
Folger Library 66
Fontana, Bernard "Bunny" 104, 111–112, 126–127
Fonteyn, Margot 18
Food Administration, U.S. 120
Ford Foundation 14
Fortune & Friendship, Powell ix, x, xiv, xvii, xviii, 6–7, 43, 48, 56
Francis, Sir Frank x, 8, 32, 62, 73
Francis, Kitty 8
Frey, Ann 92
Frey, Judge William 92
From the Heartland, Powell 108, 110
Frost, Robert 53
Frugé, August 33

Gallup, Don 42
Galvin, Thomas 50, 105
Gama, Vasco de 25
Gammage, Grady 84
Gandhi, Mohandas K. vii
Gardner, Frank viii
Gegenheimer, Albert 95
Geiger, Father Maynard 33
Geller, William 72–73
George, Gerald 111
Gila County (AZ) Library 74
Gill, Eric 8–9, 13, 33–34, 45, 64
Gilliam, Stanley 62
Gillis, James L. 56–57
Gillmor, Frances 85; *Traders to the Navajos* 85
Gilman, Richard Carleton 83
Girdner, Margaret 56–58, 71
Gjelsness, Rudolph 73, 87
Gloss, George 51
Golden Gate Park, San Francisco **O**
Goldsmith, Joyce viii
Goldwater, Barry 112
Goodrich, Nathaniel 53
Goodwin, Fanny Coldren 34
Goodwin, John 34–35
Goodwin, Will 119
Gordan, John 30
Gotham Book Mart 44
Gould, Laurence M. 89, 112, 125
Grabhorn, Jane 124
Grauer, Ben 44
Greenaway, Emerson 43
Gregory, Lady Augusta 10, 11, 30
Grey, Zane 104
Grolier Club 114, 121
Gross, Larry 49
Guggenheim Foundation 29, 113
Guggenheim Foundation Fellowship 12, 29, 31, 32, 113

Gutenberg Bible 98

Haddock, Nita 95
Hall, Sandy 97
Hallie, Philip 40, 46
Hamill, Harold 40, 71, 73
Hanke, Lewis 116
Hanna, Phil Townsend 108
Hardy, Thomas 97
Harlow, Neal 43
Harmsen, Tyrus 78, 83
Harrison, K.C. 63, 73
Hart, James D. N
Hart, William S. 130
Harte, Bret 62–64; "Heathen Chinee," "M'Liss," "Outcasts of Poker Flat," "Truthful James" 63
Harte, John Bret 63
Hartley, Margaret 111
Hartzell, James 33, 59
Hartzell, Molly 59
Harvard University 42, 51, 53; Austin Tappan Wright papers 53; Countway Medical Library 51; Houghton Library 30; Lamont Library 51; Widener Library 51
Harvill, George 55, 79–81
Harvill, Richard A. 55, 59, 74–75, 77–81, 84, 89–94, 100, 102, 104, 106, 120
Harwell, Richard B. 41, 84
Haserot, Les 85
Havens, Shirley 43
Haycraft, Howard xi
Haydn, Joseph 8, 32, 122
Hayes, Robert xiii, 3, 129
Hayford, Harrison 51
Hemingway, Ernest 64
Henderson, John 40
Henry the Navigator, Prince of Portugal 21–25, 27, 35

Heron, David 96
Hertzberger, Menno 73
Herzog, Carl 119, 122
Hill, Peter Murray 113
Hillman, Jimmye 94
Hirth, Mary 76
Hispanic Foundation 116
Hocking, Kay 49
Hocking, Richard 49
Hocking, William Ernest 49
Hodges, Mark 51
Hoffman, Richard 116, 122–124
Hoffman, Ruth 122
Hogg, Frank 17
Holman, David 113, 122
Homage to Yeats, Powell 8, 10, 34
"Home Thoughts from the Sea," Browning 21
Honeyman collection 104
Hoover, Herbert 120
Hoover Institution 97
Horgan, Paul 11, 30, 40, 46, 47, 55, 60, 119
Horn, Andrew xiii, 3, 12, 70, 73, 93, 95, 116, 121, 122, 129
Horn, Mary 129
Horses of Instruction, The [Adams, Hazard] 77
Houghton Library 30
Howell, Warren 32
Hudgins, Jane 84
Hugo, Victor 52
Humanities Research Center, University of Texas 58–59, 69, 75–77, 119
"Hunger for Heroes, A," Powell 105
Huntington, Henry E. 77
Huntington Library 33, 35, 66, 85
Hurd, Peter 119
Hutchinson, W.H. 121
Huxley, Aldous 70

Hyatt-King, Alec 8
Hyde, Don 113

Iacocca, Lee ix
"In My Craft and Sullen Art," Thomas 50
Irish Tourist Board 10
Islandia, Wright 53–54
"Islandian on the Islands, An," Wright 53
Ives, Charles 40

Jackson, Dolly 50
Jackson, Helen Hunt 41
Jackson, William A. 30, 32, 42, 50, 51, 113
James, David D. **D, E**
Janssen, Genevieve 58
Jeffares, Norman 8,11
Jeffers, Robins 15, 46, 60–70, 82, 92, 103, 128
Jeffers News-Letter 70
Jefferson, Thomas 124
Johns Hopkin University 89
Johnson, Lyndon B. 105
Johnson, Robert K. 87
Jones, Idwal 63
Jones, Lee 106
Jones, Olive 70
Jones, Wyman 72
Jones and Laughlin Steel 126
Josey, E.J. **K**
Joyce, James 61–62

Kaplan, Justin 64
Keating, Tatiana 88
Kenan, Charlotte 97
Kennedy, Robert 53
Kessel, John 113
Kew, George **I**
Kiel University 68

Kierkegaard, Preben 73
Kindersley, Cecil 34
Kindersley, David 9, 33–35, 116
Kindersley, Evan 34
King, Martin Luther 53
Kirkpatrick, John 40
Kirsch, Jonathan 109
Kirsch, Robert 109, 111, 116
Kister, Ken 50
Knopf, Alfred 97, 112, 126
Knopf, Alfred A., Inc. 2
Krips, Josef 18
Krumgold, Joseph 97; "And Now Miguel" (video) 97
Krutch, Mrs. Joseph Wood 97, 122
Kutcher, Margaret 101

L.C. Information Bulletin 116
LaFarge, Consuelo 76
LaFarge, Oliver 75
Laguna Verde Imprenta 124
Laird, David xiv, 95–97, 100–101, 104, 106, 107, 112, 127–128; *Books of the Southwest* (ed.) 128
Lakeside Press 45
Lamy, Archbishop John Baptist 40
Land of Little Rain, The, Austin 36
Larkin, Philip 63
Lassen County (CA) Library 36
Lathem, Edward C. 41, 53
Laughlin, James 126–127
Lawrence, D.H. 42, 67, 104, 121; *The Rainbow* 67
Lawrence, Guy 6, 7, 18, 37, 61, 63
Lawrence, Marcia 6, 7, 18, 37, 61, 63–64
Lea, Tom 119

Leaves of Grass, Whitman 110
Leibert, Fritz 42
Lester, Robert 66
Letters on Poetry to Dorothy Wellesley, Yeats 8
Lewis, Wilmarth S. (Lefty) 42
Liaison x
Librarian of Congress xi, 115–117, 123–124
Library Association, The (British) x, 16
Library Association Record x
Library Journal xi, xii, 7, 29, 48, 115, **N**
Library of Congress 51, 70, 124, 129; *L.C. Information Bulletin* 116
Life Goes On, Powell ix
Little Package, The, Powell 2, 30
Livesey, Rosemary 32
Lloyd George, David vii
Lockhart, Adelaide 53
Lockheed Corporation 120
London, Jack 62, 64
London Library 62, 107
Long Beach (CA) Public Library 72
Los Angeles Public Library 32, 71–73
Los Angeles State University 122
Los Angeles Times 109, 111
Loughborough Technical College 54, 65, 88, 97
Loved One, The, Waugh 76
Lubetzky, Seymour xiii, 12
Lummis, Charles Fletcher 120, 122
Lund, John J. 35
Lycée Carnot 4
Lycoming (PA) College 42, **A**
Lyle, Guy R. viii

McColvin, Lionel viii
McDonald, Edward 42
McDonald, John 42
McGarry, Sarah 121
MacIntyre, C.F. 15, 33, 122
MacIntyre, Marian 33
McKeon, Newton F. 41
MacLeish, Archibald 115, 117, 123–124
McNamee, Dorothy 55, 106
McNiff, Philip 51
Magee, David 73
Magellan, Ferdinand 25
Maggs, John 37
Mailer, Norman 47; *Armies of the Night* 47
Malibu, The, Powell 86, 108
Manahan, Patrice 37
Manly, William Lewis 56; *Death Valley in '49* 56
Marengo Literary Leader 124
Markić, Lela 12, 15
Marks, Lillian 34
Marks, Saul 34, 116
Marquess of Anglesey 4
Marshall, John David 113; *Books Are Basic,* Powell 113
Masselos, William 45
Massey, Dudley 19
Mathews, Douglas 62
Maxwell, Margaret 106, 107, 125
Melcher, Daniel xi, xii
Melville, Herman 4, 51, 64, 104
Merton of the Movies, Wilson 70
Mestrović, Ivan 13
Metcalf, Keyes 51, 73
Meyer, Larry 37, 108
Middletown (CT) Public Library 41
Miles, Paul 3
Milhaud, Darius 5

Miller, Henry 2, 4, 6, 17, 19, 33, 89, 100, 111, 126-127, **D, E** 80th birthday tribute, UCLA 100; keepsake of writings about LCP 17; papers 33; *Tropic of Cancer* 4
Milles, Carl 54
Mills College 56
Mink, James 70, 120
Mishkin, Solly 85
Mission Santa Barbara 33
Mitchell, Robert vi, 133-164
Moon, Diana 43
Moon, Eric, "Foreword," vii-xvi; xvii-xviii, 7, 29, 43
Moore, Anne Carroll 98
Moore, Everett xiii, xiv, 3, 84-85, 116
Morgan (Pierpont) Library 66, 113
Morin, Richard 53
Morrill, Claire 58
Morse, Cliff 85
Mortensen, A.R. 111
Mortimer, Roger 68, 97, 115
Mountain Bell 85
Mowat, Charles 3-4
Mowat, Jo 4
Mowat, John 4
Mozart, Wolfgang Amadeus 8, 15, 18, 32, 122
Muir, John 42
Muirhead, Arnold 8
Muirhead, Dorothy 8
Mumford, Quincy xi
Munby, A.N.L. (Tim) 37, 113
Municipal Gallery, Dublin 10
Munson, Gorham 41
Munthe, Wilhelm 14
Murphy, Franklin 16, 58, 94, 119
Musée de Dijon 52
Museum of Fine Arts, Boston 52

Museum of New Mexico 103
Myers, Winifred 7-8, 19, 73, 113

Nabakov, Vladimir 65
National Endowment for the Humanities 102, 111, 112, 121
National Gallery (London) 7
National Library (Wales) 17
Nesheim, Kenneth 42
Nevin, Allen 70
New Directions 126
New Mexico 100, 111
New Mexico Historical Society 119
New Mexico Library Association 100, 119
New Mexico State Library 101
New York Public Library 30, 32, 98
New York Times Book Review 32, 42, 44, 64, 70, 111
Newell, Eleanor 121
Newell, Gordon 33, 82-83, 108, 121
Northern Arizona University (NAU) 84, 102, 195, 121
Northland Press 108, 110
Northwestern University 74
Nourissier, François 109
Nouvelles Littéraires, Les 109
Nureyev, Rudolph 18
Nyholm, Jens 115

Occidental College 15, 32, 33, 39, 70, 73, 78, 82-83, 85, 122
Olch, Peter **P**
Oldman, C.B. 8
"On the Grindstone," Powell xii, 30
Overland Bookshop 55, 106

173

Oxnard (CA) Public Library 55

Pacific Northwest Library Association–Mountain Plains Library Association (PNLA-MPLA) 78
Pack, Arthur 82
Pack, Phoebe 82
Panizzi, Sir Anthony viii
Papago reservation library 88–89
Parker, Wyman 11, 41, 60
Passion for Books, A, Powell xii, 2
Patchen, Kenneth 127
Paulson, Robert 81, 87, 92, 93, 101
Payne, Robert 33
Perceval, Don 86
Perkin, Robert 78
Perry, Jessica 98
Perry, Jim 98
Pessoa, Fernando 21; *English Poems* 21; "Epithalamium" 21
Philosopher Pickett, Powell 117
Phoenix Public Library 121
Photographs of the Southwest, Adams 111
Pierre, Melville 4
Pilling, George 122
Pinto, V. de Sola 67
Plantin Press 34
Plas Newydd 4
Popejoy, Thomas 80
Portrait of My Father, Powell 108, 113, 118
Pound, Ezra 126–127
Powell, Clark 6
Powell, David 6
Powell, Donald M. 87, 91, 93, 97, 127
Powell, Fay xiv, xviii, 2, 5, 7, 11, 15–16, 18–19, 28, 30–31, 33, 37, 42–44, 47–50, 52, 58–59, 61–62, 64–65, 67, 72–73, 80–83, 86, 88, 91–92, 106–107, 112, 119–120, 122, 124, 128, 130–131, **B, P**
Powell, Lawrence Clark: Arizona legal residence 106; awards and honors 42, 43, 92, 121; charities and special gifts 31–32, 33, 35, 82, 122; clubs 104, 114, 121, 122, 127; courses, seminars, and conferences 17, 41, 48–49, 54, 62, 65–68, 74, 88, 93, 95, 97, 99, 107, 120; dogs 5, 13, 55, 81–82, 99, 131, **B**; family visits 6–7, 36, 37, 39, 44, 55, 120; discusses father 117–118; 119, 120; hospitalization 106; lectures and speeches 12–14, 17, 32, 35, 42, 50, 51, 53, 56, 58, 70, 71, 72, 74, 77–78, 82, 84, 89, 98, 100, 105, 115–116, 119, 120, 121, 124, 129; library postcard collection 51; musical interests 5, 8, 15, 18, 19, 32, 40, 45, 52, 53, 55, 58, 103, 111; oral history session 70, 120; religion 46; roots 3, 17; 70th birthday festschrift 107; UCLA's Powell Library 16, 34, 128–129, **C**; UCLA retirement 1, 31; University of Arizona retirement to emeritus status 108; **WRITINGS**— *The Alchemy of Books* xii, 42, 98; *Arizona, a Bicentennial History* 102, 106, 111–112, 117; "Bibliographers of the Golden State" 32, 35; *The Blue Train* 2, 5, 6, 52, 108, 109, 117; *Bookman's Progress*

44; *Books Are Basic* 113; *Books in My Baggage* 2; *California Classics* 55, 90, 108; "California Classics Reread" 37–38; "Connecting Up" 116; "Daphnis and Chloë in Literature and Art" printed as *The Enchanted Couple* 121; "Desert Sunset" 124; *El Morro* 68, 108; *The Enchanted Couple* 121; *Farewell to the Encinal* 32; *Fortune & Friendship* ix, x, xiv, xvii, xviii, 6–7, 43, 48, 56; *From the Heartland* 110; *Homage to Yeats* 8, 10, 34; "A Hunger for Heroes" 105; *The Little Package* 2, 30; *The Malibu* 86, 108; "On the Grindstone" xii, 30; *A Passion for Books* xii, 2; *Philosopher Pickett* 117; *Portrait of My Father* 108, 113, 118; "The Purple Dragon" 124; *The River Between* 52, 108; "Shoe on the Other Foot" 77; *Southwest Classics* 101, 106, 108; "The Three H's" 13; *Where Water Flows* 104, 110, 124; *Winter Crossing, 1952* 113; on book in progress 70; in *New York Times Book Review* 32, 42, 64, 70; in *Sunset* 32; in *Westways* q.v.
Powell, Mason 44
Powell, Norman **O**
Poynter, Noel 32
Princeton University Library 76, 117
Prokoviev, Sergei 18
"Purple Dragon, The," Powell 124
Putnam, Herbert viii

Putnam Publishing Group 2

Rainbow, The, Lawrence 67
Randall, David 64, 113; *Dukedom Large Enough* 64
Random House 69
Ransom, Harry 58–59, 75–77, 80, 91, 119
Ray, Gordon N. 29, 32, 58, 113
Ready, Will viii
Redmond, Pamela 62–63
Redmond, Terry 62–63
Redwood Library 48
Renthal, Helen 88
Rexroth, Kenneth 33, 37, 127; "The Classics Revisited" 37
Ridgeway, Anne 70
Rieber, Winifred 45
Riley, Elizabeth 110
Rilke, Rainer Maria 33, 123
Ring, Frances 108
Ritchie, Ward 33, 44, 45, 71, 78, 82–83, 108, 109, 122–124, **J, N, O**
River Between, The, Powell 52, 108
Roberts, Warren 76–77
Robinson, Will W. 32, 38, 108, 116
Rocky Mountain Bibliographical Center 78
Rogers, Brian 41
Romero, Orlando 103
Roosevelt, Franklin D. 115, 123
"Rose of Solitude," Everson 46
Rosenberg, Betty xiii, xiv, 133–164
Rosenblatt, Paul 100
Rosenstock, Fred 78
Rosenzweig Award 121
Ross, Birdie 1
Ross, Larry 1
Rota, Anthony 68

175

Rota, Bertram 68, 76
Rounce & Coffin Club 121, 122
Roxburghe Club **N**
Royal Ballet 18
Rushton, Peters 42
Rutgers library school 43, 106
Ryf, Robert S. 83

St. Gallen Library 61
Saint-Saëns, Charles Camille 45
Salazar, Antonio de Oliveira 22
Saltus, Elinor 88
Sambin, Hugues 52
San Diego Public Library 71
San Francisco Examiner 109
San Francisco Public Library 40
San Joaquin, Everson 45
Sanders, Marilyn **J**
Sanders, Mark 108, 110, 122, 127
Santa Fe Opera 55
Santa Monica Unified School District 32
Sarber, Mary 119, 121, 122
Saturday Evening Post 30
Saturday Review 37
Savage, Ernest viii
Saxton, Mark 54
Sayers, Frances Clarke xiii, 32, 118
Scarecrow Press viii, ix, xvii, xviii
Schaefer, Jack 90; *Shane* 90
Schaefer, John P. 89–90, 91, 93–94, 96–97, 99–102, 103–106, 108, 111, 112, 122, 127–128, frontispiece, **G, H, I**
Schmied, François-Louis 122
Scruggs, Charles 125, 130
Seelye, John 42
Serra, Junípero 33

Shaffer, Kenneth 50
Shane, Schaefer 90
Shank, Russell 129
Shaw, Mary Andrews 99
Shaw, Ralph viii, x, xii, 98–99
Shera, Jesse viii, x, 98
Sherrill, Leicester 85, 89
Shields, Wilmer 71
"Shoe on the Other Foot," Powell 77
Shoemaker, Norman 32, 39, 60, 82
Shoemaker, Otie 36
Shoemaker, R.K. 36
Shore, Emily 26–27
Short Title Catalog (STC) 50
Shuman, Marilyn 78
Sigmund, Helen 95
Simmons, Marc 113
Simmons College library school 47, 50–53, 66, 68
Singing Wind Ranch 97
Smith, Bill x
Smith, Dick 67
Smith, Eldred 96
Smith, Lawson 85
Smith, Mark 106
Smith, Sally 7
Smith, Stanley 7, 73
Smith, Watson 125
Smuts, Jan Christian vii
Snow, C.P. 41
Southern California Quarterly 53
Southwest Classics, Powell, 101, 106, 108
Southwest Museum 55, 120
Southwest Review 111
Southwestern Book Trails, Powell 105
Splendid Idle Forties, The, Atherton 50
Sproul, Robert Gordon 34, 94, 96

Stacey, Joseph 86
Stampara, Andrea 13
Stanford University 96
Starkey, Walter 8
Starr, Ernie 50
Starr, Kevin 109–110
State University of New York, Buffalo 96
Stein, Johann Andreas 15
Steinbeck, John 30, 64
Steloff, Frances 44
Stelter, B.R. 122
Stevenson, Robert Louis 41–42
Stokes, Jeff 67
Stokes, Roy 54, 66, 67, 73
Stone, Irving 64
Strauss, Richard 55
Stravinsky, Igor 18
Sullivan, Peggy **K**
Sunset 32
Swaim, Elizabeth 41
Swallow, Alan 78
Swank, Ray 73, 94
Swarthmore College library 41
Swift, Patrick 24
Sykes, Paul 67

Tallman, Johanna ix, 3, 120
Tanaka, Shigeo 85
Taos Book Shop 58
Targ, William 2, 5, 6, 44, 109, 110
Taylor, Alexander S. 32, 33
"Tendril in the Mesh," Everson 47
Tesla 13
Texas Library Association 119
Tezać, Bozo 13
Thomas, Alan 7, 37, 73
Thomas, Dylan 50, 97; "In My Craft and Sullen Art" 50
Thoor Ballylee 10, 30
"Three H's, The," Powell 13

Times Mirror 2
Tin Drum, The 46
Tito 13
Toombs, Kenneth 69, **F**
Tor House 15, 70
Tortilla Flat, Steinbeck 63
Traders to the Navajos, Gillmor 85
Trejo, Arnulfo 87, 103
Trinity College, Dublin 10
Trinity College, Hartford (CT) 41
Trollope, Anthony 128
Tropic of Cancer, Miller 4
Truffaut, François 130
Tucson Literary Club 104, 121, 127
Tucson Public Library 121
Tucson Zoological Society 122
Tulloch, Gert 82
Tulloch, Ken 82
Turner, Patricia 95
Twain, Mark 62, 64, 104
Two Years Before the Mast, Dana 61

Unesco 117
United States Department of Agriculture (USDA) 99
United States Embassy, Tokyo 96
University of Arizona xiv, 4, 74–75, 79–81, 84–107, 111, 122, 125, 127, 130, **H, I**; Graduate Library School 75, 80, 81, 87–88, 97–98, 100, 102–103, 122; Library 91, 93, 103–104, 112, 122, 125, 126, 127; University of Arizona Foundation 85, 89, 93, 101–102, 104, 110, 122
University of Arizona Press 96, 100

177

University of British Columbia Library 43
University of California 89, 111
University of California, Berkeley 64, 70, 96, 102, 103, 104; Bancroft Library 32, 55; School of Library and Information Studies 32, 56, 94
University of California, Davis 47, 70, 95
University of California, Los Angeles: ix, xvii, 1, 3, 4, 6, 7, 30, 33, 45, 48, 53, 58, 64, 71, 76, 84, 86, 88, 93, 99, 100–103, 106, 107, 111, 127, 128–129, **B, D**; Graduate School of Library and Information Science 2, 3, 8, 12, 29, 32, 40, 48, 54, 59, 87, 88, 95, 116, 117, 127; Library xiii, 8, 12, 15, 33, 43, 51, 55, 58, 59, 70, 71, 72, 77, 85, 87, 94, 95, 96, 99, 109, 114, 116, 118, 120, 123; Powell Library 16, 34, 128–129, **C**; William Andrews Clark Memorial Library 1, 3, 4, 8, 9, 10, 11, 13, 30, 33–34, 45, 66, 67, 95, 114
University of California, Riverside 70
University of California, San Diego 94
University of California, San Francisco 70
University of California, Santa Barbara 35
University of California, Santa Cruz 35
University of California Press 33
University of Chicago Graduate Library School 45
University of Colorado 77–78

University of Denver library school 78
University of Georgia 49
University of Hawaii library school 99
University of Illinois 64, 104
University of Indiana library school 106
University of Judaism, Los Angeles 109
University of Kansas 96
University of Kentucky 120
University of Maine, Orono 49
University of Melbourne 129
University of Michigan 66, 87
University of Minnesota 96
University of Mississippi 74
University of Nevada 96
University of New Mexico 4, 101, 111
University of North Wales 4
University of Nottingham 67
University of Pittsburgh library school 105
University of South Carolina 69, 115, **F**
University of Southern California (USC) 108
University of Texas 58–59, 69, 75–77, 82, 91, 119
University of Texas Press 112
University of Utah 95
University of Zagreb 12, 13
Utah Historical Society 111

Van der Veer, Judy 71
Van Doren, Mark 70
Vaughan Williams, Ralph 19
Veaner, Allen 101
Voices from the Southwest, Dickinson, et al. 107
Voigt, Mel 94

Vosper, Robert 3, 16, 45, 73

Waddell, John 103
Wagman, Fred 73
Wagner, Henry R. 32
Walker, Franklin 64
Walkup, J. Lawrence 84
Walpole, Hugh 8
Ward Ritchie Press 44
Warde, Beatrice 34, 67
Warren, Althea 71–72, 118
Washington University, St. Louis 69
Waters, Frank 101
Waugh, Evelyn 76; *The Loved One* 76
Wayne, John 130
Weaver, Albert 94–95
Weaver, Paul 107–108, 110, 122
Webster, Daniel 53
Weinreb, Ben 68–69
Weismiller, Edward 41
Welsh National Library School 16
Werner-Bas, Juan 93
Wesley, Clarence 74
Wesleyan University, Middletown (CT) 11, 39–47, 52, 53, 66, 88, 101, 112, **B**
Westergaard, Waldemar 36
Westminster Cathedral 9
Westminster Public Library 63; Central Reference Library 7
Weston, Edward 70
Westways 32, 37–38, 62, 63, 71, 82, 85, 86, 91, 100, 106, 108, 110, 111, 126
Wheeler, Benjamin Ide 89
Wheeler, Joseph viii
Where Water Flows: the Rivers of Arizona, Powell 110
Whistler, James A.M. 14
Whistler, Rex 4
White, Stewart Edward 55
Who's Who [in America] xiv
Wiegand, Wayne A. 120
Wilbur, Richard 41
Wildcat 85
Wilkie, Dr. 42
Wilkinson, Roy 65
Williams, William Carlos 65, 107, 126–127
Williams College 41, 44, 45
Wilson, Charis 70
Wilson, Edmund 40–41, 45
Wilson, Harry Leon 70; *Merton of the Movies* 70
Wilson, H.W., Company xi
Wilson Library Bulletin 78
Wind River Press 113
Winding Stair and Other Poems, The, Yeats 11
Winsor, Justin viii
Winter Crossing, 1952, Powell 113
Woolf, Virginia 104
World Publishing Company 2
Wright, Austin Tappan 53; *Islandia* 53–54
Wright, David 24
Wright, John K. 53
Wright, Sylvia 54
Wright, Wyllis E. 41
Wyer, Malcolm Glenn 73, 78

Yale University 41, 47; Beinecke Library 42, 66
Yeats, W.B. 8–11, 34, 69, 97, 123; "After Long Silence" 8; "Coole Park, 1929" 11; *Letters on Poetry to Dorothy Wellesley* 8; *The Winding Stair and Other Poems* 11; *Homage to Yeats*, Powell 8, 10, 34

Yilmaz, Huseyn 41
Young, Noel 6, 109
Young, Ralph 41

Zamorano Club 121, 122, **N**

Zeitlin, Jacob Israel xiii, 30, 32, 78, **J**
Zeitlin, Josephine Ver Brugge 32
Zimmerman, Grady 74